NO PLACE FOR
BULLYING

NO PLACE FOR
BULLYING

Leadership for Schools That Care for Every Student

JAMES DILLON

CORWIN
A SAGE Company

CORWIN
A SAGE Company

FOR INFORMATION:

Corwin
A SAGE Company
2455 Teller Road
Thousand Oaks, California 91320
(800) 233-9936
www.corwin.com

SAGE Publications Ltd.
1 Oliver's Yard
55 City Road
London EC1Y 1SP
United Kingdom

SAGE Publications India Pvt. Ltd.
B 1/I 1 Mohan Cooperative Industrial Area
Mathura Road, New Delhi 110 044
India

SAGE Publications Asia-Pacific Pte. Ltd.
3 Church Street
#10-04 Samsung Hub
Singapore 049483

Acquisitions Editor: Jessica Allan
Associate Editor: Allison Scott
Editorial Assistant: Lisa Whitney
Permissions Editor: Karen Ehrmann
Project Editor: Veronica Stapleton
Copy Editor: Lana Arndt
Typesetter: C&M Digitals (P) Ltd.
Proofreader: Dennis W. Webb
Indexer: Molly Hall
Cover Designer: Glenn Vogel

Printed in the United States of America

Library of Congress Cataloging-in-Publication Data

Dillon, James (James E.)

No place for bullying : leadership for schools that care for every student / James Dillon ; foreword by Kevin Jennings.

p. cm.
Includes bibliographical references and index.

ISBN 978-1-4522-1669-0 (pbk.)

1. Bullying in schools—Prevention. 2. Educational leadership. I. Title.

LB3013.3.D57 2012
371.5'8—dc23   2012011687

This book is printed on acid-free paper.

12 13 14 15 16 10 9 8 7 6 5 4 3 2 1

Contents

Foreword

"Effective bullying prevention is not just instituting a program in a school. It will require educators to significantly change the culture of most schools."

—From *No Place for Bullying* by James Dillon

A fter finishing the manuscript of *No Place for Bullying*, all I could think was "Where was this book when *I* needed it?"

The time when I needed this book most was from 2009 to 2011, when I served as Assistant Deputy Secretary of Education for Safe and Drug-Free Schools and led the Obama Administration's antibullying initiative. Numerous high-profile "bullycides" (suicides apparently linked to bullying) had created a fever pitch around the issue of bullying. Nearly-panicked school officials often turned to us at the Education Department and implored us to give them a simple program they could use to make sure their schools were safe places. The pressure was on. Kids' lives were at stake and people wanted answers.

Sadly, I knew I could not give them what they wanted. The pressure to, as Jim Dillon puts it, "jump to solutions" when it comes to bullying is immense: everyone in the field of education cares deeply about the well-being of young people and wants to do their utmost to protect them. But I knew from experience that there was no easy fix to the problem of bullying—that, instead, bullying prevention had to be part of a larger effort to examine and reform school cultures so that treating others with respect became a norm. As one of my graduate school mentors, the brilliant Linda Darling-Hammond, puts it, "Change is a process, not an event." There was no easy guide to help educators understand how to undertake such a process of change, however, so I felt at a loss as to what to tell these well-intentioned folks.

Well, now there is. And you're holding it in your hands.

No Place for Bullying is the most sensible guide I have yet read as to how to "bully-proof" your school. While useful for any reader, I believe it will be most helpful for administrators who are seeking to drive a process of change in their building or district on the subject of bullying. Jim walks school leaders through the process of leading change, using his own experience as principal himself as a guide, and offers easy-to-use tools such as training exercises to help school leaders develop their own change initiatives. Grounded in the real world of schools, *No Place for Bullying* offers the best guide I've yet found on how to actually change your school culture and make respect the "fourth R" taught in your school – and one just as fundamental as reading, writing, and arithmetic.

That this book offers practical, useful advice did not come as a surprise to me. In my second month in the Obama Administration, the horrific beating of a student on a school bus in Belleville, Illinois, captured the media's attention and put pressure on us at the Education Department for specific programs that addressed bullying on school buses. In my search for such programs, I came upon Mr. Dillon's earlier book, *The Peaceful School Bus*, which offered practical advice for school leaders on how to make sure their buses were safe places. We brought the Peaceful School Bus Program to the attention of educators across the nation, and innumerable ones adopted it, testifying to its usefulness and practicality. I knew I'd found in Jim Dillon someone who—unlike so many education "experts" who have never actually worked in a school—*knew* how schools really worked and had the practical wisdom needed to devise programs that would actually create meaningful change.

With *No Place for Bullying*, the author continues his track record of offering schools his unique brand of practical wisdom. He also challenges us with the statement that "When it comes to bullying prevention, no one is to blame and everyone is responsible." In the past, even well-meaning school officials could rightfully say there was no guidebook as to how to create a school where bullying was minimized. With the publication of *No Place for Bullying*, that guide now exists. I urge you to read *No Place for Bullying* closely: each page offers advice that you can put to work when you come back to school tomorrow morning. And remember—it's your responsibility to do so. Kids' lives depend on it.

by Kevin Jennings

Acknowledgments

I am very grateful to all the students, parents, teachers, paraprofessionals, and administrators who have taught me so much about what it takes to make school a place where students feel safe, cared for, and valued. It is my hope that this book reflects the collective wisdom of all of our experiences and that it can make a positive contribution toward that mission.

I would like to especially acknowledge the Lynnwood Elementary School community where I made my home for seventeen years. It was a special place where we led each other and learned what it meant to be a caring and learning community. Although I hesitate to single out any colleague, I would like to acknowledge the special partnership I had with our school social worker, Maureen Silk-Eglit. We worked together for seventeen years solving problems and helping those with the greatest needs. All school leaders should have as skilled and dedicated teammate as her.

I would also like to thank Measurement Incorporated, who supported me in so many ways as I wrote this book. Dr. Tom Kelsh, the vice president of the Albany/White Plains Office, believed in the need for such a resource and provided the encouragement and support I needed to put my experience and ideas into book form. I would also like to thank all the staff in the Albany office who listened to me and stimulated my thinking in the process of writing this book.

I would like to thank the dedicated professionals I have met through my association with the Olweus Bullying Prevention Program, especially Susan Limber, Marlene Synder, and Jane Riese. Their support and encouragement gave me the confidence to lend my voice and efforts to their work. I also owe a special thanks to Sue Thomas at Hazelden, who took a chance to publish the Peaceful School Bus, a program that emerged from an elementary school's attempt to tackle the difficult problems on the school bus. By helping us share its success, the school bus is a safer place for many children.

I am grateful to Jim Collins and the School Administrators Association of New York State (SAANYS), who gave me the opportunity to tour New York State and present to school administrators on the topic of leadership and bullying prevention. Many ideas for this book were a product of that experience.

I continue to learn from my friend and colleague Nancy Andress. We were administrative colleagues in the Guilderland Central School district and were cochairpersons of the district steering committee on bullying prevention. We were trained as trainers in the Olweus Bullying Prevention Program, and we continue to work together on many educational topics. She is always there to listen to me and offer her guidance, direction, and support.

A special thanks to Mary Sise who helped me take the step from leading one school to believing I could lead and contribute to the greater field of education.

I am grateful for the support and guidance of Jessica Allan, Lisa Whitney, and everyone at Corwin for helping me every step of the way in making this book a reality.

I have been very blessed with a wonderful family who supported me through the challenges of over twenty years of being a school administrator and the journey of writing this book. My grown children, Ernie, Tim, Brian, and Hannah, were great kids to raise and learn from, and they now encourage and support me as I pursue new endeavors. My wife, Louisa, who has been a school social worker for over thirty years, is truly a school leader without the formal title. We have shared our stories and struggles as parents and professionals, so she is really the uncredited coauthor of this book. Her work and how she lives her life embodies what it truly means to value and care for others.

PUBLISHER'S ACKNOWLEDGMENTS

Corwin wishes to acknowledge the following peer reviewers for their editorial insight and guidance.

Robert A. Frick
Superintendent of Schools
Lampeter-Strasburg School District
Lampeter, PA

Harriet Gould
Adjunct Professor/Retired Elementary Principal
Concordia University
Lincoln, NE

Rich Hall
Principal
R. C. Longan Elementary School
Henrico, VA

Kathleen Hwang
Elementary School Principal
Loudoun County Public Schools/Sanders Corner Elementary
Ashburn, VA

About the Author

 **James Dillon** has been an educator for over thirty-five years, including twenty years as a school administrator. While he was the principal of Lynnwood Elementary in New York, he developed the Peaceful School Bus Program, designed to prevent and reduce bullying, and subsequently published as *The Peaceful School Bus* (Hazelden). The program is now being implemented in schools across the country.

Jim was named Principal of the Year in 2007 by the Greater Capital District Principal Center. He received recognition for administrative leadership for character education. In 2010, Lynnwood Elementary was recognized by New York State ASCD for Educating the Whole Child for the 21st Century. Jim was an invited participant and presenter at the first National Summit on Bullying Prevention sponsored by the U.S. Department of Education in 2010 and is a certified Olweus Bullying Prevention Program trainer.

Jim is currently an educational consultant for Measurement Incorporated. He makes presentations and conducts workshops on a variety of educational topics, including instruction, classroom management, leadership, and supervision. He has presented at many local, state, and national conferences.

He has four grown children, Ernie, Tim, Brian, and Hannah. He and his wife Louisa, a school social worker, live in Niskayuna, NY.

Introduction

It Doesn't Add Up

Here are some commonly accepted statements about bullying in schools:

1. Bullying is now universally recognized as a serious problem, not just in schools, but in our society.
2. In the last fifteen years, there has been research yielding a substantive body of knowledge about bullying and what can be done to reduce and prevent it.
3. Schools are filled with competent, caring people who do not approve of bullying.
4. It is in the best interest of the students and the entire school to substantially prevent and reduce bullying.
5. There are now laws in almost all of the fifty states requiring schools to have antibullying policies and regulations designed to stop bullying.

Those five statements added together should make bullying less and less of a significant problem in our schools. While there are some signs that bullying prevention efforts are having a positive impact on schools, in too many schools, bullying continues unabatedly. Bullying prevention programs work in some schools and significantly reduce bullying, but in other schools, the same programs are not effective.

FOLLOWING A PROGRAM OR FOLLOWING A LEADER?

I am not a researcher but have been an educator for over thirty-five years, with twenty of them as a principal. I am not surprised that many schools seem stuck and unable to make any difference in addressing the problem of school bullying.

1

It is hard to change anything in schools. There are many problems, programs, mandates, and social pressures competing for educators' attention and action. If schools are going to change, the key element for starting that change and maintaining it is the leadership of the school.

My hunch is that the programs were effective in schools that had strong leaders and weren't effective in schools without strong leaders. A Wallace Foundation report (see Leithwood, Louis, Anderson, & Wahlstrom, 2010) on school leadership stated: "To date we have not found a single case of a school improving its student achievement record in the absence of talented leadership. One explanation is that leaders have the potential to unleash latent capacities in organizations" (p. 9). If leadership is essential for any improvement in student achievement, I feel it is a safe assumption to make about bullying prevention.

Bullying prevention is less effective in schools where people are directed to just *follow a program* that they are told will solve the problem of bullying and meet the mandates and requirements imposed by the state law. The school leaders in these schools try to get compliance instead of true commitment.

Bullying prevention is more effective in schools where people *follow a leader* who empowers them with the knowledge and skills to accept responsibility for and make a commitment to stop bullying and to improve the overall school climate.

Effective leaders set a tone and standard for how all members of the school community treat each other. They are able to tap into people's moral purpose and get their commitment to keep students safe and able to learn.

MY STORY: A WINNING COMBINATION

When I look back at my time as principal, I realize that our school was practicing bullying prevention long before we knew it was bullying prevention. Our goal was to develop a positive school environment for the "whole child." As a school leader, I directed my efforts to create a supportive learning environment for everyone. As a result of this philosophy, when we became more aware of bullying as a problem, our school was ready to add specific bullying prevention practices to what we were already doing.

My experience of combining effective leadership practices to create a positive school climate with specific bullying prevention practices was like the commercial showing how Reese's Peanut Butter Cups were created: two children, one eating peanut butter and other eating chocolate, happen to collide. They discover just how good the combination of peanut butter and chocolate taste. I discovered how the best practices of leadership and bullying prevention were a perfect fit and how they enhanced each other. I stayed at our school long enough to see the long-term positive results of this winning combination.

ORGANIZATION OF THE BOOK: THE WILL/THE SKILL/THE FOLLOW THROUGH

This book describes how the integration of bullying prevention and effective leadership can meet the daily challenges of stopping bullying and improving the quality of learning in the school.

Bullying in schools is a complex and elusive problem that can resist many of the traditional approaches to solving school problems. The integration of effective bullying prevention and school leadership consists of three interdependent elements: the Will, the Skill, and the Follow Through. Understanding how these elements work together should help school leaders address bullying in an organized way and avoid the temptation of

Figure Intro 1

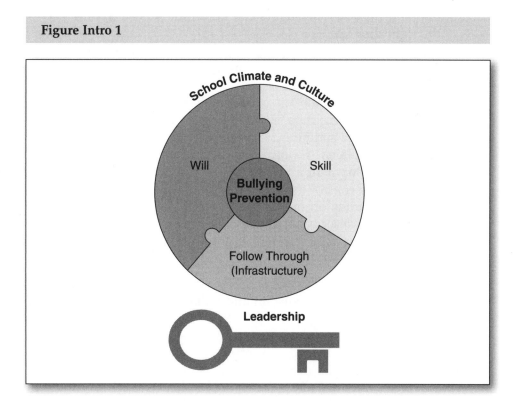

a quick fix or simple solution. This book is organized into three sections with each chapter describing the specific aspects of the essential elements.

- *The Will*: The commitment and determination to make school a safe place for students to learn to their full potential. The will entails knowing what it takes to address the problem and learning what is required to get the job done.
  - o *Chapter 1* describes the elusive nature of bullying and the difficulty that adults have in seeing it, hearing it, and understanding it.

o *Chapter 2* explains how bullying prevention requires a moral commitment from staff and why this is often hard to get.

o *Chapter 3* describes how bullying is an *adaptive* problem requiring an approach that differs from traditional approaches to school problems.

o *Chapter 4* explains how the concept of mindset can be applied to bullying prevention and compares the difference between a criminal justice mindset and an educational mindset.

- *The Skill*: The decisions, strategies, and processes that can facilitate the necessary change for effective bullying prevention.

o *Chapter 5* emphasizes how important it is for school leaders to closely examine how they use their power and authority.

o *Chapter 6* discusses the possible misdirections of bullying prevention and how school leaders can guide the school community in the right direction.

o *Chapter 7* explains the importance of working with a diverse small group of members of the community to set direction and guide the efforts of the school.

o *Chapter 8* describes the role of data in decision making and various ways of collecting data, interpreting it, communicating it, and using it for goal setting.

o *Chapter 9* explains the importance of understanding child and human development and how to work with students instead of just trying to control them.

o *Chapter 10* builds on the understanding of what we know about students and describes the type of educational approach that will empower them as bystanders and prepare them as leaders in the 21st century.

- *The Follow Through (Infrastructure)*: The structures, routines, and protocols to put in place to sustain and enhance the progress made in bullying prevention.

o *Chapter 11* offers a set of guiding principles for creating the conditions for all members of the community to become leaders. Specific leadership practices are offered to support these conditions.

o *Chapter 12* reviews the requirements and mandates that schools must follow. It offers resources for finding programs and practices that have been used effectively in schools.

o *Chapter 13* describes the approach to discipline that supports a comprehensive, principle-based approach to bullying prevention. It offers specific guidelines for supervising, responding, and intervening with bullying incidents.

o *Chapter 14* examines bullying prevention beyond the school building. Guidelines are offered for how to respond to parental complaints and how to communicate with parents of students suspected of bullying. It analyzes and offers ways to address the unique problems of bullying on the school bus and in the digital world.

o *Chapter 15* discusses the issues related to maintaining, sustaining, and enhancing bullying prevention efforts over time. Specific recommendations are made for how to integrate bullying prevention into the curricula, routines, procedures, and customs of the school.

WILL AND SKILL: DYNAMICALLY LINKED

Many schools begin their bullying prevention efforts with a high degree of enthusiasm and energy, but after a while, things seem to return to status quo. Other schools are highly organized and faithful to whatever program they select yet fail to see much, if any, progress. In the first scenario, the school might have had the will to address bullying but lacked the skill to channel that will into plans and strategies. In the second scenario, the skills and strategies were in place, but because people didn't have the will to address the problem, little progress was made.

I recall presenting our staff a video clip from the 20/20 program that showed a young child having his toy ripped away from him on the playground (Goodman, 2002). After the meeting, our staff asked me to find specific practices or programs that would help us prevent that type of incident from ever happening at our school. We had the will to stop bullying, and we went looking for something to give us the skill to stop it.

This book is designed to help school leaders understand how these two elements work together and to decide where to direct their initial efforts. The matrix below illustrates the different types of situations that can arise in a school depending on the level of *will* and *skill* present.

The *Follow Through (Infrastructure)* element can be present regardless of the degree of *will* and *skill* but will only be meaningful and fulfill its purpose when a high degree of will and skill are both present.

GOALS AND PURPOSE OF THE BOOK

There are many other readily available excellent resources (many of which I refer to in the book) that can provide accurate, thorough, and important information about bullying prevention. School leaders are encouraged to consult and use these excellent resources. I refer to research findings about bullying but only in the context of how that knowledge can be applied to specific leadership practices and strategies. This book is based on the premise that content knowledge alone about the topic of bullying is not what is lacking in bullying prevention efforts. This book is a guide for using this knowledge to change the hearts and minds of the school community to take effective action in addressing bullying.

Table Intro 1   Skill–Will Quadrant

	Low WILL	High WILL
High SKILL	• People follow rules and procedures because they have to but often don't know why or how the practice works. • People resent having more things to do, so bullying prevention becomes just another mandate. • People can question the need for the program or practice. • After a while, people wonder why they don't see any improvement. • Passive resistance can settle in.	• People see the problem of bullying in a larger context of school climate. • Members of the community commit to learning together about the problem and what works. • Community strengthens as a result of working together to address the problem. • Data are collected from multiple sources and used for decision making. • Students become educated not just about bullying but about how to be more responsible to each other. • People sustain their efforts because they see progress and feel a difference.
Low SKILL	• People generally think that things are OK. • Bullying is not seen as a problem for their school—other schools have the problem. • Schools stay committed to using traditional approaches and adjust them by increasing penalties for those who break the rules. • "Ignorance is bliss." • School is surprised when the damage of persistent bullying is revealed.	• People understand the problem and the urgency of doing something but are unclear of how to invest their time and energy. • Decisions can be made hastily without careful planning and without data. • Resources can be wasted on speakers or assemblies that are supposed to inspire people to change, yet people eventually return to old habits. • People can get frustrated when they don't see progress. (Hopes are dashed.)

This book is also not a compendium of research and practice on effective leadership. I share how I put theory into practice in my twenty years as a school administrator. I offer whatever wisdom I gained from many years of trial and error and just trying my best every day.

My primary goal and purpose is to get the reader to think a little differently about schools and the problem of bullying. It is based on the premise that people in schools can get stuck in ways of thinking and acting that prevent positive and creative solutions to problems. Thinking, however, does little good unless it is wedded to action. My goal is to support *thoughtful action* that is followed by reflection and *adjusted* action.

This book does not tell, nor should it tell, school leaders what to do, but it rather points them in the right direction and nudges them to get started with others at their side. Its main message is that school leaders cannot do it alone; they must join with others to learn about the problem and to lead together.

I have also tried to provide sticky ways of understanding the key concepts of bullying and school change. By "sticky" I mean analogies, acronyms, short memorable phrases, and stories that people are more likely to remember and use in their day-to-day practices. I urge the reader to use any or all of my stories, analogies, or phrases as often as needed—it is all for a good cause.

CHAPTER ACTIVITIES

I have provided activities for the group meetings that school leaders typically plan and facilitate. The activities can be used for any type of group: students, staff, parents, and any combination of these groups. I leave it to school leaders to decide what activities fit their particular school community. Most of these activities are designed to get people to think a little differently about things and to share their thinking with each other. They are meant to be springboards for further discussion followed by specific plans and actions.

I deliberately made generous use of video clips since they are effective ways to gain people's attention and to touch their emotions. Change is not an intellectual experience but must involve touching people's hearts and minds. School leaders must tap into both to get the type of commitment needed to address the problem of bullying.

DEFINITION OF KEY TERMS

When I refer to bullying in this book, I am using a combination of these two similar definitions. I added the second one to emphasize the social nature of bullying.

Definition 1

Bullying is when someone repeatedly and on purpose says or does mean or hurtful things to another person who has a hard time defending himself or herself (Olweus, 1993).

Definition 2

Bullying is a relationship problem in which an individual or a group uses power aggressively to cause distress to another (Pepler, 2007). According to Morrison and Marachi (2011)

- The child who bullies is learning to use power and aggression to control others.
- Bullying occurs repeatedly over time rather than a single act of aggression.
- The child who is victimized becomes trapped in an abusive relationship and needs help to stop the bullying.

School Climate

I refer frequently to *school climate* or *school culture* in the book. This definition of school climate includes the concept of culture.

School climate refers to the character and quality of school life. It is based on the patterns of people's experiences of school life and reflects: norms, goals, and values; interpersonal relationships; teaching, learning, and leadership practices; and organizational structures (Pickeral, Evans, Hughes, & Hutchinson, 2009).

The two concepts are very similar and are interrelated: school culture is what a school believes and values, and school climate is how it feels as a result of how those beliefs and values are practiced.

BULLYING PREVENTION AS AN OPPORTUNITY

Being a school leader is a demanding and at times an almost impossible job. With bullying, school leaders are often the first people blamed for the problem and its consequences; they are the last to get help and support. Although I am retired as an active principal, I still devote my time and energy to providing support to the unsung heroes of education: school leaders.

All educators should stand together with the goal of making school a safe place for all students. I hope that this book will help school leaders get started in the right direction and use this problem of bullying as an opportunity to renew the school community's passion and commitment to improving the lives of our students.

> When passion comes alive—when it turns out to be a powerful driver—it is in situations where we actually accomplish something of high moral value, which in turns energizes us to do even more . . . It is the being in the moment of a successful endeavor that fuels passion, not the dreaming of it . . . The establishment of new practices and experiences galvanize passion. This is the essence of the change leader: the capacity to generate energy and passion in others through action. (Fullan, 2011a, p. 23)

I hope that this book can help school leaders do what I know they *want* to do: make schools safe places for learning.

Section One

The Will

1

The Blind Spot of Bullying Prevention

"Far from being a sign of intellectual inferiority, the capacity to err is crucial to human cognition... Thanks to error, we can revise our understanding of ourselves and amend our ideas about the world."

—Kathryn Schulz (2010, p. 5)

I once had a minor fender bender accident because I failed to adequately check my blind spot while driving my car. It was an accident that could have been easily avoided with a quick and simple glance backward. Why didn't I do this? I know that checking is important, and I usually do check, but there are times when I don't. For over forty years of driving, this lapse in the habit of *checking* caused no accidents. Ironically, it was this *success* at not having an accident that caused the accident. Now I always check and double-check the blind spot before changing lanes. I just wish I didn't have an accident to learn this lesson.

This anecdote serves as an analogy to the current state of affairs regarding bullying prevention in our schools. Most schools keep students safe every day. School staff, like competent and safe drivers, are conscientious and skillful in managing student behavior. Schools have policies and procedures for dealing with student misconduct and rule infractions. School staff are effective in implementing the rules and maintaining an orderly school environment. When a student acts violently toward self or others, school staff feel shocked and *blindsided*, wondering why and how it happened. When persistent and frequent bullying is revealed to be a major cause for that act, they say they were unaware of the extent of the bullying. If they were aware, they say that they didn't have enough evidence to do anything about it. They didn't know what they did wrong or what they could have done differently: everything was working as it should work.

Like competent drivers experiencing many accident free years, school staff become victims of their many years of success in providing a safe environment for students. Unlike a driver who knew about blind spots and forgot to check them, school staff don't know that there are blind spots: places where bullying flourishes beyond their detection. They think they see everything that they need to see to keep the school safe. For them, checking their blind spot was not a habit they forgot; it was a habit they never had nor thought they needed.

PUBLIC PERCEPTION AND REACTION

A school's highest basic priority is its responsibility to keep students safe. In the eyes of the public, any failure to meet this responsibility is unforgiveable and weakens trust and respect for public education. Bullying in schools has been a prominent issue for many years now, so the public expects schools to be able to prevent and reduce it. The public can interpret any failure to keep students safe as a sign of indifference or incompetence, or both. To ensure that schools are safe places for students, more federal and state laws are enacted with mandates for addressing the problem of bullying and consequences for failing to do so.

These laws provide guidance and direction for schools to develop policies and regulations that define the problem and require specific actions for a school to take in addressing bullying. Laws, regulations, and policies are necessary and serve a useful purpose; however, they alone are not sufficient in effectively addressing the problem. Laws and policies do not keep students safe: people do.

THE MISSING PIECE

The people who work in schools care for students. They are skillful and competent in doing a difficult job. They do not want nor approve of bullying and would do whatever is necessary to reduce or prevent it. Parents and students do not want bullying in schools. If the school community feels like this, why does bullying persist to the degree that it does in schools?

The school community shares a collective sense of "we would, if we could, but we can't" when trying to answer that question. The blind spot, where bullying thrives undetected in schools, is the missing piece of knowledge that school staff need to reduce and prevent bullying. They need to know the blind spot exists, where it is, and how it works. When they know this, they can check it and address the problem in an effective way. It is as simple or hard as that.

THE BLIND SPOT DESCRIBED

Although the blind spot is invisible, it can be described through the data that have been collected in schools. The blind spot is also a product of how schools traditionally function in lives of students and school staff.

Numbers Tell the Story

- Adults are aware of about *4 to 5 percent* of the bullying that occurs in schools, or *95 percent* of the bullying that occurs in schools goes undetected by school staff (Cohn & Canter, n.d.; Kazdin & Rotella, 2009).
- Adults think that they are aware of over 70 percent of the bullying that occurs in schools and that they intervene all the time (Olweus, 1993).
- Only 35 percent of students who are bullied tell an adult about it. This percentage decreases as students age (Petrosino, Guckenberg, DeVoe, & Hanson, 2010).
- About 60 percent of the students who witness bullying think that sometimes the bullied student deserves to be bullied. Many of the students who are bullied think they have brought it on themselves (Hoover & Oliver, 1996).
- Bullying *is* observed by over 85 percent of the students (Hawkins, Pepler, & Craig, 2001).
- Twenty-seven percent of bullied students report that it happens in the classroom with the teacher present (Olweus, 1993).
- Many students who bully are well liked by others, including the staff. Staff can often not believe that these students bully other students (Rodkin, 2011).

Other Factors to Consider

- Students learn how to bully in those blind spots and become more skillful in not being seen or heard doing it by adults.
- Many acts of bullying are not against the typical school rules.
- The longer bullying goes unseen and unheard by school staff, the more frequent and prevalent it becomes. School staff can easily give tacit approval to bullying.
- School staff and students often don't know what bullying is; they confuse it with other inappropriate behaviors.
- Traditional consequences do not act as deterrents because students feel confident that they won't get caught (95 percent of the time they won't).

- The social rewards gained by students from bullying outweigh the potential consequences of getting caught.
- Peer pressure is such a strong force developmentally that students are emotionally driven to bully without thinking of the consequences involved.
- Bullying is a "crime" that is easy to commit; easy to deny; and hard to prove. If it is only seen as a crime, and a *criminal justice* approach is the *only* one used, adults will not do a good job in policing it.

THE CONSEQUENCES OF THE BLIND SPOT

Students and school staff share the same space and time, but they have extremely different experiences in that shared time and space. For students, bullying in schools is front and center, loud and clear. For school staff, bullying is unseen and unheard, not central to their experience, and a minor problem competing with many more pressing and prominent issues. The existence of these two separate experiences of school have consequences that only strengthen the existence and persistence of the blind spot:

- If students perceive adults as being out of touch with what happens in school, thereby, failing to keep them safe, then they will be less likely to trust those adults. Students can also interpret the adults' apparent obliviousness to bullying as a lack of caring.
- Students feel disconnected from their school if they think that most adults don't care about them.
- Student will not report bullying to people they don't trust. They will not trust adults who don't seem to care or are perceived to be ineffective in keeping them safe. They may also be afraid that they might get in trouble for reporting bullying.
- If students do not feel supported and empowered by school staff to intervene or report bullying, they will be more inclined to support bullying or be indifferent to it. They stay quiet because they are afraid of being a target of bullying themselves. They also lack the skills to handle bullying situations as bystanders.

THE UNDER/OVER BARRIER

This blind spot and its consequences create a barrier that keeps a school from taking effective action against bullying. I have termed this the *under/over barrier*:

> School staff tend to underestimate the amount and prevalence of bullying in schools and overestimate the frequency and success of their intervention efforts in addressing it.

This barrier creates an immunity against the changes needed to effectively prevent and reduce bullying. This immunity against change works for the following reasons:

- If staff don't see or hear the problem of bullying, it is hard for them to believe that bullying is a problem in their school. Tragic events happen in other schools. School staff will resist efforts to address a problem they don't think exists.
- School staff could be skeptical of programs or initiatives that come from laws, mandates, or high-level administration. They could be seen as only a reaction to a problem created in the media and designed to placate the public.
- If school staff think they are doing their best, and bullying persists, they could attribute the cause and solution to the problem to external factors, e.g., the failure of parents to teach their children not to bully.
- There are many other real problems that are seen and heard that also require time and energy.
- It is hard to admit to *not* seeing such a serious problem or to be wrong after years of feeling right.
- If administration mandates that a bullying prevention program be implemented, school staff can interpret such actions as an implicit criticism of their current efforts.
- School staff need sufficient autonomy and input into any initiative that will require their own time and effort and investment. Without a true commitment and investment from school staff, any plan or program will ultimately fail.

SCHOOL LEADERS' ROLE

Since so many of the issues related to the under/over barrier are about how staff perceive the problem, a school leader is in the best position to create the conditions for the staff to break through the barrier to change. These conditions require a high level of trust between administration and staff and a sense of shared leadership.

What school leaders can do about blind spots and the under/over barrier to effective responding to the problem of bullying is the following:

- Invest time in learning about the elusive and insidious nature of bullying. Lead staff in learning about blind spots.
- Act on the assumption that staff do want to prevent and reduce bullying. Attribute resistance to them not understanding the complexity of the problem and the blind spot.
- Acknowledge and accept how dependent school staff are on the *eyes and ears* of the students to get an accurate picture of how much bullying is happening. Help others learn this fact.
- Make trust and communication a priority in bullying prevention efforts. Students cannot be forced to trust—*adults must become trustworthy.*

- Welcome complaints of bullying. Thank those who complain for helping the school meet its responsibility.
- Reframe the problem of bullying so that any new efforts to address it are perceived as a continuation of the current efforts rather than a criticism of them.
- Make "being wrong" understandable given the complexity of the problem of bullying.

SUMMARY

- Bullying happens in the blind spots of adults. Most adults, however, don't know this and think that they have the problem of bullying under control.
- Bullying is not in the blind spot of students—it is loud and clear, front and center.
- School leaders must know and understand the elusive nature of bullying and how it thrives in blind spots.
- Adults in a school must become trustworthy to students. When students trust enough to share what they see and hear with adults in the school, the blind spot starts to fade, and bullying weakens it grip on a school environment.
- School leaders play the key role in connecting the student experience in school to the adult experience so that they can work together to make their school safe. They must facilitate the change of how bullying is understood and the approach to addressing it.
- School leaders are in the best position to reveal the blind spot to staff in a positive and safe context. They have the best knowledge of what conditions their staff need to build their knowledge and capacity to effectively address bullying.

ACTIVITIES TO ADDRESS THE BLIND SPOT PROBLEM WITH STAFF OR OTHER MEMBERS OF THE SCHOOL COMMUNITY

Staff might have difficulty accepting that they are not accurate in their perception of the problem of bullying. Merely telling staff that they are not seeing it all is not enough for them to change their beliefs about the problem of bullying in the school.

These activities can help staff to accept being wrong as something to be expected and an opportunity for adjusting their view of this problem. This adjustment is an important first step in addressing the problem of bullying more effectively. These activities will provide a soft landing for making this necessary adjustment in perceptions and actions.

ACTIVITY 1: LOOKING BUT NOT SEEING

Purpose

Have staff experience *blind spots* in a safe environment. *Show, not tell.*
In staff meetings, use a visual phenomenon that simulates the experience of looking at something without seeing it.

Content

Put the FedEx logo up on the screen.

Procedure

Ask your staff to find the arrow in the picture. Some will and some will not. They are all looking at the same thing, yet some see it and some don't.
(The arrow is between the uppercase *E* and lowercase *x* in the *Ex* part of the logo.)
Allow for discussion about why some can see it and some can't. What of the implications of this phenomenon in school?

ACTIVITY 2: THERE IS TOO MUCH TO SEE

Purpose

There are many things happening is a school besides bullying. There are many students interacting in many ways at rapid speeds. Adults in charge of supervising students have many things to observe besides bullying. Even with the best intentions and a determination to spot bullying, bullying can easily blend into the busy environment of a school.

Content

To illustrate this, use a film clip from the Marx Brothers' *A Night at the Opera* (Wood, 1935). The clip is available on YouTube at www.youtube .com/watch?v=l0xHIFtLzp0&feature=youtu.be.
There is a scene in Groucho's room on the ship. It is a very tiny space. Over the course of three minutes, a variety of people come knocking at his door, and he welcomes them in. Soon, there are twenty-five to thirty people, including plumbers, janitors, waiters, manicurists, as well as the other brothers, all jammed into the small room. They are all doing their jobs, so this is a chaotic scene that ends abruptly when someone opens the

door from the outside, and the entire mass of people literally pour out of the room.

This is obviously an exaggerated view of the busyness of an environment. To even exaggerate it more, I used the IMovie application to speed up the three minutes into less than thirty seconds and put a loud crowd noise as the background sound.

Procedure

When the scene is over, ask how many actions in that room would have been against the rules or how many actions could be considered as acts of bullying. It is almost impossible to answer.

This would be a good starting point to discuss what parts of the school are hard to monitor because of the number of students, the noise level, and degree of movement. Staff could be broken up into small groups with a recorder, reporter, facilitator, and timekeeper for the discussion. Each group would be asked to agree on that time and place and then list three to four descriptions of what is going on in that environment.

ACTIVITY 3: THERE IS TOO LITTLE TO SEE

Purpose

This activity explores how bullying happens under the radar and is often not against the rules. It illustrates how traditional disciplinary approaches often fail to sufficiently address the problem of bullying.

Content

Use a clip from the movie *Forrest Gump* (Zemeckis, 1994), also available on YouTube (www.youtube.com/watch?feature=endscreen&NR=1&v=nK ubwgJK8q8), to illustrate this point. It is the scene where the young Forrest Gump gets on the school bus for the first time. As he walks toward the back of the bus to find a seat, different students, some nonverbally and others verbally, indicate that he can't sit next to them. He is clearly being excluded, which is a type of bullying. Finally, a young girl welcomes him and invites him to sit.

This video clip can be used in various contexts. In this activity, it would illustrate the subtlety of bullying and how bullying is not against most typical rules. (This same clip could be used to show how discipline alone cannot manage bullying, and it can also be presented emphasizing the empathy shown by the little girl toward Forrest.)

Procedure

Following the clip, ask staff to discuss (break into small group and assign roles as in the previous activity) the following:

Why does the bus driver have a difficult time spotting bullying?

How would a parent of the one of the students excluding Forrest react if his or her child were disciplined for bullying him?

To whom did they pay more attention? To the students who did the excluding or the girl who welcomed him?

ACTIVITY 4: SOMETIMES YOU JUST CAN'T SEE AT ALL OR THE INVISIBLE GORILLA

Purpose

This activity allows staff to dramatically experience not seeing something blatant and obvious even when they are looking right at it.

Content

To experience this before using it with others, go to the www.invisible-gorilla.com website or YouTube at www.youtube.com/watch?v=IGQmdoK_ZfY. It is also called "The Monkey Business Illusion." Initially, refer to it as "The Monkey Business Illusion" and avoid the *invisible gorilla* term until after the activity (Chabris & Simons, 2009; Simons, 2010).

Procedure

There is a brief video to watch that shows two teams of people passing a basketball. The directions to the audience are to count the number of times the white team passes the ball. (These directions are given as an introduction right on the video.)

SPOILER ALERT! Do not read until after you have viewed the video and followed its directions.

About halfway through the video as the basketball is being passed, someone in a gorilla suit walks through the circle where the two teams are passing the basketball. The gorilla even stops and pounds his chest and then walks out of the scene. When the video concludes, staff are asked to share the number of times the white team passed the ball. The viewers offer answers like fifteen, sixteen, or seventeen, and the correct answer is sixteen. After asking for the number of passes, the viewers are asked if they saw the gorilla. About half of the group typically sees the gorilla; the other half looks puzzled by that question: they did not see the gorilla.

Many find this hard to believe, so it is important to show the same video clip again and tell them not to count the passes. This time everyone sees the gorilla.

This is a vivid and dramatic example of how we miss so much that is right before us. If the gorilla is unseen, it is not surprising that bullying can easily fly under the radar, unseen and unheard.

Have staff sit in small groups and respond to the following:

What does the Monkey Business Illusion tell us about bullying in schools?

How did it feel to not see the gorilla? If you saw the gorilla, were you surprised that others did not see it? What are the implications of half the people seeing it and the other half not seeing it when applied to the school environment?

What can we do about overcoming the problem of not seeing even when looking?

OUTCOMES

1. Staff share a common learning experience and engage in the discussion that follows.

2. The activities are designed to stimulate thought and discussion. They illustrate the importance of thinking differently and sharing that thinking. This problem of perception applies to issues other than bullying, so allow for a wide-ranging discussion, should it develop.

3. The principal is established as a leader of learning rather than an imposer of policy or program.

4. Activities like these will play a role in changing the hearts and minds of staff just by stimulating thought and discussion. They can be an effective first step in building the knowledge and capacity for staff to commit to working on this problem.

2

The Moral Purpose and Obligation of Bullying Prevention

"Emotion is, in this way, also a moral signal. It alerts us that something demands our attention, that something has gone wrong, that action is required ... And it is our empathy and compassion—our emotions—that compel us to act."

—Barry Schwartz and Kenneth Sharpe (2010, p. 75)

A few years ago, I accepted an invitation to speak to a high school faculty on the topic of creating a caring community. As I stood in front of a skeptical audience sitting as far away from me as possible, I suddenly doubted my prepared remarks wondering, "Who am I, an elementary principal, telling them, a high school staff, what to do?" Then I looked at them and posed the following statement: "Raise your hand if you care for the students in this school." Every hand went up. I paused, looked out at them, and replied, "I thought I would see every hand go up; you are already a caring community. You don't really need my presentation."

I picked up my notes, turned, and walked toward the exit. As an apprehensive silence filled the auditorium, I stopped and slowly walked back to the lectern. Looking out at now more attentive faces, I said, "I just thought of another thing to ask you: raise your hand if you think every student in this school knows that every one of you cares." No hands went up. Waiting until everyone saw that no hands were raised, I replied, "All you have to do now is let the students know that you care, better yet, relentlessly *advertise that you care*. There is no greater tragedy in life than having someone think that no one cares when in reality everyone does care."

This is perhaps the most perplexing part of bullying prevention in schools today. How is it that there are people in schools who started their career to help students, yet they end up failing to help students who need not just their care but their protection? Why is it that some people ask "Why?" when asked to address the problem of bullying when the question really should be "Why not?"

"Why not, why not?" is a hard question to answer. Although schools need to act without knowing an answer, school leaders should at least consider the question as they approach bullying prevention. Bullying prevention is more likely to succeed when staff commitment and determination are a key element of the school's efforts. The will does help a school find a way to effective bullying prevention. Surface compliance to any program is a weak substitute for a staff's commitment to keeping all students safe.

REASONS FOR STAFF RELUCTANCE AND STRATEGIES TO ADDRESS THEM

A staff's reluctance and resistance to bullying prevention is not necessarily a lack of moral purpose and obligation. School leaders must believe that staff have it and then clear the way for it to emerge. The blind spot described in Chapter 1 is one reason why staff might be reluctant to address the problem. There are other reasons that can significantly prevent staff from making the commitment needed for effective action. School leaders need to recognize and understand these reasons and the way they affect how staff view and do their job.

1. The Power Issues Between Staff and Administration

People don't resist change but rather resist being changed by someone else.

Here are some ways to avoid unnecessary power struggles:

If teachers are used to top-down decisions and feel little control over what happens to them, they are more likely to exercise power by resisting or subverting any change. Involve staff in learning about a problem and give them input into how to address the problem. This will avoid having bullying prevention perceived as another imposition or exercise of power from administration.

Leadership is getting people to do things when they have the freedom not to. Avoid exercising your power and authority as the way to get people to change (Collins, 2005). Leadership may take longer with this type of problem, but it is the only way to lasting and meaningful change.

Ask for staff just to be open to learning about the problem of bullying. This is very different from telling them to accept and implement a program. Learning along with your staff builds trust among all participants and develops a greater sense of shared leadership in approaching the problem.

Avoid jumping to solutions. Once the solution to a problem is presented to a staff, it is easy for them to shoot it down either overtly or covertly.

If there are mandates that you have little control over, use them as an opportunity to join with staff—you are in the same boat. Provide staff opportunities for input and choice with the limits of what you can or cannot do.

Clearly state the purpose of each meeting devoted to the issue. If the purpose is unclear, staff might assume that the discussion will determine an important decision. When the stated purpose is to ask for their input rather than make a decision, there will be less competition among differing perspectives.

Bullying prevention can be viewed as adding a new responsibility to a teacher's job description. Teachers may think it will mean involving them in time consuming disciplinary procedures or meetings that pertain to administrative duties. Knowing what changes will be expected of them will become clearer as the process of change proceeds. Make it clear that it won't be adding administrative responsibilities to their job.

Welcome opposing points of view. Accept resistance that occurs during the process of problem solving and decision making as useful information to have. Staff can accept and support change if they feel that their voice was heard in the change process.

2. The Everyday Press of School Life

Teachers can experience weariness from the press of daily demands and responsibilities. This press of school, according to Humberman (1983), draws teachers' attention to a short-term perspective, limits meaningful interaction with peers, exhausts energy, and limits time for reflection. People are reluctant to even discuss anything new or different, regardless of its value, in order to avoid adding to this press.

Here are some ways to address this issue:

Having staff being involved in exploring the problem, learning about it, and planning first steps assures other staff that those who "live the press" will account for it in any proposed change. Make sure that staff know how the problem is being addressed and who is involved in that process.

Create time during the school day for at least a small group of people to meet. Tacking on extra meetings at the end of the day will add to the weariness.

Provide some amenities for meeting times: snacks, a comfortable room, an offsite location, etc.

Acknowledge the press in your discussions without letting it determine decisions. The press can influence the pace of change or the amount of change being implemented.

Make it clear to staff to that all decisions are subject to modification or amendment. Include specific dates and times when staff will reconvene to evaluate how things are going. Staff can commit to short-term change open to modification much more easily than they can to a perceived permanent change.

3. "Path Persistence" or Old Habits Die Hard

Routines are necessary for structure and order but can also decrease staff sensitivity to new issues or topics. This is also related to "path persistence," that is, doing something a certain way just because it has always been done that way.

Here are some strategies to consider in addressing this reason:

For some staff, any change, for any reason, is a loss of something. Acknowledge this upfront. Don't pretend otherwise.

Let people know that the change can be discussed and evaluated along the way. Let everyone know that anyone can signal a time-out to discuss how things are going.

Give people the option, if possible, of not changing. Let staff who are comfortable with the change try things out and share their experiences with others.

4. Increased Pressure on Teachers to Perform With Their Evaluations Now Being Tied to Test Scores

People who are under siege are reluctant to do anything new. Teachers are "under siege" in many ways. There is less respect toward the teaching profession in the eyes of the public. Many educators are angry and resentful about the criticism directed toward them.

Schwartz and Sharpe (2010) explain it this way: "People can be put in institutional settings . . . that can discourage emotions like empathy and encourage other emotions like fear, embarrassment and anxiety about pleasing superiors" (p. 79).

Consider the following strategies:

Use the moral purpose and obligation connected to keeping students safe to remind teachers of who they are and why they do what they do. Don't let public perceptions of who they are affect how they do their job.

Discuss how preventive and positive approaches to bullying demonstrate to the public that staff do care about all the needs of students.

The process of committing to bullying prevention and planning the school's strategy is a great way to bring parents and teachers together. This teamwork is an opportunity for parents to see educators in action. These actions can contradict many of negative images of teachers in the media.

Do not use guilt or the threat of being blamed for some future tragedy and potential lawsuits as a way to get staff support for bullying prevention. Teachers need to be affirmed, and their commitment to students has to be acknowledged. The urgency for addressing the problem shouldn't stem from fear but rather from wanting to improve the school community for everyone.

5. Change and Anxiety

As Kegan and Lahey (2009) state, "It is not change that causes anxiety; it is the feeling that we are without defenses in the presence of what we see as danger that causes anxiety" (p. 49). For teachers, that danger is often the fear of failure or appearing to be incompetent in the eyes of others. This is particularly true if the change requires teachers to do something that might expose them as incompetent or place them in a situation where they might feel vulnerable.

Edmondson and Nembhard (2009) offer some strategies to address this reason:

- Make sure that resources are available for professional development for learning new skills if teachers are being asked to do something new and different.
- Have staff work in teams where the individuals trust each other and will help each other.
- Acknowledge your own apprehension and anxiety about the proposed changes. A staff's insecurity is lessened when the expectation is just to try rather than to perform immediately at a certain level of competence.

PRIMING: PREPARING THE SCHOOL COMMUNITY TO COMMIT TO BULLYING PREVENTION

A school leader can do and say things differently that influence the readiness of staff to consider certain ideas, which they might otherwise dismiss or reject. There are many changes that school leaders can make in their own behavior and leadership style that can create a greater receptivity to bullying prevention, when it is ultimately presented as a topic to the staff.

Here are some ways of priming or preparing a staff for bullying prevention:

The blind spot activities in Chapter 1 can be done without connection to the topic of bullying. They involve interesting ideas and concepts related to learning in general.

Devote some time to each faculty meeting to discuss ideas and concepts outside the typical list of agenda items. This sends a message about what a school leader values.

Distribute short, thought provoking articles or chapters of a book that will stimulate interesting discussion. This helps get staff ready to think about things that are not currently problems or issues. These readings and discussions can later provide a reference and context for discussions related to keeping students safe and ready to learn.

Ask for help in planning faculty meetings so that they are faculty meetings and not principal meetings. Involve staff in picking short articles or video clips on intriguing topics for the meetings. If this is too radical a change, start by having even ten minutes of the meeting devoted to small-group professional discussion.

Try to have individual, informal conversations with staff where you can share your thoughts and solicit their reactions. This can give you an assessment of how people think about topics. It will also give the staff an opportunity to think about topics they have never thought about prior to any group meeting.

Make use of videos that present topics not directly related to bullying prevention but to learning and education in general. TEDTalks is a great website with free downloadable fifteen- to twenty-minute talks by excellent speakers.

If you haven't used shared decision making on meaningful issues in your school, don't use bullying prevention as a place to start. Learn to work as a team with problems or issues with less impact on the school. Invite some people who are typically the greatest resisters to change to help with the group.

Don't be afraid to ask for help on a problem you are facing. State what your concerns are, what you have done so far about it, and where staff could help. Shared ownership of the problem leads to shared leadership in addressing the problem.

Things to Remember as You Start This Change Process

There is an understandable tendency to address the problem with a quick or step-by-step plan that will take care of the problem and allow the school to get back to business as usual. Bullying in schools is a complex problem that is far reaching in its implications and impact on the school environment. Any successful approach will require time, knowledge, teamwork, and ongoing monitoring. Even successful efforts will be filled with stress, uncertainty, and doubt. A school leader will also have these feelings while at the same time helping to navigate staff through them.

The first chapters explain two key elements often overlooked in bullying prevention efforts. The issues of the blind spot and moral purpose and obligation, when recognized and understood as necessary parts of any effective bullying prevention approach, can provide a strong and lasting foundation to all subsequent efforts.

Since every school is different, and the course and timeline of bullying prevention efforts will vary from school to school, school leaders can get lost, sidetracked, and discouraged, despite their best efforts. School leaders need to accept this as part of the process of change and stay optimistic and confident in themselves and their staff.

Things to Remember: Keeping Your Bearings on the Journey

As a school leader, give the benefit of the doubt to staff when it comes to commitment and moral purpose. It is better to act on the positive assumption that staff do care and be proved wrong than act on the negative assumption and be proved right.

A school leader's job is not to create the moral purpose and obligation, or "pull it out" of staff, but rather to clear a path and create a safe place for it to emerge on its own.

Staff can help each other with this task. It is not the school leader's job to change the school but rather to create the conditions where staff can influence and support each other to change what needs to be changed in the school.

For some staff, their moral purpose lies close to the surface and will spring up at any hint that it is needed. They are just waiting to be asked and will embrace being empowered to act on such a problem.

For others, it rests just below the surface and needs the prompting of peers and the safety of emerging on its own terms to come out.

For some, the moral purpose and obligation is buried pretty deep and might be forgotten; it might take a very long time to come out. For these individuals, the best-case scenario would be that they refrain from actively blocking the actions of others in addressing the problem. As others become more invested and engaged in the effort to make the school a safer place, the influence and impact of those who resist become less and less of a factor in the change process.

A staff's moral commitment to addressing this problem does not happen dramatically but is a process that takes time. School leaders need to get the process started and point it in the right direction.

A school leader's passion and values are keys to setting direction and communicating priority. A leader, however, has to respect those who are not yet at the same level of commitment and passion.

Express to staff not just hope and confidence but a sense of inevitability for making school a safer and more supportive environment for all students.

When in doubt, remind yourself and your colleagues about what really matters: having even one student walk through the school day a little less afraid and more hopeful than the day before.

SUMMARY

- School staff care and want to keep every student safe, but not all students know that, and it is crucial that they do. Staff need to advertise their caring to students. That is what bullying prevention is really all about.
- A school's staff moral purpose and obligation is present, but sometimes, for various reasons, it can be dormant.
- There are several reasons why it lies dormant. A school leader needs to know these reasons and can do many things to help moral purpose and obligation emerge.
- There are many activities or decisions a school leader can make that appear unrelated to bullying prevention but prime the staff for it later on.
- Effective bullying prevention is not a product but a process that happens over time. School leaders need to know this and know their role in the process. They can refer to certain key points about the process to keep themselves on track and encouraged.

ACTIVITIES TO STRENGTHEN MORAL COMMITMENT AND PURPOSE

ACTIVITY 1: PERSONAL MISSION STATEMENT— "WHAT'S YOUR SENTENCE?"

Purpose

The purpose is to provide an opportunity to personally reflect on values and accomplishments tied to the role of educator.

Content

Present the short two-minute video called *Two Questions That Can Change Your Life* (Pink, 2010b). It can be found on the websites danpink. com, vimeo.com, and YouTube (http://www.youtube.com/watch?v=0-MYeEb3eoE). The video presents the scenario of Clare Booth Luce telling JFK, "A great man is a sentence." She thought he was trying to do too many things and needed to focus on fewer and clearer goals. An example of a sentence for Abraham Lincoln would be "He freed the slaves and won the Civil War."

The video asks the viewers, "What is your sentence?" and gives examples from different careers, for example, "He taught generations of students to read." The second question is "Was I better today than yesterday?" The video states that, if you combine the two questions, you will find your true motivation for your work.

Procedure

The staff should sit in small groups while watching the video. Your presentation does not have to be tied to bullying prevention. You can just say you found an interesting video to share and talk about.

Show the video. Ask staff to write down their initial reaction to it. After giving them time to reflect, they can each share briefly their reaction. Each group could select one to two common reactions of the members and then share them with the whole group at the end.

Ask staff to think about what their sentence would be. This is more of a homework assignment since it could be difficult to share this in public so soon after seeing the video.

Follow-up

Ask staff to share anonymously their sentence on paper and then compile the sentences on a sheet and share them at a future time.

If staff are willing, they could share their sentence at the next staff meeting. As the school leader, you should strongly consider sharing your sentence.

ACTIVITY 2: COLLECTIVE MISSION STATEMENT— GIVING AND RECEIVING

Purpose

The purpose is to reflect on the personal experiences of giving and receiving with individuals. Use those positive experiences to reflect on the type of school they want to have.

Content

Have staff reflect on and share personal experiences related to helping and caring. This will help them discover positive connections with each other they might not have known. They can use these experiences to think about the type of school they want to have.

Procedure

Version 1: Ask staff to personally reflect on a time when they felt they helped someone who really needed help. This can be in or out of school. Have them write down the basic information of the situation. Answer the following two questions: How did the person feel about the help you gave? How did you feel about the help you gave?

After staff have had time to reflect, they can briefly share with the others in their small group. Designate someone as a recorder and a reporter.

After everyone has shared, the recorder jots down common elements of what was shared. After the group reviews these common elements, the reporter briefly shares two to three common elements with the whole group.

Version 2: Follow the same procedure, but this time, ask people to reflect on a time when they received help or support in a time of need.

End Product (you can do versions 1 and 2 or just one of them.)

Ask the group to review the common elements of the helping situation and how that applies to their school. Translate the personal experiences everyone has had into common experiences for members of the community.

Ask each group to complete one of the following sentences (you can design your own sentence stem to fit your school):

School is (or should be) a place where _____.

School is (or should be) a place where staff _____ and students _____.

Have the recorder write the sentence on a piece of chart paper and post it on the wall.

After all the sheets have been posted, staff can do a gallery walk: invite them to walk around the room and read each group's sentence.

Following the walk, each group could have a brief discussion about what they saw. Give staff an opportunity to volunteer their thoughts to the whole group.

ACTIVITY 3: "THINK OF ONE"—WITNESSING AN ACT OF BULLYING NORMALLY NOT SEEN

Purpose

It gives staff an opportunity to see an act of bullying that is not seen and share their thoughts and feelings about it.

Content

This would be an excellent activity to do as a follow-up to the Invisible Gorilla activity from Chapter 1. It uses a video clip taken as part of the research of Dr. Wendy Craig (2007) from the University of Toronto. Her research used hundreds of hours of video taken by a concealed camera of students during outdoor recess. A short segment of the video was featured on the *20/20* program with John Stossel (Goodman, 2002). The DVD version can be purchased or viewed on YouTube at www.youtube.com/watch?v=gSh2uBM2cSA&feature=youtu.be. The entire segment featured on this program lasts about seven to ten minutes. There is one scene in particular where a solitary student has a toy ripped from his hand by a group of students.

Procedure

Show the video clip featuring the playground scenes. Have the staff sit in small groups. Give a minute for individual reflection and then have each member share responses to the scene. Ask staff how this relates to the blind spot concept. Keep the discussion open-ended to allow people to express feelings without tying it to specific ideas for addressing the problem.

ACTIVITY 4: "WHAT GETS IN THE WAY"—REFLECTING ON WHY PEOPLE DON'T ACT

Purpose

Give staff an opportunity to reflect on the barriers to taking action on serious problems.

Content

Use a TEDTalks video (about seven minutes long) by Dave Meslin called *Antidote to Apathy* (TEDxToronto 2010), available at www.youtube.com/watch?v=LuHNVYW4tW0. In this video, he attributes apathy not to people's insensitivity but rather to what gets in the way of people acting. It discusses issues similar to the ones described in this chapter. Since the issue of commitment or apathy is a sensitive one to address directly, this video raises questions about our society's culture and how many aspects of the culture work against people working for positive change.

Procedure

Have staff view the video in small groups and follow a similar sequence of time for individual reflection, uninterrupted sharing, and then, group discussion.

That can be as far as the activity goes or you can decide to take it step farther and ask them to discuss the barriers to change that they see in the school community. Each group could be asked to recommend one action that the school community could take to increase people's commitment and energy toward improving the school community.

OUTCOMES

1. Staff are treated as thinking and caring people who do and can make a difference in the lives of children. This counters the prevailing concepts of teachers being the problem rather than the key people in the solution.

2. It presents the problem of bullying prevention as being connected to larger issues of climate, culture, and community.

3. Staff can explore issues in a safe way without any direct expectation for making changes in the school. The activities can provide the necessary food for thought to prepare staff for future discussions on the topic of bullying prevention.

3

How We See It Is How We Solve It

"Two roads diverged in the wood, and I—
I took the one less traveled by,
And that has made all of the difference."

—Robert Frost, "The Road Not Taken"

At the conclusion of a workshop I conducted on leadership for bullying prevention, one principal asked me: "If we establish a bullying prevention program in our district, won't we be announcing to the public that we have a problem with bullying?" I was a little taken aback by the question, for I assumed that bullying was an acknowledged problem in every school, but I responded, "Yes, but so does every district; at least you can say you are doing something about it." My answer didn't seem to relieve his anxiety.

On another occasion, after a similar workshop, a principal with an exasperated look on his face raised his hand and said, "So just tell me now, what do I need to do?" Because I had just spent two hours explaining "what to do," I was again taken aback but replied, "You are doing it. You invested your time and energy to learn more about this problem." He looked even more exasperated; I did not give him what he came looking for.

I was caught off guard by the two questions because those principals and I had come to that moment having walked down totally different roads, or ways of viewing the problem. Our perspectives colored and influenced all of our experiences with the problem: it made all the difference in how we looked for solutions, and then, how we understood and evaluated them.

CHOICE GIVES US A BETTER CHANCE

Our perception of problems becomes so ingrained in us that "we live inside them. We do not 'have them'; they 'have us'" (Kegan & Lahey, 2001, p. 6). When most people look at a problem, they are not aware that they see it through a *lens* or a perspective that influences their understanding of it. To avoid being caught in our perspective, we need to

- know that there are different ways of seeing problems
- articulate and describe what those different perspectives are

Heifetz and Linsky (2004) have proposed that there are two types of problems: technical and adaptive. The two principals mentioned above viewed the problem of bullying as a technical problem and expected a response to match that perspective. I viewed bullying as an adaptive problem, and all of my recommendations were based on that perspective. These two basic ways of viewing problems to a large extent determine all subsequent decisions and actions related to them. School leaders need to know they have a choice in what road to take: there is more than one way to view a problem.

Two Main Types of Problems

Technical Problems

Technical problems can usually be fixed, corrected, or controlled with solutions that have been used successfully with similar problems. These problems sometimes require expert knowledge from outside sources. They can be figured out, thereby restoring the status quo and improving the functioning of the organization.

When technical problems are resolved, they bring order and predictability to situations that were causing disruptions and distractions to the normal routines, activities, or events of an organization. These problems are often viewed as nuisances. Most people in the organization are happy to see them resolved, regardless of who does it (Heifetz, Grashow, & Linsky, 2009).

In schools, most of these problems are ultimately the responsibility of the principal. These are examples of technical problems:

- The school lunch line taking too much time
- Fire drills not running smoothly

- Bus schedules that are out of sync, so buses arrive at different times
- Legal issues regarding special education compliance
- Students running in the halls

Adaptive Problems

Adaptive problems have no clear cut or easy solutions. They cannot depend on the knowledge of experts to be solved. Solving them does not mean eliminating them. They are social problems that involve people's needs and interactions. These problems require ongoing attention and analysis.

People must learn about adaptive problems and work together to find new and different ways of addressing them. Solving adaptive problems involves changing people's hearts and minds (Heifetz et al., 2009).

These problems require leadership, not just management, since everyone in the school needs to change in some way. Leaders set the direction for the change process but rely on the commitment of others to create the needed change. The process of learning and working together changes the entire school for the better.

These are examples of adaptive problems:

- Improving collaboration among teachers
- Increasing parent involvement and participation in the school
- Developing a new teacher evaluation system
- Making sure students continue to read over the summer break
- Increasing student attendance

Schools are filled with both technical and adaptive problems. An effective leader knows how to accurately identify problems and match the right type of approach to the right type of problem. Applying a technical solution to an adaptive problem usually is not effective.

BULLYING: TECHNICAL OR ADAPTIVE PROBLEM?

There is common agreement that bullying is a problem in schools. Judging by the different approaches schools take in addressing bullying, there is no common agreement on whether it is a technical problem or an adaptive problem.

Chart 3.1 illustrates the differences in how bullying is understood and addressed depending on the two basic perspectives on school problems.

Technical and adaptive problems are not mutually exclusive of each other; many complex problems require a variety of strategies that are both technical and adaptive. Chart 3.1 highlights these differences to illustrate

Chart 3.1   Bullying and the Two Basic Perspectives on School Problems

Bullying	Technical View	Adaptive View
Nature of the problem	Can and should be fixed Similar to any other inappropriate behavior If it was learned, it can be unlearned. Discipline problem Problems get in the way of the real purpose of school (learning subject matter), and they should be fixed or eliminated.	Unacceptable but related to human development and interaction Very different from other inappropriate behaviors because of its social nature and the power differential involved Educational problem Problems are opportunities for learning and source of creativity/learning.
Approaches	Effective disciplinary procedures that work for other inappropriate behaviors need to be applied. Finding the right way to prevent and intervene based on antecedents and consequences is the key.	Disciplinary procedures alone are not sufficient for dealing with the unique elements of problem related to power and social status. A comprehensive approach is more effective and should address social and emotional learning.
Students	Need to know bullying is wrong and inappropriate in relation to rules Can be reinforced to be appropriate and follow rules Need to know consequences for bullying. Deterrence is a critical element for changing behavior.	Need to know bullying is wrong and why it is wrong. Need to know how bullying affects others. This is a very important part of changing behavior. Are wired to be empathetic and responsible. A key element of change is tapping into that.
Staff	Must be on board with consistent interventions and consequences Individual judgmental and discretion can be detrimental.	Need to know that bullying is a relationship/power issue. This knowledge is critical to their effectiveness. Relationships with students imply that each situation is different and requires judgment and discretion.

(Continued)

Chart 3.1 (Continued)

Bullying	Technical View	Adaptive View
School climate and culture	Will improve once bullying behavior is under control School can return to normal functioning.	Must be examined as contributing factor to the problem Changing relationships critical to addressing underlying issues of bullying
Role of leadership	Clearly define the problem. Find appropriate solution based on established procedures effective for other inappropriate behaviors. Ensure that all staff are on board and consistent.	Understand the problem and its relationship to larger issues and values. Change how people think and feel about the problem. Work with staff to find unique solutions.
Outcome/ Goal	Solve the problem of bullying to allow the school to function as it is supposed to. School will be a better place because the problem is under control.	Solve the problem of bullying by changing the way people interact with each other. The school will be a better place as a result of working together on the problem.

how each perspective dramatically affects the manner of addressing the problem. There can be serious conflicts among staff because of differing perspectives on problems. Unless staff are aware of these differences, they will be talking a different "language" to each other without knowing it.

DEFAULT MODE OF MOST SCHOOLS

Problems have a bad reputation in schools. They are viewed as obstacles to learning. Most teachers would like a problem-free classroom where the students are attentive and comply with all of the rules. In this type of classroom, they could *really* teach and the students could *really* learn. Many of the interventions that are used in schools today are designed with the elimination of problems as an ultimate goal so that schools can function as they are meant to.

If there are going to be problems, technical ones are better to have. School leaders are skilled in solving technical problems, and with experience, they become even more skilled. Technical problems have numerous solutions. A skillful leader relies on experience to pick the best solution to fix the problem and has the skills to implement that solution. Fritz (1984) summarizes this initial approach to solving problems:

> A common rule of thumb in life is to have a formula about how things should work, so that if you learn the formula, you will always know what to do. From a reactive-response orientation, this notion is very appealing, because with such a formula you would hypothetically be prepared to respond appropriately to any situation. (p. 73)

There is an understandable resistance to see bullying as anything other than a technical problem. As explained in Chapter 1, bullying is a problem school staff mistakenly believe is under control. There is no reason to try another way if you think that what you are doing works.

I empathize with the two principals who attended my workshops. One was hoping that the problem of bullying didn't exist or at least wanted parents to think that it didn't. The other principal came looking for a solution and only heard that the problem was an even harder one to solve than he had previously realized. For them, attending my presentation was like taking their car in for an oil change and being told that they needed an engine overhaul. I was only making their professional lives even harder by telling them there was a problem and that the problem was not a technical one; it was much more complex and difficult than they had realized. I was considered the *expert* with the knowledge to solve a technical problem, and I came up short in their minds.

BULLYING IS AN ADAPTIVE PROBLEM

Bullying is a complex adaptive problem. It involves how people interact and treat each other. Students bully other students for many reasons, some related to social status and popularity, but it is clear that bullying impacts every student and the entire school climate.

Stopping bullying depends on caring and skilled people working together. There is no blueprint or recipe that can be universally applied to addressing the problem. Bullying manifests itself differently in different environments, so each school must collect reliable data and develop a unique set of interventions and initiatives tailored to its particular culture.

Bullying does not occur just in schools that are in trouble or need to be turned around. It happens in the best schools where a high percentage of students graduate and go on to college. These schools have competent and caring teachers and high levels of parent involvement. Bullying is not a by-product of dysfunctional schools; it occurs in every school. It can be difficult for school staff to accept the results of school surveys on bullying. The data don't match their perceptions. It adds another "serious" problem to their checklist of problems. They will often respond to the data by questioning if students understood the definition of bullying or say that students are not really reliable sources of information. Accepting the results would undermine their sense of competence in being able to meet one of their most important responsibilities of keeping students feeling safe and ready to learn. Accepting the results would also mean that the strategies they have been using *do not work*.

THE TECHNICAL SOLUTION THAT'S NOT COMPLETE

Traditional school discipline policy and procedures rely on clear rules and consequences consistently applied by all staff when inappropriate behavior occurs. This approach can be effective for many of the challenging behaviors that students demonstrate. Bullying, however, is a different type of behavior that is more complex and is influenced by many factors that do not lend themselves to this type of control. Perhaps the strongest argument against traditional school discipline approaches is that they haven't worked so far in schools. Students typically report much higher rates of bullying than most staff believe is possible. Staff often think that disciplinary procedures are sufficient for controlling bullying, but the data (when they are collected) tell a different story.

SUMMARY: WHAT SCHOOL LEADERS NEED TO KNOW AND DO

"Leaders are continuously faced with problems, many of which have to be quickly resolved. That's the managerial side of leadership . . . Leaders can invite every teacher and administrator to have a learning relationship with at least one good problem . . . The ones we can learn from are the ones we don't solve as much as they 'solve us.' They change us . . . That is particularly important in schools, which are after all first and foremost about learning."

—Robert Kegan (As cited in Sparks, 2002)

- Technical problems can be solved through the knowledge of experts. Traditional solutions can be used effectively to solve these problems. Managerial skills are effective in solving technical problems.
- Adaptive problems are primarily social and cannot be permanently fixed. There are no existing solutions to apply; new ways of thinking and acting are needed to effectively address them. Leadership is needed to mobilize people to face these problems and develop creative solutions to them.

- These two perspectives influence how people think and feel about bullying.
- Staff need to learn about these perspectives and discover what their perspective is on bullying.
- Most schools have a default mode of putting all problems into the technical category and using traditional approaches, such as disciplinary procedures, to address them.
- The source of staff conflict and resistance to addressing bullying often stems from the lack of awareness that there are two perspectives on problems.
- Knowing why bullying is an adaptive problem is an important first step in the process in mobilizing staff to face and address the problem.
- There are certain strategies that lend themselves to a certain type of problem. Technical type solutions alone cannot sufficiently meet the challenges and complexity of the adaptive problem of school bullying.
- It may be very difficult for staff to let go of technical tried and true strategies and develop adaptive ones that require time and collaboration.
- Leadership is essential to the process of changing people's hearts and minds. This change is essential for success in facing adaptive problems.

ACTIVITIES ON PERSPECTIVE AND PROBLEMS

The following activities are designed to get staff to think about problems. Many of them use video clips that can be found on YouTube. The focus is less on the content of problems and more on staff's thoughts and feelings about problems. The activities should also introduce the two main categories of problems and how they differ. The activities will show rather than tell about the concepts presented in this chapter.

ACTIVITY 1: THE BROKEN ESCALATOR

Purpose

The purpose of this activity is to reflect on the nature of problems and how people react to them and to introduce the concept of technical problems.

Content

Present a short video available on YouTube (www.youtube.com/watch?v=47rQkTPWW2I), titled *Broken Escalator* (Piper, 2006), of two people on an escalator in a sparsely populated shopping mall. In the video, there is a businessman with briefcase and cell phone and a woman who has been shopping. All is going fine until the escalator comes to an abrupt halt with the two people stranded in the middle of it. They both bemoan their situation, and the businessman immediately uses his cell phone to get help but is unable to reach anyone. After shouting out for help, they give up. A good amount of time passes. Out of nowhere, an escalator repairman arrives on the lower escalator apparently coming to the rescue of repairing their broken one. The two stranded people are relieved and happy to finally have their problem fixed. As they watch the repairman use another escalator below them, their relief quickly vanishes when that escalator also stalls.

Procedure

Prior to showing the video: Ask staff to take thirty seconds to write down any/every word that comes into their head when they hear the word *problem*.

(*Warning*: Not everyone who watches this video immediately senses the absurdity of it, so you will hear some laughter at different moments from different people. Eventually, everyone quickly gets the absurdity of the situation.)

The staff should sit in small groups while watching the video. This does not have to be introduced as an activity related to bullying. It is about problems in general and could be applied to any problem.

Show the video. Ask staff to write down their immediate response to it without discussion. After they have had this time to reflect and respond, they can go around the group reading/sharing their initial response.

Guide Questions

Assign the roles of facilitator, recorder, reporter, and timekeeper to each group. Distribute a sheet with the following questions to each member of the group:

How did the two people on the escalator react to their situation?

Have you ever experienced a similar problem when you were totally dependent on the expert help of someone? How did that feel?

Describe a situation where you initially thought that the answer to the problem was from some outside expert but later found out that the expert wasn't needed.

Describe a problem in school where you worked with someone to solve a problem that you couldn't have solved alone. How did that feel?

Review the list of words associated with the word *problem*. What are the connections between the list and your response to the video?

What problems at school do you think require expert knowledge to solve them effectively? Where does the expert knowledge come from: within the school or outside the school?

Each small group can choose the questions that they want to discuss. Have the reporter share two to three key discussion points (limit the sharing to no more than two minutes per group).

Whole-Group Processing

After small-group discussion, open up the discussion to the whole group to see if there is anything else to share or contribute. Following the whole-group discussion, ask each small group to write down one or two "takeaways" (statements, ideas worth remembering) from the meeting and write them down on an index card. Later on, have the takeaways compiled and distributed to staff. This list can be used at a subsequent meeting.

Introduce the definition of technical problems. Provide staff with a definition of it. Discuss what problems in a school are technical.

ACTIVITY 2: RESPONDING TO AN URGENT PROBLEM—APOLLO 13

Purpose

The purpose of this activity is to reflect on the nature of problems and how people react to them. Introduce the concept of adaptive problems.

Content

Present a scene from the movie *Apollo 13* (Howard, 1995), available on YouTube at www.youtube.com/watch?v=hLZZ_y1xdJg. Use the scene where Gene Kranz, played by Ed Harris, presents the crisis to a skeptical staff (this scene is approximately one hour and seven minutes into the film). He accepts their technical advice and their misgivings about being able to use systems that were not designed for the problem they are facing. After listening, he states the goal: "failure is not an option." He also empowers his team to experiment and create new ways of achieving their goal. This video illustrates the importance of reframing the problem, setting goals, listening to all points of view, working together, and creating new solutions. (Video clips from this film can highlight and demonstrate many different aspects of decision making, leadership, teamwork, and mindset.)

Procedure

Prior to showing the video, ask staff to write down whatever comes to mind when they hear the word *leadership*.

Staff should sit in small groups while watching the video. This does not have to be introduced as an activity related to bullying. It is about problems in general and could apply to any problem.

Show the video. Ask staff to write down their immediate response to it without discussion. After they have had this time to reflect and respond, they can each share within the small group.

Guide Questions

Assign the roles of facilitator, recorder, reporter, and timekeeper to each group. Distribute a sheet with the following questions to each member of the group:

How did the members of mission control feel when they discovered the problem?

Describe the leadership style demonstrated by the Ed Harris character. Was it effective or not? Explain you answer.

What was the relationship between Ed Harris and the staff? How do you think they felt about him? How did he feel about them?

Describe at least two essential elements of his leadership style. What exactly did he say and do to demonstrate that style?

What role did emotion play in solving the problem?

Describe two lessons that the staff learned as a result of this experience.

Are there any similarities between the problems that the staff faced in the movie and what school staff face every day? Explain.

Think of a problem at school that required creativity and teamwork. Describe how that problem was addressed. What were the results of the problem solving? How did it affect how future problems were addressed?

Review the list of words associated with the word *leadership*. What are the connections between the list and your response to the video?

Is failure not an option in schools? Explain your answer.

Each small group can choose the questions that they want to discuss. Have the reporter share two to three key discussion points (limit the sharing to no more than two minutes per group).

Whole-Group Processing

After each group sharing, open up the discussion to the whole group to see if there is anything else to share or contribute. Following the whole-group discussion, ask each small group to write down one or two takeaways from the meeting on an index card. Later on, have the takeaways compiled and distributed to staff. This list can be used at a subsequent meeting.

Introduce the definition of adaptive problems. Provide staff with it. Discuss what problems in a school are adaptive. How do they differ from technical problems?

ACTIVITY 3: ONE FOR TWO (TECHNICAL FOR ADAPTIVE)

Purpose

The purpose of this activity is to reflect on what can happen when an adaptive problem is only addressed with a technical solution.

Content

Present the *I Love Lucy*, episode "Job Switching" (Asher, 1952). A video clip available on YouTube (www.youtube.com/watch?v=8NPzLBSBzPI) shows Lucy and Ethel as newly hired employees at a chocolate candy factory. They are given instructions on how to do the job of wrapping each piece of candy as it comes down a conveyer belt. At first, the job appears easy, but as the belt speeds up, they soon become overwhelmed and resort to various methods of wrapping the candy, none of which succeed.

Procedure

Prior to showing the video, ask staff to reflect on a time they felt frustration while trying to solve a problem. Ask them to briefly jot down why they were frustrated.

The staff should sit in small groups while watching the video. This does not have to be introduced as an activity related to bullying. It is about problems in general and could apply to any problem.

Show the video. Ask staff to write down their immediate response to it without discussion. After they have had this time to reflect and respond, they can go around the group reading/sharing their initial response.

Guide Questions

Assign the roles of facilitator, recorder, reporter, and timekeeper to each group. Distribute a sheet with the following questions to each member of the group:

Describe Lucy's and Ethel's initial reaction to the job once the conveyer belt started to roll.

What did the boss do to make sure they met the expectations for the job?

How did they react when the conveyer belt went faster?

How did they respond when the boss returned? Explain.

Describe the relationship of the employees to the supervisor.

What could they have done to be more successful in getting the job done?

What prevented them from changing the basic setup of the job?

What was the boss's response to their work?

How does this work situation compare with your experiences in your job?

Why is the scene so funny?

Why would you consider the problem to be an adaptive one?

Develop an alternative strategy for getting the job done. Have the reporter briefly share their recommendations of improving job performance.

Whole-Group Processing

After each group sharing, open up the discussion to the whole group to see if there is anything else to share or contribute. Following the whole-group discussion, ask each small group to write down one or two take-aways from the meeting on an index card. Later on, have the takeaways compiled and distributed to staff. This list can be used at a subsequent meeting.

Discuss other possible situations where technical solutions are applied to adaptive problems.

ACTIVITY 4: TAKING INVENTORY

Purpose

The purpose of this activity is to reflect on problems in the school and determine if they are primarily technical ones or adaptive ones.

Content

This activity is designed for staff to share their perspective on current issues in the school. Staff should not start to discuss how to solve the problems but rather decide if they are adaptive or technical.

Procedure

Have one slip of paper for each person participating.
On half of the slips, write the word *technical*.
On the other half of the slips, write the word *adaptive*.

If there were forty people, half of the slips (twenty) would have the word *technical* and the other half (twenty) would have the word *adaptive*.

Number the "technical" slips for one half of the total number of people (one number on each slip); e.g., if there were forty people total, there should be twenty slips with the word *technical* numbered 1 to 20.

Number the "adaptive" slips for one half of the total number of people (one number on each slip); e.g., if there were forty people total, there should be twenty slips with the word *technical* numbered 1 to 20.

Distribute the slips randomly.

Tell the participants that, if their slip has the word *technical*, they should take a moment to think of a technical problem that they recall having; if they have the word *adaptive*, they should think of an adaptive problem that they recall having. They can briefly jot down the problem on their slip of paper.

After they have had time to do that, signal them to stand up and find the person with the matching number. Once they find their partner, they can begin to share with each other the problem that they wrote down on their slip. For example, someone with a technical slip no. 5 would find someone with an adaptive slip no. 5. They would form a pair and remain standing.

Partners can discuss why the problem is technical or adaptive. They can also discuss if the solutions applied to the problem have been a good fit.

The facilitator of the activity could record examples of technical problems and adaptive problems on a sheet of chart paper.

OUTCOMES

1. These activities should help staff reflect on the type of problems that schools face. If staff are aware that there are different types of problems and that each type requires a different response, they should be more open to addressing the problem of bullying.

2. Show staff that they can engage in conversations about problems without automatically looking for solutions.

3. Encourage reflection and professional conversations as critical elements in the change process.

4. Reframe the concept of *problem* with a positive context: as an opportunity for learning.

4

Changing Your Mind(set)

"Problem solving is taking action to make something go away; creating is taking action to have something come into being."

—Robert Fritz (2010)

NO WAY OUT

Many principals have presented me with the following scenario:

> *"I receive a complaint from parents about their child being bullied. They share information about who did the bullying and when and where it occurred. I take their information and say that I will investigate and get back to them. When I speak to the student accused of bullying, he denies it. I can't find any evidence that it happened because no adult witnessed it, and there are no bystanders who report seeing or hearing it. I get a sense that the complaint is true, but it is one student's word against another student. There is not much I can do at that point. I get back to the parents who made the complaint and indicate that there is nothing I can do because I can't find any evidence of bullying. The parents are not satisfied with my response and are angry that I am not doing anything about the problem. What can I do?"*

These principals sincerely wish there was something more that they could do. They do not like having to tell any parent that there is little to be done regarding the safety of their child. They are doing their job in a responsible way and being as fair as possible, but they don't see any other options, and they know that their efforts are coming up short.

I wish that I could give them *the* answer that would solve this problem, but I can't. They are looking for a different way to make traditional discipline work more effectively. They are looking for answers to these questions: How to get the evidence needed? How to get the student to admit to the bullying? What is the right consequence that will effectively deter most students from bullying? They are not asking "Is there a different way?"

This situation they are in is similar to trying to build something with only a hammer and discovering that the hammer isn't getting the job done. A hammer might be the only tool they have ever used. They have been trained in using the hammer and have been successful with tasks that only require a hammer. When the hammer fails to get the job done, they look for other ways to use the hammer or to find a different type of hammer. It would also be hard for them to let go of the hammer completely.

If traditional school discipline is like a hammer, the problem of bullying is the task that needs more than a hammer. It requires a variety of tools or approaches that work together to get the job done. Before school leaders can let go of the hammer/discipline and consider additional tools to use, they have to change how they see the problem and understand why more than one tool is needed to be effective. They need to change their mindset toward the problem of bullying. This is not easy to do, but it is the only way out of the frustrating scenario in which they too often find themselves.

MINDSET: DEFINITION AND EXAMPLE

> *"A mindset is a set of assumptions, methods or notations held by one or more people or groups of people which is so established that it creates a powerful incentive within these people or groups to continue to adopt or accept prior behaviors, choices, or tools. This phenomenon of cognitive bias is also sometimes described as mental inertia, 'groupthink', or a paradigm', and it is often difficult to counteract its effects upon analysis and decision making processes."*
>
> —"Mindset," (n.d.)

Through her research, Carol Dweck (2006) has described two main mindsets for learning: *a fixed mindset* and *a growth mindset*. In the fixed mindset, people attribute success to an innate ability or talent. In the growth mindset, people attribute success to the effort and time devoted to learning or mastering a skill or completing a task. These two mindsets determine how individuals approached tasks and their persistence when faced with a challenge.

Those with a fixed mindset tended to avoid challenging tasks. Having difficulty or struggling with a problem was an indication to them that they weren't smart. They would also be concerned that others would interpret their struggle as an indication that they weren't smart.

Those with a growth mindset persisted on challenging tasks. For them, having difficulty had no bearing on whether they were smart or not. They focused on their efforts on figuring out the problem or challenge. Their success was dependent on the effort and energy they devoted to their work, which resulted in their growth over time.

Mindsets color almost every decision, action, and evaluation related to a problem. A student's mindset and subsequent actions are highly influenced by the teacher's verbal feedback. If a teacher offered praise that attributed success to innate ability, "You're so smart," the student seemed to develop a fixed mindset. If a teacher offered feedback on the student's effort and persistence, "You really put a lot of effort into that," the student usually developed a growth mindset.

Although Dweck's work focused on a mindset for learning, the concept of mindset can be applied to many other aspects of education. Different mindsets lead to different opportunities and options for addressing problems. The current (default) mindset on the problem of bullying in schools often presents limited options to school leaders when responding to complaints of bullying.

THE DEFAULT (CRIMINAL JUSTICE) MINDSET ON BULLYING

According to Heifetz, Grashow, and Linsky (2009), "organizations fall back on defaults because they are familiar and they have proved useful for explaining reality and solving problems in the past" (p. 64).

The default mindset for bullying in most schools is a criminal justice mindset. This mindset conceives of bullying as a technical problem that can be fixed with applying appropriate consequences to those students who bully. Traditional school discipline with an emphasis on rules and consequences is the typical approach used with all behavior problems, including bullying.

The traditional disciplinary approach used in schools mirrors that of the criminal justice system in the world outside of school. The criminal justice system consists of law enforcement where violations of laws are considered crimes. In this system, every crime must be proved in order for action to be taken against the person who committed the crime. Those who commit crimes face some punishment that is sufficiently negative to help deter future crimes. The scenario presented by the principals earlier in this chapter reflects the limits of the criminal justice mindset when it comes to bullying in schools.

Here is a typical sequence of events using the criminal justice mindset to address bullying:

Bullying is a crime because it is violation of the school rules (provided bullying is defined and there are school rules against it).

School officials must investigate any complaint of bullying.

They must have enough evidence to prove that the crime was committed.

Without corroborating testimony of witnesses, bullying cannot be proven. One person's word against another is not sufficient evidence.

If a crime was committed, consequences can be given to the person who bullied.

If a crime was not proven, there are few, if any, actions that can be taken.

This criminal justice mindset in a school environment severely limits the response to bullying. In school, bullying is a crime that is easy to commit, easy to deny, and hard to prove, yet it has very negative consequences on the lives of each member of the community. This mindset definitely handcuffs school leaders in what they can do about the problem. It also inadvertently contributes to the problem rather than prevents or reduces it. Bullying stays in the blind spot, under the radar, and more entrenched in the school.

EDUCATIONAL MINDSET ON BULLYING

As quoted in the foreword to *Zero Tolerance: Resisting the Drive for Punishment in Our Schools* (Ayers, Dohren, & Ayers, 2001), Marva Collins states that "an error means that a child needs help, not a reprimand or ridicule for doing something wrong."

An educational mindset is one that views bullying prevention as a complex challenge that requires changing the knowledge, skills, and attitudes of all members of the school community. An educational mindset directs all members of the school community to invest time and energy in improving how they treat each other, thereby, improving the climate of the school.

An educational mindset is the appropriate way to address the adaptive problem of bullying. Bullying is a violation of school rules, and more importantly, it is against the cultural and social norms of how people are supposed to treat each other. Students are in the process of learning and practicing behaviors that are consistent with these norms of behavior.

Any student is capable of bullying and can do so for many reasons. With an educational mindset, adults accept the responsibility for helping students gain the knowledge and skills necessary to deal with all aspects of bullying. Part of this responsibility includes setting limits and having

consequences for exceeding those limits. Traditional disciplinary procedures continue to play a role, but they are integrated into a more comprehensive and multifaceted approach reflective of an educational mindset.

School leaders and staff are educators, not law enforcement officials.
They are better equipped to work on the problem of bullying with an educational mindset than with a criminal justice mindset. Education works in
changing people for the better; it does not need to be set aside for social
and emotional issues. Chart 4.1 illustrates the key differences between the
two mindsets.

Chart 4.1   Criminal Justice and Educational Mindset Toward Bullying

Bullying: A Criminal Justice Mindset	Bullying: An Educational Mindset
Discipline alone is the main method of addressing the problem. Rules and consequences properly and consistently used should sufficiently address the problem.	Discipline is one part of a larger comprehensive approach with strong emphasis on climate and culture as key elements.
Responds to bullying primarily after it happens	Tries to prevent bullying by educating students about bullying and the socioemotional world of schools
Administrators are the ones responsible for dealing with bullying.	All staff need to be involved in addressing problem and promoting positive skills and attitudes.
Accepts status quo of the school environment	Assumes growth and change in the school environment as part of the solution
Primarily concerns perpetrator and target	Concerns everyone including bystanders
Event specific. Case opened and closed	Ongoing process of learning about how people treat each other
Most reports involve severe cases that have escalated over time.	Greater likelihood of minor incidents being reported
School leaders limited in responding and often on the defensive when not able to act	School leaders are key people in changing the culture and school climate.
Doesn't involve knowledge and skills needed to deal with the problem	Acknowledges that students need social and emotional skills

Bullying: A Criminal Justice Mindset	Bullying: An Educational Mindset
Ideally, violations should never happen.	Students are "works in progress" and learn through trial and error. Developmental issues must be understood.
Parents can think that the school doesn't care if the school is unable to prove who committed the crime of bullying and subsequently takes no action.	Parents are educated about the problem. They can see the school's commitment to addressing the problem even if a particular situation is unclear. Much can be said and done with students without an overreliance on consequences.
If students know that consequences are the main response, it decreases likelihood of bystanders reporting.	Students can be taught the importance of reporting and how it is a responsibility of everyone.
Goal of stopping bullying and returning to the status quo	Goal of preventing and reducing bullying and improving how people treat each other

Changing the mindset for effective bullying prevention would look like this:

From a *Criminal Justice* Mindset   to an   *Educational Mindset*

From a *Criminal Justice* Mindset to an *Educational* Mindset

The shift in mindset is from that of just eliminating a problem to a mindset of creating a better school, as articulated by the Massachusetts Department of Health's *Guide to Bullying Prevention*: "Schools where bullying is less likely to happen and, when it does, more likely to be corrected, are schools that promote caring, compassion, and sense of responsibility among students and staff" (Parker-Roerden, Rudewick, & Gorton, 2007, p. 33).

EDUCATIONAL MINDSET IN ACTION

Many people might be skeptical of trying a different approach because it is difficult to envision how it would actually work. For some, a different approach could be interpreted as being too lenient or not tough enough with the students who bully. Letting go of traditional discipline as the main solution to the problem of bullying could be seen as tantamount to doing nothing about the problem.

An educational mindset focuses on the social climate of the school, not just individual incidents of bullying. The work done to improve the climate and culture of a school affects the amount of bullying that occurs in the school. With a positive and trusting climate established, students are more likely to report the bullying that staff cannot see. The groundwork that is done to improve the school's culture and climate increases the range of options (including discipline) to address bullying in way that is consistent with the values and social norms of the school.

The following sequence illustrates an *educational mindset response*, in contrast to a *criminal justice/discipline only mindset* response:

Key Preexisting Conditions That Support a Response to Bullying (created by an educational mindset)

- Knowledge of the dynamics of bullying by all members of school community
- Bystanders knowing their role and responsibilities
- Clarification of school values on how people should be treated
- Strong message that bullying is inconsistent with those values
- Preventive efforts sending strong message that the school cares about the problem

An Outline of an Educational Mindset Response to a Complaint of Bullying

- Bullying is against the rules, and the students understand what it is and how it is also inconsistent with social norms and values.
- Although investigating complaints is a necessary part of the process, gathering sufficient evidence is not a prerequisite for responding and acting assertively.
- Even without enough evidence, a school leader can meet with the students involved and talk about what happened according to the student's role in the incident.
- The primary goal of discipline should be to help students learn from mistakes. Punishment is not always required for that learning to happen. School leaders can assert that bullying is unacceptable and

is against the rules and values of the school. There can be account-ability without an overreliance on consequences alone to address the problem.

- When *consequences* are not the *primary* and *the only* response to the incident, the school leader can keep the focus on the incident itself and the impact of it on the students involved and the school com-munity. The student who bullied is less likely to deny it to avoid certain punishment and is more open to accepting responsibility for it. This is especially true if that student trusts the school leader and feels connected to the school.
- If a student accepts responsibility and shows remorse for bullying, and it is not a chronic problem for that student, the school leader can use judgment to determine the appropriate response that will keep the bullied student safe and help the student who bullied to stop that behavior.
- Other actions can include closer monitoring of the students, check-ing in with the students involved on a regular basis, alerting staff to the problem, and providing additional training on social and emo-tional skills.
- Parents of the student who was bullied are more likely to support the school's actions if they think that the school does not view their child as a criminal. These parents need to see the school actions as helping and supporting their child. It is in the school's, the student's, and the parents' best interest to help that student learn from this mistake. If a consequence needs to be applied, in this context, paren-tal support of the school's action is more likely.
- Parents of the student who was bullied can be informed of a variety of actions that were taken in response to the complaint. This demon-strates that the school cares and does respond even if the crime of bullying was not proven.
- Parents of students who were bystanders can also be contacted. School leaders can ask them to echo and support what the school has been telling students about their responsibility to report bullying.

The educational mindset works by integrating the groundwork that has been done on bullying prevention with the response to an incident after it has happened. Individual interventions are more meaningful and effective if the students already know and understand the problem of bul-lying and how it affects others. Once an incident of bullying happens, it can't be undone, so the best outcome for any intervention is to increase the chances of it not happening again. The educational mindset does not accept or condone the act of bullying but does accept the responsibility of helping all students learn from their mistakes.

SUMMARY

- Effective school leaders not only must change their own mindset toward bullying, but they must begin the process that will change the mindsets of all members of the school community. This is an essential part of any effective bully prevention approach.
- Effective bully prevention requires leadership that moves people beyond just addressing that one problem. Effective bullying prevention involves a significant shift in how members of the school community think, feel, and act about the problem, and over time, it creates a positive change of the school's climate and culture.
- The concept of mindset can be applied to the issue of bullying prevention. A mindset is a set of implicit assumptions that affects a person or group of people's perception and interpretation of any experience or aspect of life.
- The predominant approach to the problem bullying in most schools is a criminal justice mindset. This mindset is compatible with traditional school discipline that relies on using consequences as a way of changing inappropriate behavior.
- A more accurate and effective mindset toward the problem of bullying is an educational mindset. This mindset includes school discipline as one part of a larger comprehensive approach to the problem. It relies on the collective learning of all members of the school community: understanding the problem and their role and responsibility in preventing and reducing it.
- Effective bullying prevention needs to address issues of school climate and culture. Schools need to increase the level of trust between students and staff. They also need to reflect in word and action the values of caring, compassion, respect, and trust.
- An educational mindset assumes that students can learn about bullying, and with adult guidance, make better choices in how they treat each other. With an educational mindset, there is an acknowledgement that many factors influence student behavior. Staff then have many options for preventing and reducing bullying and responding more effectively when it happens.

ACTIVITIES FOR "CHANGING YOUR MIND(SET)"

These activities are for staff to become familiar with the concept of mindset and how it affects perception, understanding, and reaction to a problem. Staff will discuss their own mindset for different aspects of education. After reflecting on their own mindset, they can discuss the difference between the criminal justice mindset and the educational mindset on the problem of bullying in schools.

ACTIVITY 1: MINDSET EXAMPLE—CAROL DWECK AND MINDSET EXPERIMENT

Purpose

The purpose is to see a mindset in action and how students respond differently to a task based on their mindset. Discuss implications of mindset on learning and how they interact with students.

Content

Show the video titled *Carol Dweck: The Effect of Praise on Mindsets* (vooktv, 2010), available on YouTube at www.youtube.com/watch?v=TTXrV0_3UjY. In this clip, students are given tasks to do with different types of feedback. The students demonstrate either reluctance or eagerness to do a different task depending on how they view the task. The perception of the task is highly influenced by the feedback given by the teacher after they had completed a simpler task.

Procedure

Prior to showing the video clip, ask staff to write down what the term *mindset* means to them. Ask them to write down an example of a mindset.

Staff should sit in small groups while viewing the video.

Show the video clip. Ask staff to write down their response to the clip and how this presentation of the concept of mindset compares with the one they wrote down. After the staff have had this opportunity to reflect, they can share with the rest of the group their reflections.

Guide Questions

Assign the roles of facilitator, recorder, reporter, and timekeeper for each small group.

Distribute a sheet with the following questions to each member of the group:

Have you observed anything similar to what you observed in the experiment?

What type of verbal feedback do you give your students?

How does it affect their mindset toward learning?

What are some other mindsets that students can have?

What are some mindsets that teachers have?

Can a mindset change or be changed? How?

Describe any experiences you have had with changing mindsets?

What implications do you see the research in mindsets having for our school?

Ask staff to respond to this statement by Carol Dweck (2006):

"When people believe their basic qualities can be developed, fail-ures may still hurt, but failures don't define them. And if abilities can be expanded—if change and growth are possible—then there are still many paths to success." (p. 39)

Each small group can choose the questions they want to discuss. Following this discussion, the reporter for each group can briefly share two to three of the ideas they discussed.

Whole-Group Processing

After each group has shared, open up the discussion to the whole group and invite general comments that people might want to share.

Present to the group that there can be a mindset toward how to approach the problem of bullying. Explain the criminal justice mindset and the educational mindset.

ACTIVITY 2: MINDSETS TOWARD BULLYING—CRIMINAL JUSTICE MINDSET COMPARED TO EDUCATIONAL MINDSET

Purpose

The purpose is to apply the concept of mindset based to the problem of bullying and contrasting two different mindsets: criminal justice and educational.

Content

This activity can be done following the general one described using Carol Dweck's research at the same meeting. It could also be done at a subsequent meeting. Review the concept of mindset and how it applies to the problem of bullying.

Present Chart 4.1 given in this chapter. This can be projected on a large screen or distributed on a sheet of paper to each person (or both). Have the left-hand column labeled "Criminal Justice Mindset" and the right-hand labeled "Educational Mindset."

Leave some items in the chart. It is your choice as to which ones would be most relevant to the staff.

Procedure

Have staff sit in small groups. Distribute a sheet of chart paper and markers to each group. Instruct each group to work together to complete the chart. Have each group post the chart paper with their completed chart.

After each group has posted the chart, have the entire group do a gallery walk, where they silently move around the room to view each completed chart. They can take notes on what they see. After each person has had the chance to view all the completed charts, signal everyone to return to their small groups and discuss what they observed on the other charts.

Ask each group to assess the school's mindset on bullying. How much of it reflects the criminal justice mindset and how much reflects an educational mindset?

Ask each group to recommend one change and/or addition that the school should consider making regarding its approach to bullying prevention.

Whole-Group Processing

Have a general discussion with the entire staff. Make sure that someone records the recommendations made by each group. Indicate that the appropriate school committee assigned to this issue will consider these recommendations.

ACTIVITY 3: LEADERSHIP AND MINDSETS— *HOOSIERS* AND ELECTION

Purpose

The purpose is to reflect on the influence that mindsets have on how we face problems or challenges.

PART 1

Content

Present the video clip from the movie *Hoosiers* (Anspaugh, 1986) available on YouTube at www.youtube.com/watch?v=9Cdc13CU9Fc. The clip (approximately at 1:30 minutes into the movie) shows the underdog high school basketball team from a very small town entering a large arena where they will play for the state championship against a team from a much larger school. The coach, played by Gene Hackman, leads the team into the empty, cavernous arena. The players look overwhelmed not just by the arena but by the challenge they face. The coach takes out a tape measure and hands it to one of the players and instructs him to measure the length of the foul line to the basket and the height of the basket from the floor. He tells the student to state the measurements out loud. The coach points out to the players that those measurements are the same ones that they have been using all along. He reminds them that the game is the same no matter where they play.

Procedure

The staff can stay as a whole group and watch the clip together. Distribute a sheet to each person with the following questions:

What were the players thinking as they walked into the arena?

What was the coach trying to do by asking them to take the measurements?

How did this relate to their mindsets?

Was this an effective strategy on the part of the coach? Explain.

How does this example of trying to change a mindset apply to the problem of bullying at school?

Ask each person to briefly write down his response to the questions and any other response he might have had to the video clip.

After each person has written down her responses, lead a whole-group discussion based on the questions related to the video clip.

PART 2

Content

Present the video clip from the movie *Election* (Payne, 1999), available on YouTube at www.youtube.com/watch?v=tcgvP8v3W54&feature=youtu.be, which takes place approximately forty minutes into the movie. The clip shows a student (Tammy) who is running for high school class president at a school assembly. In her speech, she said that if she were elected, she would dismantle student government so that no one would have to sit through another assembly. She gets a standing ovation much to the dismay of the administration. The administrators retreat to the principal's office where they try to think of an appropriate response to her speech. The assistant principal suggests that the best response is to suspend her. The next scene shows her riding her bike on the day she is suspended, and in a voice-over, we hear her reaction to being suspended.

Procedure

The staff can stay as a whole group and watch the clip together. Distribute a sheet to each person with the following questions:

Why does Tammy get such a reaction from the students?

Why did the administration react the way they did?

How effective was the consequence of being suspended?

What was the mindset of the administration in responding to her speech?

How accurate is Tammy's perception of the effectiveness of suspension?

Ask each person to briefly write down her response to the questions and any other response she might have had to the video clip.

After each person has written down his responses, lead a whole-group discussion based on the questions related to the video clip.

OUTCOMES

1. Staff can reflect on how their mindset affects their words and actions. They can also reflect on how their words and actions affect the mindsets of others.

2. Staff will have a better understanding of how mindsets affect the range of options available in addressing problems.

3. Staff can rethink how to approach the problem of bullying.

Section Two

The Skill

5

You Can't Bully Your Way to Bullying Prevention

"Nearly all men can stand adversity, but if you want to test a person's character, give him power."

—Abraham Lincoln

THE FEAR OF THE PRINCIPAL

I had two perennial goals as principal: to know every student by name and to spend as many days as possible in front of the school to greet or say goodbye to all of them. The second goal always put the first one to the test.

One day, early in my tenure as principal, a father walked by me with his son at dismissal time. As they passed me, I smiled and said goodbye to the student addressing him by name. The father abruptly stopped and looked at his son and said, "What have you done wrong? How come the principal knows your name?" The boy was startled and was unable to answer. I quickly interceded and told the father that his son had done nothing wrong and that I knew a lot of the students' names. The boy looked relieved, and the father commented on how things have changed since he went to school.

THE PRINCIPAL AS ENFORCER

"True leadership only exists if people follow when they have the freedom not to."

—Jim Collins (2005, p. 13)

While I was principal, there was a districtwide professional development initiative called *curriculum mapping*. It required staff to use technology and work collaboratively to implement curriculum standards. Most staff were supportive and willing to learn the new skills required of them, but some were resistant.

At a faculty meeting, one of the resistant teachers raised her hand and asked me, "Do we *have to* do this?" Suddenly the room became quiet, and I could feel the entire faculty becoming focused on my reply. A *yes* response would increase the resistance to the initiative, while a *no* response would give permission to ignore it. Sensing that it was a loaded question, I calmly said, "I don't believe in forcing professionals to do anything, but I expect professionals to be open to any idea that has the potential for improving our professional practice. This initiative was determined to have such potential, so I am confident that everyone here will be open to learning about it and trying it out." The tension in the room broke, and we returned to discussing how we were going to implement it. The question never came up again.

These two scenarios illustrate the dilemma and challenge that school leaders face as they use the power and authority of their position. They inherit the stereotype of principal as *chief enforcer* who has to maintain order and discipline for the school. They are also expected to implement the mandates from those who have power over them, i.e., central office administration, school boards, and state and federal governments. They are perceived to have power and authority by those they lead, but as "middle managers," they often can have very little.

Leaders are expected to and often praised when they aggressively use their power to get things done or maintain order. The marine drill sergeant, the tough football coach, and the "no nonsense" CEO are culturally approved and admired stereotypes. Although often a source of humor in television and movies, these cultural stereotypes represent models of behavior that can influence the words and actions of students who observe them. School leaders, when they assume these traditional role expectations, run the risk of modeling the type of behavior they say is not acceptable for others. Adult bullying of students or staff in the school environment can trump and undo the best bullying prevention programs and initiatives.

Since bullying involves the abuse of power in human relationships, school leaders are in a very precarious position in how they do their job.

For them, the line between the use and abuse of power is often not clear, as they confront challenging problems that demand action. Effective bullying prevention, however, needs school leaders who have the courage to reflect on and monitor their use of power and authority when interacting with students, parents, and staff.

LEADERSHIP STYLE AND BULLYING PREVENTION

Effective bullying prevention is not dependent on radically changing the organizational structure of a school. Schools are not structured to be democracies and not all decisions can or should be shared with others. Leadership styles and approaches do, however, affect the culture and climate of a school. A top-down, or autocratic, style affects a school differently than a more collaborative/democratic style. School leaders need to know where their school is on this continuum and examine how their leadership style might affect bullying prevention efforts.

There are two critical and related elements of bullying prevention that are influenced by the overall leadership/decision-making structure of a school:

- The degree of ownership/connection that students and staff have with the school
- The degree responsibility that students and staff have for reporting incidents of bullying

A recent Secret Service report investigating bystander behavior provides a good description of the type of climate needed in schools:

> Schools should ensure a climate in which students feel comfortable sharing information they have regarding a potentially threatening situation with a responsible adult . . . Developing meaningful social and emotional connections with students and creating a climate of mutual respect are essential to keeping schools safe . . . Students in this study felt connected to the school when they believed that someone in the school knew them and cared for them. Schools demonstrate their commitments to such climates by promoting social and emotional connections between students, staff and teachers in everyday interactions and activities. (Pollack, Modzeleski, & Rooney, 2008, p.8)

Schools with autocratic leadership, especially when it is *too* managerially efficient, are less likely to have students and staff feel responsible for schoolwide problems. In these schools, problems like bullying often belong to the administration to solve. Often a person's reluctance to help others is not from a lack of empathy or caring but from the perception that it is someone else's job to help. People who work in schools with auto-cratic leadership are reluctant to take risks, make mistakes, or do any-thing outside of their job description. Effective bullying prevention needs the eyes and ears of everyone and the type of leadership that welcomes new ideas, questions, and complaints. Schools need to be places where problems and mistakes are viewed as opportunities for learning, not criticism.

THE BEST (ONLY) PLACE TO START

"Example is not the main thing in influencing others. It is the only thing."

—Albert Schweitzer

School leaders need to help all members of the school community view bullying prevention as part of a larger goal of improving how people treat each other. For this goal to have credibility, school leaders should be very circumspect and sensitive to how *they* treat others. They need to set high standards of behavior and consistently meet those standards. They have to practice what they preach.

Of course, most school leaders will say they already treat all people with respect, but unfortunately, not all the students and staff always agree with that perception. School leaders make a serious mistake when they assume that others need to change, and not themselves. The change *has* to start with them, but this has many advantages:

- It doesn't cost anything.
- It can start immediately.
- It doesn't require professional development or training.
- It doesn't require "staff buy-in" from the outset.
- It doesn't need to be called bullying prevention.
- It can happen without being announced or recognized.
- It requires no timetable or action plan.
- It doesn't need approval from supervisors or school boards.
- It is, however, the most important thing a school leader can do or not do.

FIVE-POINT LEADERSHIP INSPECTION

School leaders who accurately inspect themselves will be better prepared to lead the school community in bullying prevention efforts. Here are five key areas to check as part of reflecting on their use of power:

1. Check Under the Hood

Many of the decisions that school leaders make are guided by the implicit or hidden assumptions that they make about those they lead.

For a school leader, *checking under the hood* means being aware of these assumptions and how they influence all their interactions with staff and students. (See Chart 5.1.)

Question to ask: Do my decisions reflect Theory X or Theory Y assumptions?

2. Check Your Power Source

Leadership is changing people's hearts and minds by not throwing one's weight around but by getting people to pay attention to the right things. It is important for leaders to ask themselves why people should follow them.

People listen to leaders whom they trust and think are acting to support them rather than trying to control or manipulate them. People listen to leaders who listen to them and respect leaders who respect them.

Change might take longer when leaders give people the freedom not to follow. Effective bullying prevention requires staff commitment, not just compliance. When the school community has the will to change, they will find the right way to do it.

Question to ask: What is the main source of my authority— the power of my position or respect for my ideas, values, skills, and knowledge?

Chart 5.1   Comparison of Underlying Assumptions about People

Theory X	Theory Y
Most people don't like work and will avoid it if they can.	Most people will make a commitment to an organization if they find the work satisfying.
People need to be controlled and manipulated in order to work hard and achieve.	Most people will learn and achieve given the right conditions. They will also accept responsibility given respect and support.
People basically prefer the security of being controlled and directed.	People thrive when they can be creative and solve problems together with others.

Source: Adapted from McGregor (1960).

3. Monitor Your Comfort Index

Bullying is a complex and challenging problem that manifests itself differently in each school. School leaders are most effective when they promote a sense of shared leadership with the entire school community. Bullying prevention is a process rather than a final product; therefore, there will always be problems and challenges. The input and feedback from all members of the school community are essential to making the right adjustments and modifications in the school's ongoing efforts.

Questions to ask: How comfortable am I with

- Asking for help
- Being uncertain at times
- Admitting mistakes
- Accepting ideas that might differ from my own

4. Check Your Alignment and Balance

School leaders are in the spotlight and under the microscope at the same time. Their words and actions need to be in alignment with their own values and the mission and values of the school. They should be wary of any justification for words and actions that do not reflect a high standard of respect for all.

There should be an urgency to all bullying prevention efforts, yet using fear or panic to motivate others is counterproductive. Effective school leaders convey urgency not out of fear or panic, but from a desire to do what is right and necessary for the school community. They should project a calm confidence that the school community will work together and do what is necessary to make school a safe place for all students to learn.

Questions to ask: Do I consistently treat others the way I want to be treated regardless of what others have done? Do I convey the importance and urgency of keeping students safe while also expressing confidence in the school's ability to respond to that challenge?

5. Decide on How to Use Your GPS

A Wallace Foundation report summarizing the research on educational leadership stated that the two essential roles of a school leader are to *set direction* and to *influence others* to move in that direction (Leithwood, Louis, Anderson, & Wahlstrom, 2010). Effective school leaders help others understand the goal and purpose of bullying prevention. They involve all members of the school community in planning, implementing, and evaluating all bullying prevention efforts.

Question to ask: Do my words and actions point others in the right direction and influence how they think and act, or do I decide what needs to be done and then manage others to follow my plan?

THE POWER OF BABY STEPS

School leaders have less control and more influence on the people they lead than they probably realize. They can start to change the culture of their schools (the only way to change it) with what they say and do in their everyday interactions.

Here are some small individual changes a school leader could try:

- Make a habit of using "please" and "thank you" every time you give a direction to anyone—especially students.
- Show up someplace in the school where you don't usually go and help out there.
- Invite students to eat lunch with you and ask for their thoughts and opinions.
- Make an effort to find something in common with staff who give you the most trouble.
- Walk around the school after the students leave and pop in a classroom just to chat with the staff there. Ask them how they are doing.
- Make a list of decisions that you typically make alone and find ones that you can share and make with others.
- Write thank you notes on a regular basis to students and staff for even small gestures that they do to make the school a better place.
- Make your own list of little things you could do that can make things a little better and then pick one and do it.

SUMMARY

- Since bullying is about how power is used in human relationships, school leaders need to be aware of the power that comes from their position and how they use it.
- School leaders inherit a stereotype of leadership that can often be interpreted as institutionalized or sanctioned bullying. School leaders who accept and adopt this stereotypical behavior send a contradictory message to the school community about bullying prevention.
- Leadership styles do affect the school community and how it responds to the challenge of bullying prevention.
- School leaders need to have the courage to reflect on their use power in their relationships. They must accept the responsibility for improving their own behavior, if it does not meet a high standard for respect for all.
- Bullying prevention can and should begin with how school leaders interact with others.

- School leaders can reflect on how they use their power using a five-point inspection consisting of the following:

  o Check under the hood.
  o Check your power source.
  o Monitor your comfort index.
  o Check your alignment and balance.
  o Decide on how to use your GPS.

- School leaders should lead by example. They can make many small gestures that can significantly change in a school's culture for the better.

ACTIVITIES TO REFLECT ON THE USE OF POWER

ACTIVITY 1: KINDNESS FROM ABOVE VS. THE WRIST SLAP

Purpose

The purpose is to reflect on personal experiences related to a supervisor's response to a mistake or problems.

Content

Sometimes people who are in positions of power over others forget how even the slightest word or gesture can affect those they lead. Teachers inherently hold such power over students. This activity is designed to provide reflection and discussion on how vulnerable people are to messages from above.

Distribute a sheet of paper divided into two columns. On the top of one column have the heading "Kindness From Above" and on the other "Wrist-Slap Moment." Give time for reflecting on past experiences with superiors. Superiors can be defined as anyone who has either formal or informal power over someone else, i.e., parent, teacher, coach, supervisor, police person, clergy, supervisor, or any other similar type position.

For the "Kindness From Above" column, they should recall a time when they made a mistake or created a problem and their superior responded in a kind, forgiving, and understanding manner.

For the "Wrist-Slap Moment" column, they should recall a time when they made mistake or created a problem and their superior responded with a reprimand or criticism.

Ground rule: Do not use the names of any person or use the activity as an opportunity to grip or complain about a current supervisor.

Ask each person to recall and reflect on the following questions under each heading:

Remember a time when you made an error, mistake, or something that you had responsibility for that went awry. Write down a brief description of the situation and the superior involved.

Write down the feelings you experienced after the mistake or error. Include the response you anticipated from the superior.

Write down how the superior actually responded to the situation. Did the response match the anticipated response? Explain.

Describe how you felt after the superior's response.

Write down how that response affected future actions that occurred with the superior.

Add any other thoughts or reflections.

Procedure

Staff should initially work individually without conversing. Depending on the time available, each person could respond to the questions under each heading. If time is limited, half the group could respond to the "Kindness From Above" and the other half to the "Wrist-Slap Moment."

After staff have had enough time to reflect and write down their thoughts, they can find one person to share whatever moment they want. (There are various ways to pair people—use whatever has worked for you in the past.)

After the pairs have shared, have the whole group reconvene and ask for volunteers to share any experience with the whole group. Invite thoughts and insights for the whole group.

Ask the group if this activity made them rethink how they interact with others.

ACTIVITY 2: THE BREAKFAST CLUB MOMENT— WHAT PUSHES YOUR BUTTONS

Purpose

The purpose is to reflect on situations that trigger emotional responses that could lead to the abuse of power and a justification for it.

It is understandable and expected that there will be times when people lose it in response to a conflict or problem. This activity is *not* designed to invoke remorse for the times when they lost it. It is designed to affirm people's best efforts to deal with trying situations and to offer support for staff when they face similar situations. It is also designed to help staff decide about when to back off from situation and seek help rather than continue to deal with a student who is especially good at pushing their buttons.

Content

Present the video clip (approximately at 1:30 minutes) from the movie *The Breakfast Club* (Hughes, 1985), available on YouTube at www.youtube. com/watch?v=bTeYncx1xmI. In this clip, the vice principal, Mr. Vernon, is in charge of Saturday morning detention and has a confrontation with the student Bender. Make sure that the clip includes as the final scene a close-up of Mr. Vernon on the other side of the door immediately following the heated confrontation.

Procedure

Prior to showing the video, clarify for the staff that the clip is not meant to criticize the vice principal, but to reflect on challenge of disciplining students. Ask them to view Mr. Vernon as a dedicated professional trying to do a difficult job.

Staff should sit in small groups while watching the video.

Show the video. Ask staff to write down their immediate response to it without discussion. Ask them to describe their reaction to Mr. Vernon, Bender, and the other students.

Guide Questions

Assign roles of facilitator, recorder, reporter, and timekeeper to each group and ask the following:

Why did the conflict escalate between Vernon and Bender?

Why do you think Bender did what he did?

What role did the other students play in the conflict?

How do you think you would have reacted to Bender?

Who won between Vernon and Bender? Did anyone? Explain.

Explain the look on Vernon's face after the confrontation is over. What do you think is going through his mind?

What do you think will happen on Monday morning when they all return to school?

How do you think the head principal would respond to what happened?

If you were mentoring Vernon, what would you say to him?

What would happen if you showed this clip to high school juniors and seniors? How do you think they would react?

The movie is from the early 1980s. Have schools changed since then? Explain your answer.

Each small group can choose the questions that they want to discuss. Have the reporter share two to three key discussion points with the whole group (limit the sharing to no more than two minutes per group).

Optional Activity: The Letter at the End of the Movie

Here is the letter written by one of the Breakfast Club students to Mr. Vernon:

> *Dear Mr. Vernon,*
>
> *We accept the fact that we had to sacrifice a whole Saturday in detention for whatever it was we did wrong. But we think you're crazy to make us write an essay telling you who we think we are. You see us as you want to see us ... In the simplest terms, in the most convenient definitions. But what we found out is that each one of us is a brain ... an athlete ... a basket case ... a princess ... and a criminal ... Does that answer your question?*
>
> *Sincerely yours,*
>
> *The Breakfast Club*

Read the letter to the staff. Solicit staff reactions to the letter in the light of the previous activities.

Discuss the letter and how it relates to the issue of bullying prevention.

Activity 3: "Please" and "Thank You" and the Golden Rule

Purpose

The purpose is to reflect on the effect of small acts and gestures in the school culture and climate.

Content

The best way to present this activity is after school leaders have tried it themselves. They can share their own experiences as part of the introduction to the activity.

Present the concept that many small actions and gestures done by enough people have a dramatic impact on a school environment. Point out how these actions have no cost and don't require professional development or extra time. *Make it clear that it is an optional exercise but would work best if everyone was on board.*

Present these two options to staff:

1. Commit to consistently using "Please" and "Thank you" when speaking to anyone in the school or to any group of people.

2. Commit to using the Golden Rule as a guide for all interactions with others.

(Substitute any other simple gesture that could have a positive impact if enough people did it on a consistent basis.)

Procedure

Assign roles of facilitator, recorder, reporter, and timekeeper to each group. Have staff sit in small groups and have each group decide on one gesture they commit to trying for at least one week. Ask each group to make a prediction on what (if any) changes they foresee if the gesture was consistently used by all staff for one week? One month? One school year?

For the sake of time, indicate that the gesture that is recommended by the most groups will be the one that is tried for one week. The other gesture could be implemented simultaneously or tried later on.

Have each group share their choice of gesture and reasons why they chose it and what they predict will happen.

Emphasize that changing habits, especially patterns of speech, is very difficult. The commitment is to try their best.

Designate a time to meet again to share on how it is going and decide on next steps. (For example, continue the gesture? Discontinue the gesture? Modify it? Add to it?)

OUTCOMES

1. These activities should help staff see the connection between adult modeling and bullying prevention.

2. They should also raise awareness about how hard even simple changes in speaking or acting can be.

3. They can also bring the staff together in a social experiment that could turn out to be fun.

4. They send the message that bullying prevention is more than just implementing a program; it is people working together toward a common goal.

6

Leadership for Bullying Prevention

What Not to Do and Not to Think

"Sometimes, he who hesitates is wise."

—Malcolm Forbes

There once was a businessman who was very late for an important meeting. His daily commute included taking a ferryboat that ran every half hour. He knew that if he was late for the ferry, he would miss his meeting and suffer serious consequences. As he entered the ferry slip, he panicked because he saw the boat ten feet away from the dock. Determined to be on time, he ran as fast as he could and leaped off the dock and crash landed on the ferry deck. Although he was quite bruised and in pain, he was very relieved that he would not miss this meeting. A surprised deckhand quickly came over to him and said, "Mister, are you OK? If you had only waited a few seconds, we would have pulled into the dock."

This story is analogous to the reaction that many schools have to the current problem of bullying. With many dramatic and tragic news stories on television, harsh criticism of schools being almost a daily occurrence, and new legislation being imposed, schools can feel under siege and pressured to do something to stop bullying. In response to this type of environment, school leaders often feel forced to act without having devoted sufficient time to understand the scope and complexity of the problem they are facing. They are also surrounded by a tremendous number of products, programs, and resources, all claiming to be the answer to solving the problem of bullying. No wonder there can be a tendency for school leaders to do something, anything, rather than appear to do nothing and indifferent or callous to the public.

The problem of bullying is an urgent one and affects the lives of all students. Clearly, schools need to act, but they also need to know what they are doing. They need to make sure that their time and resources are used wisely and that they are heading in the right direction. In times of diminishing school resources and greater pressure on all school staff, the choices that school leaders make (or don't make) can have significant and lasting impact on all subsequent bullying prevention efforts. Not only will misdirection waste time and energy; it could increase the problem and the damage it does.

COMMON MISDIRECTIONS IN BULLYING PREVENTION

"If you don't know where you are going, you will probably end up somewhere else."

—Yogi Berra

There are several common misdirections in bullying prevention that have emerged through research and are included as part of the basic information on bullying prevention. School leaders should know these, but more importantly, should be able to articulate why they are misdirections and answer the questions or objections about not using them.

Here are the common misdirections with a brief description, the reasons for the practice, and the reasons why it is a misdirection. Since these misdirections often appear to make a lot of sense, school leaders should have commonsense responses to the defense of such practices; I have added a response to many of the common defenses of them.

Zero Tolerance Policies

Description

These are policies that have an automatic, predetermined consequence for any proven instance of bullying. Typically, these consequences involve some type of suspension from school.

Reasons for Using

- Sends a strong message that bullying is unacceptable
- Provides a deterrence for bullying
- Provides a high degree of predictability
- Removes possible accusations of unfairness because of different consequences for different students

Reasons Why It Is Misdirection

- It treats all incidents of bullying as equal without considering the students involved and the circumstances of the incident.
- Students who bully for the first time could be treated the same as students who have bullied repeatedly.
- It only addresses "proven" cases of bullying.
- Students who bully are more likely to deny it. They have a lot to gain by denying and a lot to lose by being honest.
- Parents of students who bully are more likely to challenge the consequence and criticize the school. Students who bully benefit from the school and parents agreeing and supporting the corrective action.
- It fails to acknowledge that bullying prevention is also about helping the students who bully. Consequences alone don't teach alternative behaviors.
- It decreases the likelihood of the bullied student reporting it. These students primarily want bullying to stop and don't necessarily need or want the student who bullied to be punished as the way of getting it to stop.
- Bystanders could have more sympathy for the student who bullies and less for the student/target who reported it.
- Reporting is also diminished because adults appear less trustworthy and more threatening to students in general.

Response to the Defense of the Practice

- Not supporting zero tolerance can be viewed as tolerating or accepting bullying. *(Reframe the issue as "zero indifference" to bullying. Having more flexibility in responding to bullying will be more productive in preventing and reducing it.)*
- Not having the same consequence for bullying means not being fair or consistent. *(Being fair does not mean doing the same thing for every student. Instead, being fair means doing what is necessary to make sure all students are safe. Since each situation of bullying is not the same, consistency will not be achieved by responding in the same way to different situations. Consistency is most important in aligning words and actions with values.)*

- Suspension will at least keep the student who bullied away from the student who was bullied. *(Suspension can be an appropriate consequence is some situations, but not all. There may be more effective and lasting ways to keep that student safe.)*

Conflict Resolution and Peer Mediation

Description

Conflict resolution is a commonly used strategy for helping students resolve conflicts in an appropriate way. It also provides them with skills that can help them avoid and resolve future conflicts. Peer mediation involves training students in how to mediate conflict situations. These trained students facilitate the discussion between the two students in conflict.

Reasons for Using

- These programs are often well established in a school and have been successful.
- Students should not view themselves as victims.
- They empower students to solve their own problems without being dependent on adults to intervene.
- Independence and leadership in students are promoted.
- It is not helpful to always rescue students when they have problems.

Reasons Why It Is Misdirection

- Fails to acknowledge and distinguish bullying as different from conflict.
- Treats individuals with a significant disparity of power between them as equals or having similar power.
- Implies an equal sharing of responsibility for bullying. The student who bullies has the responsibility to stop and must stop.
- Can reinforce the notion that the student who was bullied was deficient or unskilled in defending himself or herself. Victims of bullying can often then blame themselves.
- Will deter students who were bullied from reporting bullying because they will then have to face the person bullying them.
- Will deter bystanders from reporting since they know it could make things worse for the student who was bullied.
- Implies that peer mediators, not adults, bear the primary responsibility for keeping all students safe.

Response to Defense of Practice

- Adults shouldn't rescue students from problems. Learning to solve life's problems is an essential part of education. *(Students should learn how to solve problems. The skills to resolve conflicts are not the same skills needed to prevent or reduce bullying. Bystanders do need to learn a variety of strategies for responding to bullying, but ultimately, they must tell adults if a student is at risk of being harmed. Many students who are bullied are not always lacking in skills but are bullied for things they cannot control, such as their physical appearance, disability, or ethnic background.*

- Why start a new initiative to address bullying when there are well-established and effective programs in place that can do the job? *(These programs can and should continue, but they are not designed for the particular problem of bullying. Different problems require different tools, and bullying requires a special set of tools.)*

Chart 6.1 compares and illustrates how the two behaviors differ.

Reliance on Motivational Speakers or One-Time Training or Programs for Students or Staff

Description

There are many experts and speakers in the field of bullying prevention who have information that could be helpful to a school's bullying prevention efforts. Many have very moving and inspirational stories that could change people's hearts and minds. School assemblies can raise student awareness about the problem. In addition, one-time staff workshops can provide important information on bullying and how to prevent and reduce it. These are traditional methods that schools have used for many other issues/topics over the years.

Reasons for Using

- They have worked before and are usually very well received by all members of the school community.
- They demonstrate to the community that bullying is a problem that the school takes seriously.
- They take little time away for all of the other things that are going on in school.
- They can generate goodwill in the community and get positive publicity for a school.
- Teachers are not given more things to put on their already full plate.
- Most schools are doing a good job at bullying prevention, so all they need is a little boost to awareness rather than have to make any significant changes.

Chart 6.1   Differences Between Bullying and Conflict

Conflict	Bullying
Equal power between participants	Unequal power between perpetrator and victim
Issue or problem at center of conflict	No apparent issue or contention between perpetrator and victim
One incident or isolated incident	Pattern of behavior
Usually not a targeted action toward hurting someone	Victim is selected by perpetrator
Does not produce great fear and anxiety	Victim experiences fear and anxiety
Each person involved can defend or protect himself or herself	Victim can lack skills, resources, relationships for defending/protecting himself or herself
Goal of actions is not to control or intimidate another	Goal of actions is to control or intimidate another
Issues are between participants. Audience is not a key factor	Perpetrator seeks audience for words and actions
Willingness to solve problem	No desire to solve problem
Participants usually want resolution to conflict	Perpetrator denies that there is a problem or claims it was "just a joke"

Source: Adapted from Garrity, Jens, Sager, Porter, and Short-Camilli (2000).

Reasons Why It Is Misdirection

- Although there is still a lot of research to be done on effective bullying prevention, the research is very clear that this type of approach does *not work* (Farrington & Ttofi, 2009).
- With limited resources, schools cannot afford to invest in approaches that do not work.
- The research on successful change indicates the need for shared leadership and commitment from all members of the school community to change the culture and climate of the school.
- It will only postpone or even prevent the initiation of more effective and proven approaches.
- These events or activities can be most effective when they are *part* of a more comprehensive and schoolwide approach.

Response to Defense of the Practice

- Change comes from touching people's emotions, not just words. (*Emotions play a key role in changing how people think and respond to problems. They are one ingredient that is most effective when combined with a multifaceted approach.*)
- Nobody wants bullying, so once they are aware of the problem, people will do what is necessary to stop it. (*Nobody wants bullying, but it is a complex problem that occurs in the blind spot of school staff. Developing the knowledge, understanding, attitudes, and skills of the entire school community is an ongoing process that will lead to the improvement of the culture and climate of the school.*
- The public needs to know that the school cares about stopping bullying, so having a high-profile speaker will send a strong message that something is being done. (*All of that is very true and can be a very important part of a comprehensive strategy. There are, however, other ways to send the same message. Other more evidence-based approaches are even more efficient and effective and have longer-lasting positive effects.*)

Misconceptions of Bullying Prevention

Here are some misconceptions about bullying prevention and how they can confuse the issue for the school community:

Bullying prevention will eliminate bullying.

This is an admirable but unrealistic goal for the following reasons:

- It might be realistic if there were a stable population of students that attended the same school every year. New students enter schools every year; there is a changing population of students interacting in different ways all the time. Relationships change over time based on many factors; students treat each other differently from year to year and even from day to day.

- Students are "works in progress," and learning how to relate to others is part of maturing. Students will make mistakes in the socioemotional domain just as they will in the academic domain. Schools need to view bullying prevention as an ongoing responsibility to educate, guide, and discipline students in the socioemotional domain, just as they do in the academic domain.
- Schools should have a goal of reducing and preventing as much bullying as possible. This goal requires that schools have a clearer picture of how much bullying is actually happening. Having specific goals based on the data collected on a regular basis provides staff with the feedback they need to adjust their efforts to the actual needs of the school. Staff can get unnecessarily discouraged if success is measured too broadly or in vague and general terms.

Bullying is too negative a term, so it should be replaced with another term.

I knew of a school that changed the wording of the rule *we will not bully others* to *we will not hurt others*. The reasoning behind this change was that the word *bully* was too negative. This avoidance of the term *bullying* is misguided for the following reasons:

- The verb *to bully* is a negative term because it is a negative and hurtful act.
- Avoiding this fact does not help students learn what they need to learn about bullying, and ultimately, what is expected of them.
- Bullying is not just hurting someone: it is deliberately hurting someone who cannot defend himself or herself. This is very different from two students who get into a fight and hurt each other.
- Children need adults to differentiate certain behaviors indicating degrees of severity. For example, a toddler needs to be taught that going near the road is a more serious rule to break than playing in a room in the house that is off limits.

Bullying prevention should be just one part of a discipline program based on following rules for appropriate behavior.

This misconception is related to the previous one of minimizing the meaning of the term bullying. This misconception, however, is based on the potential confusion that students and staff can have when they have to distinguish bullying from other behaviors. This approach is often promoted because it *doesn't* require staff and students to make these distinctions or use judgment. From this perspective, staff and students are more easily trained and, therefore, will be more consistent when intervening when these distinctions are removed. There are several problems with this premise:

- Bullying *is* different from other inappropriate behaviors such as running in halls, talking out of turn, or forgetting to do homework. It is a more complex (adaptive problem) and requires a comprehensive approach that includes educating students and staff so they can make better decisions.
- Staff and students are very capable of knowing the distinctions among behaviors. Students need to learn that certain actions have more serious consequences than others. A mean look, a whispering in another's ear, or excluding someone at the lunch table are subtle acts of bullying that are hard to detect and police. Unless bullying and its relationship to power are understood, students would have a hard time seeing those actions alone as being inappropriate and would resist being held accountable for them. Bystanders without this understanding would also be reluctant to report such actions.
- Students need to learn to make judgments and to discern differences among words and actions. Students need to learn how to make judgments and decisions in the social world; simplifying expectations ultimately does students a disservice by depriving them of the opportunity to make such judgments.
- Most students follow most of the rules most of the time. Since bullying prevention is for all the students, responsible action often is not rule governed. Students who are bystanders have to sometimes make courageous decisions far beyond the expectation of just following rules. Effective bullying prevention educates all students about being responsible, caring, and empathetic to others.

Bullying prevention should primarily emphasize training students on how to resist or defuse bullying situations.

Students need to have as many strategies at their disposal to avoid and react to bullying situations. This is a key component of bullying prevention and does need to be addressed in school. This strategy is only effective when it is part of a more comprehensive and systemic approach to the problem. Here are the reasons why it should not be the primary focus of bullying prevention:

- Students who are frequent targets of bullying might feel that they have failed in using these strategies if they do not prevent or stop the bullying.
- The student who is targeted can internalize this "blaming the victim" mentality. Bystanders might mistakenly think that these students have to just learn to defend themselves.

- There is emerging research indicating that some students are bullied because of how they look and much less on how they act.
- For students who are frequently the target of bullying, the slightest hint that they failed to use the right strategy and "deserved" the bullying would only intensify their pain and sense of hopelessness.

*Bullying prevention is primarily about changing
students, not adults.*

Approaches to bullying prevention designed only to change students fail to significantly improve the culture and climate of a school. Ultimately, the entire school community must change for the better. Here the reasons for including all members of the school community in bullying prevention:

- If students learn that it is their responsibility to report incidents of bullying, school staff need to be open and receptive to such reports, or students will not continue to report them.
- Although it might be easier for a school leader to get staff to support approaches that focus on students, significant change will only happen when all members are committed to learning and changing for the better.
- Bullying prevention curricula are most effective when they are used within a schoolwide and comprehensive approach that supports the messages of those curricula.

*Bullying prevention efforts should primarily be directed toward
certain groups of students thought to be bullies or victims.*

This misconception is counterproductive for the following reasons:

- It ignores the role that bystanders play in supporting or deterring bullying.
- Bullying is a behavior that is caused by many factors, and all students are capable of and vulnerable to bullying in one form or another. Students can bully in one situation and be bullied in another and witness it, all within the same school day.
- It can also lead to labeling students, and students learn to *live up to* or *down to* the labels we place on them. It could create bullies out of students who sometimes bully. Staff get what they expect from students, so it is better to err on the side of expecting too much rather than too little of them.
- Students who follow the rules or get good grades and occasionally bully are less likely to stop bullying. In their mind, only bullies bully and since they are not bullies, what they did is not bullying.

- Students can more easily accept responsibility for bullying when they are not accused of being a bully or a bad person.
- It minimizes staff perceptions of the amount of bullying that occurs in a school. Staff can mistakenly believe that bullying is under control when certain students are more closely monitored or separated from students.

Success in bullying prevention is finding the
right program and implementing it.

School leaders need to consult current research and best practice when working with their staff in determining the best way to approach the problem of bullying. Here are some key points regarding the right message about bullying prevention:

- Ultimately, all successful change depends on people helping people learn and grow together.
- Staff need to be empowered and supported for they ultimately are responsible for starting and sustaining the change process.
- The members of the school community need to see that a program, or any element of a program, is only a *tool* in achieving its goals.
- The best program can only be effective when members of the school community are committed to learning about it and to developing the knowledge and skills needed to implement it.
- Conversely, schools without the resources to purchase a program or materials could feel that there is not much they can do to prevent or reduce bullying.

J. David Smith (2007) aptly summarizes what it really takes to address bullying in schools:

Clearly there are no magic solutions for bullying problems. No book, video, or smartly packaged program can eliminate the problem. Ultimately, effective solutions to bullying will require the hard work of educators and their commitment to fostering a school-wide climate of caring in which all students will grow and thrive.

SUMMARY

- School leaders are under pressure from many sources to do something to stop bullying.
- Schools do need to act but also need to be careful about acting without thinking and going in the wrong direction.

- There are certain misdirections that have been well articulated and disseminated in various resources on bullying prevention. These common misdirections include the following:

  o Zero tolerance policies
  o Conflict resolution and peer mediation
  o Reliance on motivational speakers or one-time training or programs for student or staff

- School leaders need to be able to explain why these approaches are misdirections and have a reasonable response for those who advocate for them.

- There some *misconceptions* regarding bullying prevention that can interfere with making substantive and long-term progress in addressing the problem:

  o Bullying prevention will eliminate bullying.
  o *Bullying* is too negative a term, so it should be replaced with another term.
  o Bullying prevention should be just one part of a discipline program based on following rules for appropriate behavior.
  o Bullying prevention should primarily emphasize training students on how to resist or defuse bullying situations.
  o Bullying prevention is just about changing students and not adults.
  o Bullying preventions efforts should be directed toward certain groups of students thought to be bullies or victims.
  o Success in bullying prevention is finding the right program and implementing it.

- Effective solutions and approaches to the problem of bullying depend on educators working together to create a more positive school culture and climate.

ACTIVITIES TO ADDRESS THE MISDIRECTIONS AND MISCONCEPTIONS IN BULLYING PREVENTION

ACTIVITY 1: BUYER'S REMORSE

Purpose

It provides an opportunity for staff to reflect on a time when they did something impulsively or felt pressured to make a quick decision that they later came to regret.

Content

People feel *driven* to make a decision. There are many reasons for feeling this way:

The decision offers an escape from a distressing situation.

The decision-making process can be too taxing and exhausting.

There is not enough time to think and analyze the decision.

Fear that hesitating in making a decision will remove an important opportunity

Pressure from others to act

Being swept away by the claims of those promoting a product or service

Procedure

Distribute to each person a sheet of paper with the following headings on top of each column:

Regretted Decision/Reasons for Making It/Outcomes or Consequences/Reflections

Give time for individual reflection and writing.

When staff have finished completing the sheet, use an activity of choice for getting them into random pairs. Have pairs compare and share their decisions with their partner. This can be done once or several times.

Have a sheet of chart paper with the same headings as the sheet distributed to staff. Call on individuals to share their decision stories and record a summary of their responses on the chart paper.

Facilitate a large-group discussion about decision making. Ask the whole group to brainstorm some helpful guidelines for making wise decisions based on what they have learned from their experiences. Record these guidelines.

Apply these guidelines to the decision for addressing the problem of bullying. Discuss the pressures schools feel to do something about the problem. How should these pressures affect their decisions? Facilitate a whole-group discussion. Ask someone to record the key ideas of the discussion. Indicate that this information will be brought to the decision-making group that has the responsibility for bullying prevention planning.

ACTIVITY 2: "I ONCE WAS LOST, BUT NOW I AM FOUND . . ."

Purpose

Most people have had the experience of thinking they were right about something but then, later on, discovered that they were wrong—sometimes very wrong. This activity will give staff the opportunity to reflect on this experience. Since many approaches to bullying prevention appear to be right, it often requires a little humility to shift one's opinion. This activity gives staff a chance to reflect on times when they had to make this shift.

Content

School leaders should be willing and ready to share a story of their realization of a mistaken notion and subsequent shift in perspective or opinion. If possible, use an educationally relevant experience. Invite staff to reflect on similar experience they might have had.

Procedure

Distribute a sheet with four columns: "I have no doubt . . ." / "I am not so sure . . ." / "How could I be so . . . ?" / "Now I see . . ."

Ask staff to reflect on personal or professional story that demonstrates a change of thinking that they had. Ask them to describe that change under the four headings. They should also indicate how this change or shift happened. Have staff share in pairs.

After they have finished sharing, have the whole group return to their seats. Present the key misdirections and misconceptions on bullying prevention listed in this chapter. On a sheet of chart paper, facilitate a discussion using the same four statements as they could apply to these misdirections or misconceptions. Record staff responses on this large piece of chart paper.

Facilitate a staff discussion on why changing one's mind is healthy activity, but why it might be viewed as a problem by others.

What are the misdirections/misconceptions that they might have regarding bullying prevention?

OUTCOMES

1. These activities help staff see that uncertainty can be part of the process of coming to a quality decision.

2. Reflecting on the decision-making process can improve the decisions that a staff can make.

7

Leading Groups to Lead

"Groups tend not be wise about their own wisdom ... Someone will have to take it on himself to champion the idea of collective wisdom, and in a way create the conditions that allow it to flourish."

—James Surowiecki (2005, p. 281)

W e called our shared decision-making group "the building cabinet." It consisted of teachers, teaching assistants, parents, and the principal for a total of about ten people. This group made meaningful decisions that affected all aspects of the school. I valued the work I did with them, so every summer I would invite them to my house for a daylong retreat. This was an opportunity for the group to get acquainted and prepared for the upcoming school year.

Our school had significant success in reducing school discipline problems by building stronger classroom communities and investing time in social and emotional learning for our students. The school bus, however, remained a source of frequent and intense behavioral problems. At our building cabinet retreat, I proposed bringing the students from one bus route into the school and working with them to build a sense of community. Since I didn't want to give another responsibility to the staff until I had a better understanding of what it would entail, I proposed that the school social worker and I pilot this idea using the bus that had the most behavioral referrals.

"Never doubt that a small group of thoughtful, committed citizens can change the world. Indeed, it is the only thing that ever has."

—Margaret Mead

After I made the proposal, there was a moment of silence that worried me. Finally, a few members said they liked the idea but had a problem with it. Bracing for their objections, I was pleasantly surprised when they recommended it for all of the bus routes, not just one of them. Soon, all the members agreed to try it with all the buses. I requested that members of cabinet share this proposal at the first faculty meeting of the school year. They agreed and quickly gained the support of the entire staff for trying it in the coming weeks.

We called it the Peaceful School Bus Program (Dillon, 2008), and within four years, it reduced the number of behavioral referrals from fifty-eight to eight. It has become a published program with a facilitator's guide and accompanying DVD and has sold over 2000 copies. It has helped schools across country make the school bus a safer place for many students. I guess Margaret Mead was right.

LESSONS LEARNED

"People want a chance to take part in something meaningful and important. There is a deep and human yearning to make a difference. People want to know that their lives mean something. A significant part of the leader's job is uncovering and reflecting back the meaning that others seek."

—James Kouzes and Barry Posner (2010, p. 66)

The problem of bullying manifests itself differently in each school. Only an empowered group of representative individuals can effectively find the creative solutions necessary to meet the challenge of effectively addressing the problem. As principal, I couldn't do it alone. When I asked for help, I discovered that people were just waiting to be asked and wanted to help.

For seventeen years as principal, I worked closely with a small representative group of people who formed a team that made the key decisions for our school. They did not make all the decisions for the school, but they were involved with the ones that impacted our overall culture and climate. Some problems were not easy to solve and challenged the team. We developed processes and procedures together that ensured that we took the necessary time to get the decisions right.

Although the decision that led to the Peaceful School Bus Program seemed to emerge effortlessly from this small group of people, it was the result of the time invested in developing positive and trusting relationships among the members of the team.

Here are the key factors of that effective teamwork:

- Team members had time to explore one another's core values and how those were connected to the stated mission of the district and school.
- They had a shared sense of pride and appreciation of their school community.
- Their focus was on the future and building on previous success. The team's default response to ideas that had merit was "Why not?" instead of "Why?"
- They had a shared confidence that the school community would support any effort that improved the education of students.
- They recognized and acknowledged the need to educate the "whole child."

It is beyond the scope of the chapter and my expertise to cover all the issues involved in group process and decision making. I will offer what I regard as some basic principles that I relied on when working with a small group. Using my many years of experience working with a small group on regular basis, I recommend practices that would support the work of the small group that is essential in gaining community support for bullying prevention.

School leaders have three essential tasks for ensuring that the group works effectively to address the problem of bullying:

1. Create the conditions for effective group functioning.

2. Establish a structure and process for deliberating and decision making.

3. Navigate through the difficult and complex problem of bullying.

CREATING THE CONDITIONS

Invest time in helping the group get acquainted.

As I previously stated, I would invite our building cabinet to my house for a relaxed environment where the members could informally talk and get to know each other as people. We would usually do an icebreaker activity that would also help people get better acquainted. I would provide lunch and ask the members to bring something to drink and a dessert to share. We would also review the role of the team, operating principles, and other procedures that we would be using.

Assign facilitator and recorder roles on a rotating basis.

The team should not be merely an extension of the principal. A principal is a member of the team and has a critical role to play in supporting its work; however, the team should not become dependent on the principal for managing the meeting. Each member of the group should have the opportunity to facilitate a meeting and record the minutes of the meeting. The principal can share a description of the roles and model them in the first few meetings. Simple guidelines for each role can be developed and distributed to the members of the group. The group can also determine the rotation schedule for facilitator and recorder assignments.

Discuss the parameters of confidentially for the group's discussion.

The minutes of the meeting should be made available promptly after the meeting to the school community. For issues related to bullying, the discussion should not include specific names of individuals. Discipline for incidents of bullying remains the responsibility of the principal, but the group can develop and adopt a discipline policy and procedures for the building that would support districtwide policy.

Make sure that the group has the opportunity periodically to reflect on and discuss how they are doing.

Every team member is responsible for how the group functions. There can be regularly scheduled times for the team to review and evaluate how it is functioning. Having a regular and predetermined time for checking in provides a sense of security to the members. This gives them the time and opportunity to raise issues and problems without feeling like they are causing trouble or throwing the team off schedule.

Allow time for the group to discuss its role and mission.

Just as a principal can be a top-down manager, so can a team. To the people who are not members of the group, a decision that is imposed from above by a team can be no different than a decision made solely by one person. The small group should function as a catalyst for school change rather than just dictate it. All new members need to understand and accept how the team is a catalyst for change in working with the entire school community.

Our team agreed that each member would not be acting as a spokesperson for the group they represented. They would bring the experience and perspective gained from doing their job but share their own ideas and perspectives, and not be bound to just represent a group. They would also make this clear to their colleagues.

Discuss the parameters of decision making.

Prior to the start of the school year, the principal should review with the team what decisions it can and cannot make. In our school, the building cabinet could not make decisions regarding personnel or those pertaining to a labor contract. The team should also know what district policies and procedures override any building-based ones. It is much better to discuss these parameters at the start of the year rather than have the team discover them in the midst of decision making.

ESTABLISHING A STRUCTURE FOR DELIBERATION AND DECISION MAKING

Facilitate the group in formulating operating principles for themselves.

Operating principles is a better term to use than *rules*. They are meant to guide professional behavior toward productive meetings and decisions. Rules imply controlling unwanted or negative behavior. The team will benefit from designing their own operating principles for reaching common goals. Our team's operating principles included phrases such as the following:

- We will listen with the intent to understand.
- We will arrive on time prepared to participate.
- We will make decisions based on the values and mission of our school.

Decide how to make decisions.

The group needs to decide how it will make decisions. Each decision can be made a different way, and consensus is just one of those ways. On important issues that impact many people, consensus can provide a vigorous process to ensure that the final decision is a quality one. The group should have a good understanding of what consensus means and should operate from a commonly agreed on definition that is printed and available for review. Consensus is often misunderstood as full agreement by all members. There are decisions that all members may not fully agree with but will support. The group should explore this critical difference. As a member of the team, I would support a decision if it seemed reasonable and didn't compromise my core principles and beliefs. I would support a decision even if I didn't fully agree with it in order to take action and avoid the alternative of doing nothing.

There are many other ways to make a decision for problems with less impact and importance. These options should also be reviewed by the group and be available as a reference as needed. The team needs to know what options it has for decision making.

Establish a method of discussing a problem with full and equal participation.

People with the strongest and most emotional opinion can dominate a discussion. Someone who has thought a lot about a topic and is very vocal in advocating a position can have great influence over someone who is less invested and has spent less time thinking about it (Surowiecki, 2005). Some people can be afraid to say what they think if they feel that they will have to defend what they say to someone who they perceive as more articulate or emotional. To avoid this situation, each person should have time to think or write down his or her thoughts before a discussion. Team members can take turns stating thoughts without challenges or objections being immediately voiced. Each idea or opinion could be written on a sheet of chart paper and posted for review. An entire meeting could be devoted to allowing each idea to be stated.

Be clear about the purpose of a discussion before the discussion starts.

A discussion perceived as leading to a decision takes on a different tone than one whose purpose is to solicit everyone's thoughts. Establishing an agenda that states the purpose for the agenda item can remove unnecessary tension from a meeting.

NAVIGATING THROUGH THE COMPLEX PROBLEM OF BULLYING

Lead the learning and make sure people know that learning is an essential part of the change process.

The best way to initiate effective bullying prevention is to have a small group of people learn about this problem together. Although it could seem too slow of a response to an urgent issue, becoming familiar with the research and best practice regarding bullying will empower the group and also make it function more cohesively. A school leader can provide a small group with a menu of resources on bullying prevention. Making this choice together is a positive way to start the learning together as a team.

Don't do too much ahead of time.

Peter Bregman (2007) recommends the Just Enough to Start (JETS) strategy as the most effective way to make change in an organization. It is the leader's role to start the process of change by putting as much of the assessing, planning, and decision making in the hands of the people who will be impacted by the change. This approach also ensures that the collective talents and strengths of members of the school community are recognized and valued as assets.

Look at underlying assumptions.

Many seemingly intractable differences among members of the school community can be reconciled eventually by allowing some time to explore the underlying assumptions of their differing opinions.

Here is an example of how this exploration of underlying assumptions led to a consensus on a contentious issue:

> *Members of our staff once had a strong difference of opinion over how students should be placed in classes for the following school year. Some staff thought that students should be matched to fit teachers with certain styles of teaching. Others thought that styles did not matter and that students should be appropriately grouped together and randomly assigned to teachers. There seem to be no reconciling these two positions. The debate was stuck between two different ways of placing students. Our building cabinet, after discussing how the staff was stuck, decided to change the discussion from debating two methods of placing students to exploring staff assumptions about the placement process itself. The staff agreed that the source of the disagreement over the placement process was the following assumption: "Every teacher is capable of effectively teaching every student." Once the discussion shifted to this assumption, people started to listen to each other rather than support one method over another. After a thorough discussion, all staff ended up agreeing with that assumption. They then worked together to build a method that reflected that common shared assumption.*

Make sure resistance is not just accepted, but welcomed.

Although people who resist the ideas that most people support are often seen as obstacles to progress, inviting their opinions and ideas is an essential part of the change process. School leaders can meet individually with people who are resistant or skeptical for the purpose of hearing what they have to say. If a leader listens well (listening is not agreeing), two important things happen:

- Important issues become known before a change is put in place.
- Those who resist lose their complaint that no one listens to them.

Since effective bullying prevention requires the commitment and cooperation of everyone, hidden resistance and complaints against those in charge can undo even the most impressive plan. It is better to listen and listen again even if it slows the process down a bit. Welcoming skepticism is the best way of avoiding cynicism.

Avoid jumping to solutions.

All of the previous points made about small group processing echo the need to understand the problem of bullying before searching for a solution and then implementing it. Taking the time to understand the problem of bullying, its scope, and complexity will ultimately produce better solutions than picking one solution too quickly and hoping it does the job.

Discuss and explore areas of agreement on a problem or issue before starting to differ.

Sometimes the perception of differences can impede decision making. If members of the team think that there are too many differences and that the gap is too wide to bridge, they can become discouraged. Investing time to discover areas of agreement can make the task of coming together seem less overwhelming.

Locate and discuss the true sources of conflict.

Realize that differing styles or temperaments for problem solving among the members of the team can be a greater source of conflict than substantive differences. Include some activities for the team members to discover how they differ in style and temperament. Miscommunication, unclear language, and fuzzy thinking on concepts could also be the source of conflict rather than the substance of the issue itself.

Remind people that nothing is cast in stone.

Sometimes new ideas need to be tried out and evaluated before they become accepted and institutionalized. People often resist change because they are uncertain of the consequences of that change. They are afraid of being stuck with something forever. Any new initiative or change can have a tremendous number of possible contingencies that resistant staff members can transform into many objections that can never be answered in advance. Acknowledging the validity of possible problems and proposing a trial period to assess and evaluate the change will often be a reasonable and acceptable alternative to a permanent change.

Michael Fullan (2010b) states that we "learn about implementation during implementation" (p. 27). People are more likely to support trying something for a trial period of time and evaluating it at predetermined time. This approach will decrease some people's resistance and create a reasonable alternative for those who are undecided. This also has practical value because it can provide information for improving the proposed change.

Recognize, monitor, and constructively use emotions to support the change process.

Sometimes a topic can be so emotionally charged that people have trouble thinking rationally about it. People who are too emotional can be easily dismissed by those with a less emotional investment in the issue. Trying to suppress people's emotions will only create greater conflicts and could damage relationships within the team. A more productive strategy is to acknowledge and affirm people's emotions as a sign of their caring and investment in an issue. People with strong emotions need the opportunity to share their thoughts, opinions, and their stories.

An effective leader helps the group accept the emotions that arise during the decision-making process but does not allow them to dominate the process. Setting aside a designated time for sharing and intentionally separating it from the decision-making process is a helpful strategy.

Here is story about how emotions, when used correctly, galvanized a large group of people into positive action:

> I was a cochairperson of a district task force to address the problem of bullying. Up until that time, the district did not have a policy on bullying or any plan on how to address it. The task force was comprised of parents, teachers, administrators, and support staff and some students. We had a productive first meeting where we outlined the scope of the problem and what we needed to do. The purpose of the second meeting was to plan and schedule how we would proceed in the fall of the following school year: developing a policy, exploring programs, planning professional development, and communicating with the public. In the time between the first meeting and the second meeting, many more parents heard about the task force and showed up at the next scheduled meeting.
>
> My colleague and I were fine with the increase in the number of people interested in helping with the problem and welcomed the new members. As we started to follow our plan for the meeting, the emotions in the room became palatable. We looked at each other and knew that our plan for the meeting would not work. We called a brief time-out and decided to see if the group was open to the idea of letting everyone tell their story about bullying. We proposed it to the group, and everyone agreed to listen to these stories. Two and half hours later, the last story was told. To their credit, every district administrator was present and heard the stories and the criticisms that came with many of the stories, and they did not become defensive—they just listened. The parents, who had felt that no one had listened to them, finally felt that they were heard.
>
> Even though we were a few weeks away from the summer break, the task force decided to work and meet throughout the summer rather than wait until fall. At our next meeting this large group of parents, teachers, students, and administrators was divided into subcommittees assigned a different task. The task force ended up learning about the problem together, and people who initially seemed to be at odds started to work together toward common goals.

LINKING THE TEAM TO THE LARGER GROUP AND SCHOOL COMMUNITY

School leaders could be very skilled in working with a small team of eight to ten people, but that is only the *first* step in facilitating positive change for the whole school community. An important part of the team's responsibility is to educate and facilitate the larger school community. This does not mean that its job is to sell the change to the larger group but rather to find ways to involve them in solving problems and meeting goals. This means creating trust and opening lines of communication. There needs to be a continuous back-and-forth and give-and-take between the larger groups in the school and smaller group or team.

Figure 7.1 illustrates how the leader, team, and larger school community need to operate.

Figure 7.1   The Flow of Information

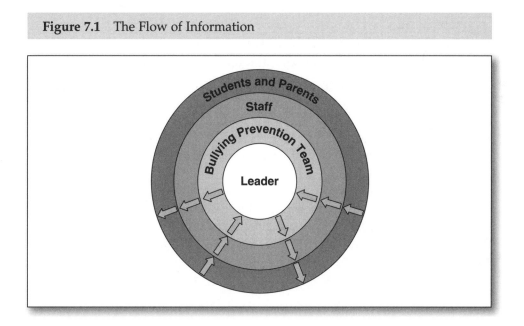

Here are some ways for linking the team with the entire staff:

Have the faculty meeting planned and facilitated by the team, not just the principal.

If the team is empowered to address the key problems and issues of the school, this team should be responsible for planning and facilitating this part of the meeting devoted to the problem. A member or members of team should present the issue on the agenda and facilitate the activity or discussion planned for that agenda item.

Here is sample of how our staff/faculty meeting's agenda looked like:

Topic	Person(s) presenting	Method	Time	Purpose/ Outcome
Cafeteria supervision	Mr. Smith and Mrs. Jones	Small group discussion	15 minutes	Brainstorming ideas for planning

Staff should receive the agenda prior to the meeting. This will tell them what they can expect at the meeting (adding predictability and decreasing surprises helps people be in a better frame of mind for the meeting). Having staff other than the principal facilitate the meeting increases the collective ownership and shared leadership of the staff. A predetermined time, decided by the team, can demonstrate a respect for colleagues' time and can keep the discussion focused and on task. Listing the outcome and/or purpose adds another element of predictability to the discussion.

Use small group discussion as a way to increase staff participation and keep the discussion on task.

We assigned a facilitator and recorder from the building cabinet for each small discussion group. It was important to have a member of our building cabinet hear each discussion so he or she could bring that information back to the cabinet meeting. Keeping notes from each small-group discussion demonstrates to staff that their ideas are important and will be considered by the team.

To ensure that every voice is heard, the small-group facilitators should decide on an organizing structure for the discussion. A simple one would be round-robin where each person gets thirty seconds to a minute to share their thoughts without interruption, until all the ideas and thoughts are shared.

View the faculty/staff meeting as a vehicle to collect data.

Sometimes, our team would need the ideas and thoughts from the entire staff to help them make a decision. They would often want to know what people were thinking and feeling about a topic or problem. They would craft a few key questions in a survey and ask staff to respond to them.

Our team would convey to the larger community that their input is valued and a necessary part of the decision-making process. Members of the team would inform staff that the notes generated at the meeting would be reviewed and analyzed by them at the next meeting. Our team would draft a proposal based on the notes and present this proposal at the next meeting or in written form prior to the meeting in order to solicit input from the entire staff.

Invite nonmembers of the team to the team meeting.

Sometimes, an issue or problem involves staff who are not members of the bullying prevention team. Inviting them to the team's meeting to solicit their thoughts is an effective way of linking the team with the entire staff.

Give People the Right Things to Think About.

The team can be a catalyst for change by putting the right things in front of the staff to think about. Adding a new element to the conversation on a problem and allowing time for discussion can be an effective way to bring staff together without concerns about a decision being made. Changing the discussion, raising awareness, and increasing the knowledge of the large school community can have a great benefit that can go beyond just solving a problem or addressing an issue.

SUMMARY

- A school leader needs to actively empower a small group of representatives of the school community in taking the lead in bullying prevention and making decisions.
- A strong decision-making team needs time to become acquainted with each other and to develop trust based on an understanding and respect of each other's values and beliefs.
- A school leader has three essential tasks for empowering and sustaining the effectiveness of the team:

  o Creating the conditions for effective group functioning
  o Establishing a structure and process for deliberating and decision making
  o Navigating the difficult and complex problem of bullying

- A school leader needs to allow time for members of the team to develop a sense of ownership and identity as a team and understand the parameters of their decision making.
- Key elements of effective group functioning include having operating principles developed by the team, having a variety of ways of making a decision, and ensuring full and equal participation of all members of the team.
- There is a variety of strategies for a school leader to use in helping a team effectively address the complex and elusive nature of school bullying. Most importantly, school leaders should welcome dissenting opinions, explore areas of agreement, and probe for underlying assumptions that could be the source of conflicts.
- Emotions can be acknowledged and affirmed as an important part of the change process.
- The team and the larger school community need to work in concert with each other in planning, implementing, and evaluating any bullying prevention effort.

ACTIVITIES TO "LEAD GROUPS TO LEAD"

ACTIVITY 1: SMALL GROUPS—WHAT NOT TO DO

Purpose

The purpose is to reflect on what small groups need in order to work effectively. Watching a negative model can be a fun way to see what happens when a group has no structure or operating principles.

Content

The four main characters in the *Seinfeld* TV series are well known to most people. They are infamous for their pettiness, insensitivity, shallowness, and inability to learn from experience, hence; they are very funny. There is a scene from the episode titled "The Comeback" (Trainor, 1997; available on YouTube at www.youtube.com/watch?v=c2eCXhbYWVU&feature=youtu.be) where George, who had just been insulted by a coworker for eating too many shrimp, finds Jerry, Elaine, and Kramer and asks them for advice on what to say as witty comeback to his coworker. This could have been a great situation for brainstorming together in support of a friend; however, George does not get the response he wants, and the situation rapidly deteriorates.

Procedure

Have staff sit in small groups to view the video clip. Show the video clip and provide a brief description of George's situation. It is a very funny scene, especially when Kramer gives his advice. Ask participants to reflect on a time they were part of a group that was dysfunctional. Have them reflect on that experience and why it was dysfunctional (*make it clear that no names of specific individuals should be used*). Ask them to go share their experience with the other members of the group. Have members assume the following roles: facilitator, note taker, reporter, and timekeeper.

Guide Questions

What made the small group experience unproductive?

How did the people in the group interact?

What type of decisions did the group attempt to make?

How did you feel about the decisions made or not made?

What could have helped facilitate the process so that the group could have worked better together?

What is your feeling now about working in groups?

If you were in charge of that group, what would you do?

As a group, agree on two essential elements of effective group decision making.

Have each group share the essential elements they agreed on.

ACTIVITY 2: COMPASS POINT ACTIVITY

This activity is adapted from *The Personality Compass: A New Way to Understand People* by Turner and Greco (1998).

Purpose

This activity can be used with the entire staff as a way of having them discover their personal style of interacting. It will give participants an opportunity to reflect on their own personality type and their colleagues' types.

Content

This activity is based on the assumption that there are four basic personality styles. Each style is assigned a point on the compass.

North (plunges into problems/"Let's do it" mindset): People with this style like to act, try things out, and plunge right into things.

East (sees "big picture"/speculating): People with this style like to look at the big picture and consider possibilities before acting.

South (caring/relationship focused): People with this style like to know that everyone's feelings have been taken into consideration and that all voices have been heard before any action is taken.

West (paying attention to detail/concerned with logistics): People with this style like to know the who, what, when, where, why, and how before acting.

Procedure

Distribute a sheet of paper listing the four compass points and their description. Ask them to individually select the compass point that best describes the way they work in a group.

After they have had the opportunity to select their compass point, have them join the other people who selected that same point. (You could have a sign posted for each direction, so they can congregate under the sign with their compass point on it.)

Each compass point group should answer the following questions and chart the responses on a piece of chart paper and be prepared to report back to the full group.

Questions to Answer

What are the strengths of our style? (List four adjectives.)

What are the limitations of our style? (List four adjectives.)

What style do we find the most difficult to work with? Why?

What do others need to know about us that will make our work together more successful?

Each direction group can share with the other groups their responses to the questions.

When groups have finished presenting, the entire group can discuss the following questions:

What ratio of the different compass points would make an effective and productive team?

What would happen if a team were made up only of one direction?

What can a team do to make sure that the different styles can work productively?

OUTCOMES

1. Diversity in a small group can lead to quality decisions, but it will not happen by chance. Each team must determine the best way for it to function.

2. Awareness of differences in styles can make a big difference in a group surviving and being productive or floundering and being unproductive.

8

The Human Face of Data

"Bring 'data' in, but in the right way."

—John Kotter (2008, p. 90)

I got very discouraged about how our school was doing in preventing and reducing bullying. After about a year implementing our bullying prevention program, I felt that our efforts were not paying off; in fact, things seemed to be getting worse. The number of phone calls from parents and student complaints of bullying seemed to be growing exponentially—it was hard for me to keep up with them. It was only after a few conversations with colleagues and some time for reflection that I realized that the complaints were actually a sign that our efforts were working.

School leaders can view complaints as negative things. Sometimes, the best feedback we can expect for our efforts is "No news is good news." When a school is running smoothly, it seems to be on automatic pilot rather than a sign that we are competent and skillful in doing our jobs. Having a lot of complaints is a sign that things are not working, so how could I interpret it as a sign of progress in bullying prevention?

A complaint about bullying made to a school leader can mean several things:

- The person being bullied knows that what is happening is bullying and that bullying is wrong and not something deserved.
- It is acknowledgement that the person receiving the complaint is someone who cares and will do something about it.
- Bystanders understand their responsibility to report bullying and know that it is not tattling.
- The true picture of what is happening is gradually emerging.
- Anything negative happening between students is viewed as bullying.

All of the above points are positive signs. Even the last one about over-reporting is positive. I viewed bullying complaints that turned out not to be bullying, as a teachable moment to explain the difference between bullying and other inappropriate behaviors. It was better to have a bullying complaint turn out to be a nonbullying incident than to have no complaints and mistakenly think that all was well.

The best analogy to reframe complaints from a negative to a positive is that of comparing bullying in schools to having high blood pressure. People with high blood pressure can feel fine and live their lives with no apparent problem or outward symptom of a problem. Unfortunately for many, the first sign of a problem could be a fatal one: a heart attack.

Schools can appear fine and run smoothly yet still have a serious problem with bullying. Unfortunately, the first visible consequence on prolonged ongoing bullying can be a violent act of revenge or self-harm. Long-term psychological and emotionally harm done by bullying negatively affecting a person's life can go undetected by the school.

Like a person discovering high blood pressure before serious damage happens, a school discovering the true extent of bullying should feel positive because knowing about the problem is better than not knowing. Knowing allows corrective steps to be taken. As with high blood pressure, the problem of bullying requires "numbers" to reveal the extent of the problem. Schools need to have a way to get the numbers (data) that will tell the real story about bullying. They cannot rely on how things look or feel on the surface. Receiving complaints is one way to *start* to get those numbers, but there are others ways that need to be used.

ASSESSING THE PROBLEM OF BULLYING

There are many options available for measuring the extent and type of bullying in a school. Many assessment tools also provide valuable information about how students feel about school in general and about the school's efforts to address bullying. In addition to identifying who is doing the bullying and who is being bullied, these measures can assess bystander behaviors and attitudes.

Here are some guidelines for selecting an *assessment tool*.

Do not reinvent the wheel.

Some schools and districts decide to develop their own student surveys or questionnaires. Unless there is a trained psychometrician on staff, it is very likely that these homemade instruments will not yield valid or reliable information. Staff can often have a difficult time accepting the results of a survey, so any doubts or misgivings about the legitimacy of the instrument will only strengthen the resistance people may have to doing something about the problem. Developing a homemade instrument also takes a lot of time and can require frequent revisions and editing. Homemade instruments also do not have built-in ways of analyzing and presenting the data, so information obtained can be difficult to interpret and use for guidance and goal setting.

Involve the bullying prevention team in selecting the most appropriate assessment instrument.

This can be one of the most important initial tasks that the team can do. The selection process is a great example of on-the-job or embedded professional development. Their task is determining the *most appropriate* instrument for meeting the particular needs of their school. Since no assessment instrument is perfect, the team will benefit from knowing in advance what information they will be getting and what they are not getting. The team should develop, articulate, and communicate the criteria for selecting an assessment instrument.

Consider how the assessment will be administered.

Even the *best* assessment instrument has to be administered in the school environment. The team needs to consider all the variables and details involved in administering it. The time and resources available to a school need to match the administrative requirements of the assessment. Schools are busy places, so any assessment must fit into the crowded schedule of the school day.

Use *Measuring Bullying Victimization, Perpetration, and Bystander Experiences: A Compendium of Assessment Tools* (Hamburger, Basile, & Vivolo, 2011) from the National Center for Injury Prevention and Control to view scientifically valid instruments that have been used in research and practice.

This is a free resource available at www.cdc.gov/violenceprevention/pub/measuring_bullying.html. It is a publication of The National Center for Injury Prevention and Control and the Center for Disease Control and Prevention. Here is how it describes itself:

> This compendium provides researchers, prevention specialists and health educators with tools to measure a range of bullying experiences . . . Given that numerous measures of bullying exists, researchers and practitioners may find it challenging to identify which of the available measures is appropriate for assessing a particular bullying experience. (p. 2)

Overall, it contains thirty-three measures that met their criteria for being scientifically appropriate for use. It does not recommend any of them. It is not an exhaustive list and is limited by measures for which they received permission to feature. It only includes one instrument that specifically measures homophobic bullying. There are two instruments that measure electronic aggression or cyberbullying.

Don't limit your assessment to just students; include parents and staff.

Although some assessment instruments are designed only for students, that shouldn't prevent assessing parents and staff. Using more than one instrument does make data collection more complicated and time consuming, but the information gathered from these groups will make the effort worthwhile. Assessing students, parents, and staff also affirms the message that bullying prevention involves the entire school community and that change needs to occur not just with the students.

Note About School Climate Assessments: Many schools want to assess their school climate. Some school climate surveys include information about bullying, but not all do. There is much overlap between assessing bullying and assessing school climate. The choice does not have to be either/or but could be doing both types of assessments. All of the considerations listed regarding bullying assessment can be made regarding school climate. It depends on the needs and goals of a particular school. An excellent resource for information on school climate assessment is at the Safe and Supportive Schools website (safesupportiveschools.ed.gov).

USING MULTIPLE SOURCES OF DATA

> *"Emotionally intelligent leaders know that their primal task is to look first to the organizational reality, identifying the issues with the full involvement of key individuals. They take the conversation to the organization as a whole, using engaging processes to get people viscerally involved in unearthing the current reality, while tapping into individual and collective hopes for the future."*
>
> —Goleman, Boysatziz, and McKee (2002, p. 201)

No matter how well any assessment tool collects information related to bullying, that information must somehow touch the hearts and minds of the school community. John Kotter (2008) described how to use that information:

> For the most part, we have been taught to tell people the facts, and as logically as possible. But there is another method and one that is arguably more powerful. Show them. Let them see with their own eyes, and not only through aggregated abstract data . . . rational misses the exceptionally important point here about the effect of thinking on behavior versus the effect of emotions on behavior. (p. 75)

I know of some school leaders who have been convinced that the data they collected on surveys about bullying would *convince* staff to support bullying prevention. Data alone cannot do the convincing. I know a committee that interpreted the data that *only 7 percent* of the students reported being bullied on the school bus to mean that the school didn't need to do anything about the problem. If one student of that 7 percent were a committee member's child, that member would feel very differently about the problem. The decision to do nothing differently would not be acceptable. *Numbers* help us see the problem of bullying, but people need to *see and feel* the human story to be moved to do something about it.

The Blind Spot Revisited

In business, the data from the external world are brought in to penetrate and inform the internal world of the company. This translates into sending people out to talk to customers or bringing customers in to share their thoughts and opinions. In schools, people of the internal world (adults) and the people of the external world (the students) share the same time and space.

In Chapter 1, I explained how bullying happens in the blind spot of adults. Bullying is *not* in the blind spot of the students. These two experiences in the same time and space are radically different, as illustrated in Figure 8.1.

Adults need to know that they only see and hear a very small percentage of the bullying that is happening right in front of them. Although it is an important first step, realizing and accepting that bullying is in their blind spot will not by itself reveal the bullying. Data from a survey by itself cannot overcome the reality of what they think their senses tell them. Adults in school need something else to help them see beyond their senses.

Figure 8.1   Two Realities of Bullying

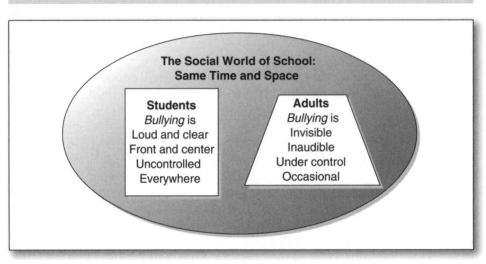

USING FOCUS GROUPS TO ADD
THE HUMAN FACE TO DATA

"It takes two to speak the truth—one to speak and another to hear."

—Henry David Thoreau

In addition to surveys or questionnaires, focus groups are another way to gather a different type of data. The information gained from them, when added to the statistical data from surveys, can create a more compelling and human description of what is happening in schools. They help schools see and hear what is happening in the blind spot.

In addition to the qualitative data they will yield, there are other positive outcomes from conducting focus groups:

- The very act of asking people to share is a tangible and outward sign that the schools care about the lives of students and take bullying prevention very seriously.
- Listening to people in a focus group can demonstrate great respect for the stories and thoughts of members of the school community.
- Having people tell their stories in focus groups creates greater trust in the school and increases the likelihood that people will feel more comfortable reporting bullying.
- People who participate in a focus group can experience a greater sense of ownership and connection with the school.
- Staff members gain greater insight and understanding about the lives of the people they serve.

- Some great and useful ideas could emerge from the responses of the participants.
- Thoughtful and careful listening can connect the adult world and the student world.

CONDUCTING FOCUS GROUPS

There are some basic guidelines for conducting focus groups. After reviewing many of them, I would recommend using a set that was designed for use in an educational setting. It is from the Bill and Melinda Gates Foundation and can be found at www.smallschoolsproject.org/PDFS/focus-groups.PDF.

Its guidelines include steps for conducting a focus group, a sample moderator's guide, suggested timeline, and sample invitation letter.

An excellent resource from the Queensland Schools Alliance Against Violence for possible questions to include for a focus group of students can be found at www.ccypcg.qld.gov.au/pdf/publications/reports/QSAAV-Student-Consultation.pdf.

This site also includes a discussion guide, group consent form, and a fact sheet for parents of students and an evaluation form.

Focus Groups

According to Wikipedia, "a **focus group** is a form of qualitative research in which a group of people are asked about their perceptions, opinions, beliefs and attitudes towards a product, service, concept, advertisement, idea, or packaging" ("Focus group," n.d.). Questions are asked in an interactive group setting where participants are free to talk with other group members.

Table 8.1 Basic Recommendations for Focus Groups

Number of participants	8–12 people
Type of group	Homogenous group
Length of time	60–90 minutes
Number recommended sessions per topic	3–5 sessions with a different group each time
Relationship of participants	If possible, no previous relationships among them, or at least avoid having friends or family being in the same group.

(Continued)

Table 8.1 (Continued)

Selection process	Depends on desired outcome: they can be invited, selected by role or job, recruited volunteers, or selected at random. Always invite more (twice) people than desired size, i.e., if you want 8 people, invite 16.
Number/role of people involved in facilitating the group	Two people: one to ask questions and one to record comments in writing or with a tape recorder.
Number of questions	8–12
Location/environment/ seating arrangement	Can be held at school or more neutral location (community center or public library); room should be large enough to fit everyone comfortably and have door for privacy; participants should sit in a circle at tables. Provide some light refreshments if possible.
Information to share regarding topic	Develop a purpose statement for the discussion and share it in the invitation and at the start of the meeting. For example, "To gain a better understanding of the community's thoughts and attitudes toward bullying prevention in our school and solicit suggestions on improving our current efforts."

Recommended Ground Rules for Participants

A good set of ground rules will ensure that all participants feel comfortable and free to express their thoughts and opinions. Those need to be reviewed prior to the sessions and could be posted on the wall as a reminder. Most recommendations for ground rules include the following:

- One person talks at a time. Avoid side conversations.
- What is said in the room stays in the room. (Confidentiality)
- There are no right or wrong answers. The ideas, experiences, and opinions of everyone are valuable.
- Everyone doesn't have to answer every question.
- No specific mention by name of anyone involved in a bullying incident. (If someone wants to report an incident, the moderator should direct that person do so in the appropriate way in a private and individual meeting.)

Role of the Moderator

The moderator has the responsibility to present the questions and encourage full participation. The essential tasks of the moderator are the following:

- Have everyone feel welcome and comfortable.
- Clearly explain the purpose of the group.
- Present the ground rules.
- Include everyone in the discussion.
- Ensure confidentiality of discussion.
- Thank the participants for their help.

Since it is so important to have an open and safe environment for expressing diverse opinions, the moderator should have some experience in facilitating group discussions. Effective moderators should be able to

- Maintain neutrality both verbally and nonverbally to not influence the opinions of the participants
- Accurately paraphrase the responses of the participants
- Ask questions to probe for additional information or clarity
- Skillfully keep the discussion on the topic
- Keep a few participants from dominating the discussion

Key phrases to use to clarify or gain additional information from participants are the following:

"Can you talk more about that?"

"Would you explain it a little further for me?"

"Could you give an example of what you mean?"

"Let me see if I understand what you are saying . . ."

"What do others think about that?"

Role of the Assistant Moderator or Recorder

The person assuming this role is primarily responsible for making sure that all the information generated during the discussion is recorded in some form. Most recommendations for focus groups require that a recording device be used. All participants should know and agree in writing to have the session recorded. The assistant moderator can take notes and use a recording device. This person can note the body language of participants and share observations with the moderator following the session.

Questions on the Topic of Bullying

Prior to the start of the discussion, the moderator should state the definition of bullying from the school's policy. If the school doesn't have a policy that defines bullying, any definition that is part of the state law governing bullying could be used. If definition cannot be obtained from these sources, the most commonly used definition is from the Olweus Bullying Prevention Program: "A person is bullied when he or she is exposed, repeatedly and over time, to negative actions on the part of one or more other persons, and he or she has difficulty defending himself or herself" (Olweus et al., 2007, p. xxii)

Questions should be open-ended to allow for a range of responses. They should be relatively short and to the point and should not contain jargon or ambiguous language. The initial questions can be very general or invite participants to share something about themselves.

The small group responsible for bullying prevention in the school should be involved in selecting the questions used.

Some questions can be designed for soliciting participants'
knowledge about bullying.

"What do you think bullying is?"

"What are some examples of bullying behavior?"

"How can you tell bullying from other behaviors like fighting or breaking school rules?"

"How much of a problem do you think bullying is in school?"

"Why do you think some kids bully other kids?"

"Why do you think some kids are bullied?"

"What do you think about students who witness bullying?"

Questions can also be designed to solicit opinions on the
current status of bullying prevention in the school:

"What do you think of bullying in our schools right now?"

"What is the school doing to prevent and reduce bullying?"

"How do you think the school is doing?"

"How important do you think bullying prevention is for the school?"

"What could be done to improve bullying prevention in the school?"

"What do you think can be done to help students who are frequently bullied?"

"What do you think can be done to help stop students who bullying other students?"

"What do you think most kids feel about bullying?"

Questions can also be designed to solicit how participants feel about reporting bullying:

"If you were bullied, what would you do?"

"If you saw or heard someone being bullied, what would you do?"

"How do you feel about reporting bullying to staff person?"

"If you were to tell someone at school, who would it probably be?"

"If you are reluctant, explain why?"

"Why do you think other students are reluctant to report bullying?"

Questions can solicit ideas for what the school should do about bullying:

"What would be the best thing the school could do about bullying?"

"How should the school deal with kids when they bully others?"

"What do you think the school can do to make kids more comfortable with reporting bullying?"

"What could the school do to help bystanders deal with bullying?"

"What do you think people need to learn about bullying?"

"What would be the best way to help them learn it?"

ANALYZING THE DATA FROM ASSESSMENT INSTRUMENTS

Some assessment instruments are computerized and process all of the data automatically and generate a report with the statistics on each item. The data are also given for gender and grade level. What the coordinating team does with the data is what is most important for meaningful change. Data must ultimately help the school community make the best use of its time and efforts in bullying prevention and positive school change.

Key Points to Consider in Reviewing and Analyzing the Data

The coordinating team should revisit their selection criteria for choosing the instrument used. The team needs to remember what information it was looking to get and why that information was important for the school. Because of time and resource limitations, a shorter and easier way to administer instrument might have been selected, so the team should not be surprised or disappointed if they didn't get the information they wanted.

Avoid comparing data to evaluate one school or grade being better than another. Bullying prevention requires the entire school or district working together. Competition creates winners and losers, which is not what your work should be about. The information should be used to improve the entire school community and support everyone's efforts.

Use the data as a support to the overall efforts to improve the school, not as a way to criticize current efforts. Staff resistance to bullying prevention efforts will only increase if they feel that they are being judged or criticized.

Progress in bullying prevention needs to be evaluated in many ways, not just by one instrument. Substantive change does not happen quickly but requires long term and sustained effort over time.

Progress in some areas is more likely to happen than in others. Since the content of the student body is always changing, it might be difficult to see progress in the percentage of students who report being bullied. This shouldn't negate progress in other areas such as students feeling more comfortable reporting bullying or students feeling more trusting of school staff.

Give significant attention to the frequency and duration of bullying experienced by some students. Students who are bullied frequently over long periods of time are at great risk. Even if the percentages are low in that category, the team should devote their attention to finding out who those students are and take steps to protect them. This means having school counselors check in with students who they feel are vulnerable and at risk.

Look for information that points to areas for immediate positive change. There are many certain areas of the school building where there is more bullying happening than expected. It might be relatively easy to reassign supervision in that area. This change could have an immediate positive impact in decreasing bullying there. If it does, that success should be shared and celebrated with the school community. People need to see their efforts paying off.

ANALYZING THE DATA FROM FOCUS GROUPS

The purpose of the focus group is to supplement the data from quantitative assessment instruments. More importantly, it allows staff involved in bullying prevention to hear firsthand the experiences, thoughts, and opinions of the school community. Focus groups can provide data that can make the issue more human and better able to touch the hearts and minds of the community. Most school leaders and members of the bullying prevention team are not researchers or professionals in the field of evaluation. Time is also a precious commodity in schools. Summarizing and analyzing the information from focus groups should reveal any pattern or reoccurring theme found in the answers and also provide specific information that could be useful in bullying prevention planning. It is important to keep the original purpose in mind and be as efficient as possible in analyzing the data.

Here is basic summary, adapted from McNamara (2006), of how to analyze information from focus groups:

Basic analysis of "qualitative" information (respondents' verbal answers in interviews, focus groups, or written commentary on questionnaires)

1. Read all the comments from those participating in the group.

2. Have leadership team develop categories for comments, e.g., concerns, suggestions, strengths, weaknesses, similar experiences, program inputs, recommendations, outputs, outcome indicators, etc.

4. Look for patterns of responses or insights that stand out.

5. Look for stories that can tell the human side of the problem.

4. Keep all commentary for several years after completion in case it is needed for future reference.

WORKING WITH THE BULLYING PREVENTION TEAM TO INTERPRET THE DATA

Since the team selected the assessment instrument and, hopefully, participated in the focus group process, they should be the key people in analyzing and interpreting the data from all of the assessments. The team should operate as they would at other meetings with the same structure and operating principles.

Here are some recommendations for facilitating the team process:

- *Let each member of the team review the data individually (maintaining confidentiality).* This will allow people to form their own ideas rather than be influenced by others with stronger opinions. It will also save time at the meeting.
- *Use a simple uniform way of responding to the data.* Each member of the team when reviewing the data can respond to each item or key finding with

  o Confirmed what I believed
  o Surprised me
  o Intrigued me
  o Concerned me

They can come to the meeting with their responses with two main purposes in mind:

- *Explore in an organized way the collective response of the team.* The team can see where members agreed in assigning the four statements. This can be a *map* for the process of coming to consensus on what to highlight or emphasize in the presenting of the information.
- *Discuss and clarify their differences in responding to the data.* Exploring and discussing the differences in their response is a good way to strengthen the team.

The team can sort the findings into three broad categories:

1. Positives to build on

2. Areas of concern

3. Uncertain

After reviewing the findings, list:

1. Current practices to maintain or strengthen

2. Needs to be addressed in the short term

3. Needs to be addressed in long term

Use this organization of information to plan and structure the presentation of the findings with the wider school community.

Hold off on more exact goal setting until the community has seen the findings and you have solicited their input.

It is important to work visually using sticky notes, index cards, chart paper, and markers. The results should be visible to all team members for their collective review and discussion. This should help the team synthesize and interpret the data and then translate it into a plan of action.

Translating Findings Into Goals and Plans

The task of the bullying prevention team is to use data to determine appropriate goals and plans of action. Since the team should be meeting regularly, there will be opportunities for monitoring progress and making adjustments and modifications while implementing the plans. The goals should reflect both the needs determined by the assessments and by the collective judgment of the team. There should be just a few goals, and they should be clear and easy to understand.

Table 8.2 is an example of a simple form that illustrates how data can be translated into plans of action.

Look for leveraging goals in setting priorities for bullying prevention. Leveraging goals are ones that, if achieved, can have a positive impact on

Table 8.2   Translating Data Into Plans of Action

Need or Concern	Goal	Key Actions	Specific Strategies	Evaluation
Students who are bullied do not consistently report it to school staff.	Increase the trust between students and staff. Students need to know that staff are receptive to hear what they have to share.	Staff need to repeatedly check in with students and explicitly state their availability to listen to them.	Once a month for 5–10 minutes at a designated schoolwide time, every teacher shares some information about bullying and reiterates concern and a willingness to listen to any student	Members of the team will check with teachers to see how the mini session went. They will keep a record of the responses they receive. Use online survey to check in with students.

Source: Survey/Focus group.

several other areas of need. For example, promoting greater trust between staff and students will lead to more reporting, and more reporting will lead to intervening more frequently.

The goals and plans should be shared with staff and reviewed at staff meetings. When appropriate, they can also be shared with students, especially on the secondary level. Goals can also be posted on bulletin boards and mentioned in newsletters. Showing specific activities designed to meet the assessed needs demonstrates a tangible commitment to bullying prevention to the entire school community. After a predetermined period of time, the team should evaluate progress on meeting that goal and share those results with the school community.

SHARING THE ASSESSMENT FINDINGS

The bullying prevention team should also be involved in preparing and sharing the findings. This is an important part of the process of establishing an effective bullying prevention program. Presenting the data gathered from different sources should paint a picture of current status in the school/district and also introduce the preliminary work of the bullying prevention team. The school community needs to understand the extent of the problem yet also see initial steps/plans to address the problem.

There are some critical components for presenting the assessment findings:

Prefacing Statement: Four C's

How you introduce the findings will have a strong influence on how they are perceived and understood by any audience. The four elements will help present the information in a positive context without diminishing the needs and concerns of the school/district.

- *Core*: Bullying prevention is not an add-on program. It is at the core or center of the school's efforts to provide the best education possible for all students. Students need an environment where they feel safe and secure in order to learn. Connecting bullying prevention to the values and mission of the school/district emphasizes that the benefits of effective bullying prevention will go beyond just dealing with a problem to improving the learning of all students.
- *Courage*: Any school/district that actively assesses the extent and scope of bullying and people's attitude toward it is taking a very positive and essential first step in preventing and reducing bullying. Regardless of what the findings reveal about the current school environment, knowing what is really happening and taking appropriate action is preferable to not knowing and thinking everything is fine. This could be where the concept of the *blind spot* could be shared. The school/district should be commended for having the courage to find out what is happening and openly sharing it with the whole school community.
- *Commitment*: Regardless of what the findings reveal, bullying prevention requires the concerted effort of each member of the school community. This presentation is an opportunity for the school community to know that bullying prevention is more than implementing a program; it is a commitment to work together to improving the learning environment for everyone. The commitment is to put the *caring* that people have for students into more visible and positive actions.
- *Continuous*: The school is not starting from scratch in its efforts to address bullying. It also doesn't have to reject or negate all that it is currently doing related to this problem. The findings provide an opportunity to develop an approach that can build on prior achievements. Bullying prevention requires ongoing vigilance. The addition of any new program or practice will only sustain and improve current bullying prevention efforts.

Explain the assessment process and the definition of bullying used. It helps the audience to know the source of the information and how it was obtained. You can also include the number of participants who took the survey and participated in a focus group.

Clarify that the presentation includes the most salient assessment information. The audience needs to know how much information they are receiving. All the assessment information should be made available somehow afterward for those interested enough to want it.

Share the basics. The *who, what, when, where,* and *how* of bullying should be shared.

Be open and candid about the concerns raised by the data. Be specific about the concerns and where the school needs to direct its efforts.

Share actual quotes from focus groups in relation to the data presented. A piece of data represented by number will only have more impact if an actual quotation from a participant in a focus group is shared.

Include the preliminary work of the team in designating long—term goals and short-term goals. Audiences need to hear that some positive action is already planned to address the needs.

Considering other options depending on the audience. It might be helpful to show brief video clips about bullying. A "homemade" video consisting of student, parent, and/or staff voices sharing their thoughts regarding bullying and indicating their commitment to help with the problem can be a great tool for enlisting support for all bullying prevention efforts.

SUMMARY

- Knowing about the bullying that is happening is always preferable to not knowing, so an increase in the number of complaints of bullying could be a very positive sign of progress.
- The bullying prevention team should be involved in all aspects of assessing the problem.
- Use multiple sources of information to assess the problem—quantitative and qualitative.
- The bullying prevention team should analyze and interpret all the data and identify areas of strength in addition to areas of concern and need.
- Translate the data into a few clear long-term and short-term goals and strategies of achieving them.
- Present the data in a way that does more than deliver bad news providing areas to build on and pointing out how bullying prevention is connected to the school mission and values.

ACTIVITY FOR "THE HUMAN FACE OF DATA": TWO SIDES OF THE STORY

Purpose

This activity will help either the bullying prevention team or larger groups (faculty, parents, and students) gain a better understanding of assessment and how it leads to positive action and change.

Content

Ask participants to describe themselves using only numbers. (If necessary provide some examples: age, height, years of experience, address, phone number.) Leave it up to them to decide on what categories to use and how many to use. The goal would be to provide the clearest and most comprehensive description of themselves. Have them record the numbers on a sheet of paper and also state what the number represents, i.e., 52 represents age and 22 represents years teaching.

After they have finished that task, ask them to describe themselves using only words or phrases that don't include numbers. This can include adjectives but also descriptions of how they act in certain situations.

Procedure

After each participant has worked independently and finished both descriptions, divide the group in half; designate one half as the words group and the other as the number group. Have one person from the numbers groups find someone from the words group. Each person takes turns sharing their descriptions. Following the sharing, ask them to discuss what set provides a better description of a person.

Facilitate a whole-group discussion on assessment.

Follow-up

The group can be divided into small groups of four to five people. Pose the following task to them.

Pretend they are a life coach and need information on a person in order to help that person set goals to improve his or her life. Develop a list of critical questions to put on a form or use to interview with the client. Choose questions that would help the coach assess the person and help the person improve. Explain why those questions were selected. If the list had to be cut in half, what questions would stay and which ones would be eliminated?

Follow-Up (Another option)

Instead of using a set of numbers and a set of words, ask each person to think of one story or experience that would best sum up who they were as a person and/or a professional. Have people share their stories.

OUTCOMES

1. This activity should help people understand how different methods of assessment yield a different but equally valid picture of a person or a situation.

2. It should also help them see the connection between assessment and goal setting.

9

"Of the Students, by the Students, for the Students"

What School Leaders Need to Know

"We never educate directly but indirectly by means of the environment.... The required beliefs cannot be hammered in, the needed attitudes cannot be plastered on ... The very process of living together educates ... Education is thus a fostering, nurturing, cultivating process."

—John Dewey (1985, p. 63)

A RARE GLIMPSE

I once had a very frank conversation with a fifth-grade student. He was a model citizen of the school: a good student who always followed the rules. On his school bus, the fifth-grade students were reportedly mean to the students in the lower grades, to the point that the younger students were intimidated and frightened of them. He agreed that this was true. He said that these students dared to enter the back of the bus that the fifth graders had exclusively claimed. I conceded for the moment that the fifth graders should sit in the back of the bus but posed this question to him: "Even if you have the right to the back of the bus, won't you agree that it doesn't give you the right to treat them so harshly? Couldn't you just ask them to move or ask the driver to help you?" He paused thoughtfully and replied: "We do have the right to treat them that way. We were treated like that for years when we were younger, so now it is our turn to do it." For so many years, the bus was an environment that was left to the students to "police," and this cycle of revenge had become institutionalized.

Looking back on that moment, I appreciated his honesty since he took a risk with someone who could have easily lectured or scolded him. It was a gift because I had been given a glimpse into the world of the students—a world that we adults have forgotten and from which we are often far removed.

Postscript: A few weeks later, this same student came to me to ask if I could convene a meeting with the bus driver and all the students on the bus to talk about this problem. This was an important sign to me that our Peaceful School Bus Program was having a positive impact. The program would not eliminate bus problems but would help students learn better ways to solve those problems.

To make real and substantive progress in bullying prevention, educators need to understand the students' world rather than automatically fight it or control it. Traditional school cultures have not been able to control bullying. The majority of students do want adults to do something about bullying. They want adults to find a way to keep them safe without feeling controlled or manipulated by them. They need adults to guide through the challenging and often frightening process of growing and maturing. They need the wisdom that adults have gained from living longer than they have. Educators need to become trustworthy so students can accept and benefit from their guidance and support.

THE NECESSARY SHIFTS

I often hesitate to advocate this different type of approach for fear of being accused of being too theoretical, laissez-faire, or out of touch with the reality of dealing with students. I am convinced from my own experience with students and from all that I have learned in my career that schools need to move in a very different direction from many of the traditional approaches that have not been effective.

There are many current initiatives in bullying prevention that are designed to bypass schools and reach students directly through social media and popular culture. There are technologies being developed that will give specific directions to students if they are being bullied when they are actually on a social networking site. Public service announcements about bullying are currently embedded into programs on MTV or the Cartoon Network.

There are two main reasons for this more direct approach:

1. The growing recognition and acceptance of the fact that schools are much more of the problem than part of the solution to bullying. When parents of students who commit suicide tell their tragic stories, the school either didn't care or didn't handle the problem the right way or both.

2. Research in human development, social psychology, and bullying prevention have converged on the key idea that the most effective way to prevent and reduce bullying is to empower bystanders since peer influence has more impact on students than direct adult actions to change them.

If schools are to become part of the solution instead of being part of the problem, they need to change first before the students can. The students will only change when the adults in their lives change how they interact and communicate with them. The students will only change when schools develop cultures that recognize, value, and respect students and their needs rather than primarily seek to control or manipulate them. School leaders are in the best position to start the process of making these necessary shifts in culture. They are the ones whose decisions and actions will either keep schools as part of the problem or actually have them become places where students can feel not just safe, but respected and valued. In their *New York Times* op-ed piece titled "There's Only One Way to Stop a Bully," Susan Engel and Marlene Sandstrom (2010) summarize what needs to happen: "Most important, educators need to make a profound commitment to turn schools into genuine communities. Children need to know that adults consider kindness and collaboration to be every bit as important as algebra and spelling."

Here are the key ideas that school leaders need about students and bullying:

- There are significant limits on how much direct control adults have on bullying behavior (Rigby & Johnson, 2006/2007).
- Developmentally, adolescents need to assert their independence from adults. As they grow older, they care more about pleasing their peers than adults. If they see adults only as people who want to control them, they will tune out any message that comes from adults.
- Educators must understand the dynamics of bullying within the social environment of students and develop an approach consistent with this understanding (Swearer, 2010).
- Educators need to find new ways to work with students and become partners with them in a concerted effort to address bullying.

All of the above will not be easy or quick, but there is no other way.

THE SOCIAL NATURE OF BULLYING

Traditional school interventions focus on controlling individuals and assume that students can make rational decisions based on the possible consequences of their actions. Students in bullying situations are caught up in a swirl of conflicting thoughts and feelings that are hard to understand. Students also lack the skills necessary for acting in the way they might want to act if they *were able* to think rationally about it (which in most cases they aren't able to).

Bullying is a social problem where individual students act differently and influence each other in many complex and interdependent ways. Bullying behavior is like a musical chord made of three notes, all played at the same time. Play the notes separately, and the chord ceases to exist—it is just three notes. In bullying, the student who bullies, the student who is bullied, and the students who observe it are like those separate notes all played at the same time. Effective interventions are designed to address the interaction of the three participants rather than focus on each individual separately.

Bystanders see the bullying that is in the blind spot of adults, so they are the source of the information about bullying. They are also the ones who have the most influence in preventing and reducing bullying or increasing and intensifying it. If that is the case, should adults just step out the way and leave the responsibility for dealing with the problem to students? That would be a serious mistake and would put a devastating burden on the very people—students—adults have the responsibility to protect. Schools need to support students and demonstrate this support by talking about these issues and moving them to the front of the school's agenda

Understanding Bystanders

In an enlightening article by Ken Rigby and Bruce Johnson (2006/2007), based on field research, students were asked about their reluctance to intervene on behalf of the victim. Their answers fell into four categories:

1. It was not their concern.

2. They were afraid of the consequences for intervening. It was safer to support the bully.

3. They felt that the responsibility was with the victim. The victim should be able to defend himself or herself. The victim sometimes deserved the bullying.

4. Any action they took would be useless or make things worse.

Other researchers such as Lazarus (2001) have suggested other reasons:

- They didn't recognize the behavior as bullying.
- They didn't want to get a friend in trouble.
- They didn't believe the adult would help.

Khosropour and Walsh (2000) found that 50 percent of sixth and seventh graders felt the victim could control the reason for being bullied and would learn something from the experience.

There are many compelling reasons for students not to tell and not to intervene when they witness bullying. Educators cannot simply tell students to tell them about bullying. They first need to understand why students don't tell and understand how they perceive adults.

Understanding the Social Dynamics of Bullying

"Placing bullying in its group context helps to better understand the individual's motivation to bully, the lack of support provided to victims, the persistence of bullying and the adjustment of victims across diverse contexts. Finally the group view is helpful in developing effective interventions against bullying."

—Christina Salmivalli (2010, p. 113)

The most effective interventions in preventing and reducing bullying are ones that focus on how all students relate to and influence each other's words and actions. Bullying is a behavior that functions as a way to gain prestige and status among peers. Bystanders, therefore, have a significant impact on the amount and the degree of bullying that occur in a school.

Here are some key findings from research in social and developmental psychology that emphasize the importance of focusing on the entire group of students rather than just the ones directly involved in bullying (Salmivalli, 2010):

- Part of the "coolness" that students who bully seem to have stems from their ability to challenge adult authority or "get away with it."
- Many students who bully have good social skills and can be popular with teachers. Many students who are bullied have poor social skills and are not popular with other students and staff. This can explain why many bystanders will actively or passively support the bullying even when they know that bullying is wrong.
- Sometimes joining in with the bullying becomes a way for less popular students to fit in and avoid becoming a target.
- Students who bully to gain prestige often are clever at picking on the student they know has few, if any, friends—the ones less likely to have defenders.
- Students who defend and support students who are victimized often have to have a high degree of empathy and self-efficacy. It is not enough to want to help; they need to feel that they will be successful if they try to help. They need to have the social skills and strategies to know how to intervene. They also have to have the confidence to intervene.

- Popular students with high status have the most influence in determining the amount of bullying that occurs in a class. If popular students appear to support bullying, it can go unchecked and even increase. If they appear to disapprove of bullying and support students who are victims, the amount of bullying can decrease significantly.
- Even if bystanders are not always effective in stopping the bullying toward certain students, the negative effects of the bullying on those students can be reduced. The student who is bullied at least feels that someone cares enough to help. Bystanders need to know that even if their intervening doesn't stop the bullying, it will make the victim feel supported and not alone. This can make a significant difference in lessening the pain of bullying.

A More Troubling Reason for Bystander Inaction

Research has also indicated that many bystanders want to help students who are bullied and know that they are supposed to but don't when they are actually in that situation. Students innately want to help others yet also want social connections, and these two needs are often in conflict. Sometimes helping a bullied student means risking membership in a desired social group. Students need adults to help them figure out what is the right thing to do, especially when life becomes complex and confusing.

Robert Thornberg (2010) research has revealed some other reasons for bystander reluctance that is related to the hidden messages that most schools give about what constitutes good and moral behavior. He suggests that students often think that helping other students who are bullied is in *conflict with* the school rules or what they perceive what it means to be a good student.

If the main message to students is that *good* behavior is following the rules set by the teacher, then situations that fall outside of the rules (where moral decisions are required) perplex students to the point of inaction. In these situations, students could view helping others as being against the rules, being none of their business and putting them at risk for getting in trouble. When rules and compliance with them are paramount to teachers, students often feel that it is the teacher's responsibility to intervene in any situation where rules are in question. Any decision a student made to solve a social problem would put him or her at risk of breaking the paramount rule of deferring authority to the teacher.

Schools also inadvertently send students the message that problems shouldn't happen and that they are only a distraction from the real business of school, the important business of academic learning. Students could also think that bringing attention to a problem would only evoke a negative response from a teacher who they assume is concerned with other more important issues.

A more troubling possibility is the bystander's perception that the student being bullied deserves it, because the teacher might not like or accept that student. An unpopular student who also breaks the rules of the class-room is getting what is deserved in the bystander's perception. Is it possible that bystanders might actually think that the teacher could even approve of the bullying because the bullied student only caused problems for the whole class and the teacher?

Thornberg (2010) concludes his article with the following observation:

> In order to educate and promote moral development and prosocial behavior among students, teachers have to consider the school culture they produce in their day-to-day interactions with each other and with their students . . . These are the significant part of the hidden curriculum in school . . . Teachers have to consider how they unconsciously might devalue and discourage students' real-life morals and instead consciously find strategies to empower them . . . Prosocial morality has to be practiced so that it can thereby become a significant part of the students' sense making and actions in everyday life. (pp. 607–608)

If teachers and schools, as Thornberg suggests, need to make these changes, who is in the best position to either help them or hinder them in making these changes? The answer is *the school leader*.

THE REAL CHALLENGE FOR SCHOOL LEADERS

Macklem (2003) defines school culture as follows:

> The culture of a school refers to the unwritten expectations that develop over time. It also involves the opinions that members of the culture develop and the way that problems are solved. It includes all of the rules that tell members of the system how to behave and interact with one another. (p. 26)

Effective bullying prevention is not just instituting a program in a school. It will require educators to significantly change the culture of most schools. This culture change means changing how staff view and treat students. The need for this cultural change is not understood and accepted by most educators.

Students will only listen to adults who take the time to understand their world and respect it. If school leaders, who are traditionally perceived as the authorities trying to control them, start to genuinely listen and understand their world, the lines of communication between the student world and the adult world can begin to open. This opening is where successful bullying prevention starts. Ironically, it is also where many other positive changes that go beyond bullying prevention can come together and start.

BEGIN WITH THE END IN MIND

"Today's life and work environments require far more than thinking skills and content knowledge. The ability to navigate the complex life and work environments in the globally competitive information age requires students to pay rigorous attention to developing adequate life and career skills."

(Partnership for the 21st Century, n.d.)

The qualities, attributes, attitudes, characteristics, values, and skills that educators and parents would describe as necessary for success in the world after school are the same ones that would describe an empowered bystander. That common picture or profile of the success of the K–12 educational system is what should guide all educational decisions. The best practices for bullying prevention are in alignment with the best pedagogical and instructional ones.

The empowerment of all students is the goal of all education efforts and decisions. The changes that are needed to prepare students for the 21st century are the same ones that are needed to effectively prevent and reduce bullying. *This is the key message that a school leader needs to convey to the entire school community in order to galvanize support in that direction.*

Here is a description from the Partnership for the 21st Century Skills website on leadership and responsibility:

LEADERSHIP AND RESPONSIBILITY

Guide and Lead Others

- Use interpersonal and problem-solving skills to influence and guide others toward a goal.
- Leverage strengths of others to accomplish a common goal.
- Inspire others to reach their very best via example and selflessness.
- Demonstrate integrity and ethical behavior in using influence and power.

Be Responsible to Others

- Act responsibly with the interests of the larger community in mind (Partnership for the 21st Century, n.d.).

Are We There Yet?

David Brooks in his *New York Times* column (2011) shared the results of a survey of young adults (eighteen- to twenty-three-year-olds) exploring their moral lives. He comments:

It's not so much that these young Americans are living lives of sin and debauchery . . . What's disheartening is how bad they are at thinking and talking about moral issues . . . Young people are groping to say anything sensible on these matters . . . They just don't have the categories or vocabulary to do so . . . this doesn't mean that America's young people are immoral. Far from it . . . they have not been given the resources—by schools, institutions, and families—to cultivate their moral intuitions, to think more broadly about moral obligations, to check behaviors that may be degrading. In this way, the study says more about adult American than youthful America.

These young people as bystanders had many opportunities to develop this moral reasoning but apparently did not. I assume that most of them were successful in school, yet this success did not include learning the 21st century skills of leadership and responsibility.

Leaders or Followers? Education or Training?

"Management (not leadership) is doing things the right way. Leadership is doing the right things."

—Peter Drucker

I have always had a problem with the statement "All children can learn" as a challenge to schools. Children are born *wired* to learn and start doing so immediately. Stating that they can learn is as redundant as saying "All children can breathe." The main concern should be *what* they are learning or not learning. The hidden assumption behind the statement "All children can learn" is that children need school to learn or need to be made to learn. With this assumption, they start out as a blank slate and need to be shaped or formed by the school. Under that assumption, schools have not been educating students but rather training them.

Training is for learning things that people are not wired to do—things that are very technical and specific to a certain task. Animals are trained to do things they would not instinctually do. Combat soldiers need to be trained to kill because most people are wired not to harm others. The goal of training is often to make everyone the same. Training makes sure that people follow the rules connected to the training they receive. Training can serve an important purpose, but it is not education.

Education is from the Latin word *educo* meaning *to lead out of*. The hidden assumption behind education is that there is something already there within the person, and it is the educator's task to lead, guide, or create the right conditions for it to come out and grow. Since everyone is unique, education should promote a natural diversity. This diversity is a source for more learning since people learn from each other.

Perhaps a better and more accurate saying should be "All children can lead." If educators believe that all children have the ability to lead (do the right things) they will educate them to lead and develop the confidence to do what is right. If adults don't think children are capable of leading, then children will think they are not capable of it. Students have empathy and a conscience, but they need the skills and confidence to use them in social situations. Over time, if students don't receive the education they need, empathy and conscience can remain inactive: they will lose them if they don't learn to use them.

Leading requires moral reasoning or the ability to do the right thing in situations not always covered by rules. A good example of this is when a person decides to drive well under the stated speed limit because the actual street has indications of young children playing. In fact, the great leaders of our times, Dr. King or Gandhi, actually broke the rules for a greater moral purpose. Conversely, there are people whose actions have done great harm to many while operating well within the rules of our society.

Here is the equation that emerges when we examine the issues from these perspectives:

Empowered bystander = 21st century learner = A leader

Perhaps this is the real choice in bullying prevention: do schools train students to be followers or educate them to be leaders?

Chart 9.1

The Basics of Bystander Empowerment	Description
About the Audience	Recognize the importance of audience (bystanders). Time and energy invested in developing the knowledge, skills and attitudes of bystanders pays dividends in the long run.
Bullying like Broadway	On Broadway a show closes if the audience stays away. Bullying is usually done for an audience, so if there is no audience the bullying will stop. Bystanders (audience) must know they have this influence and power.
Convey concern and care	Bystanders who care about their school community and what happens to its members should communicate their concerns about bullying. Even if bullying doesn't stop the victims of it still need to know people care about them.
Demonstrate disapproval	Bystanders must let their disapproval and dislike of bullying be known. They need to know that their silence in the face of bullying can be easily mistaken for tacit approval of it.

SUMMARY

- Bullying is a social problem involving the interplay of students who bully, who are bullied, and who witness the bullying. Effective interventions avoid solely focusing on individual perpetrators and instead address all the students involved.
- Students are more receptive to adults who listen to them and attempt to understand them than adults whom they perceive as only trying to control them.
- All staff need to understand the role that bystanders play in bullying and why they are reluctant to intervene and to report bullying.
- Some research has shown that many student bystanders are often reluctant to intervene because they fear that they might be breaking the rules by doing so.
- The leadership skills for 21st century learning are the same ones that will empower bystanders to intervene when they see bullying.

ACTIVITIES FOR "OF THE STUDENTS, BY THE STUDENTS, FOR THE STUDENTS"

ACTIVITY 1: BEGIN WITH THE END IN MIND

Purpose

Give staff time to reflect on what qualities, characteristics, skills, and attitudes they would like to see in any student graduating from high school. Describe the *successful graduate* or what would that graduate need to have in order to succeed in the world today.

Content

A basic tenet of Steven Covey's *Seven Habits of Highly Successful People* (1990) is "Begin with the end in mind." Since educators are preparing students for success in the world, sharing their visions will help them align their actions. Very often, educators only think ahead to the next grade level or let test results dominate their thinking. Sharing this tenet with staff can help them work together to shape a common vision of learning.

Procedure

Have staff sit in groups of four or five. Assign the roles of scribe (recorder), materials manager, reporter, facilitator, and timekeeper (if necessary).

Ask them to individually brainstorm as many ideas/descriptions as possible and write them on slips of paper or sticky notes.

After they have generated their ideas individually, they can share their descriptors with each other.

They can work as a team to create categories for those descriptors. They can stand at the table and move the slip of paper around until they all agree on the categories for their team.

They can then create an image or mind map illustrating their picture of success.

When all the groups are finished, staff can walk around the room and look at each group's picture of success.

Following the walk around, lead a whole-group discussion about what success means and the implications of this for how they teach the students.

Follow-Up

Find Richard St. John's TEDTalks (TED2005) three-minute video on eight secrets of success (available on YouTube at www.youtube.com/watch?v=vld jedAashA&feature=related) and show it following this activity. He interviewed hundreds of successful people and categorized the common elements of what they told him into eight essential qualities of successful people. Have staff watch this video and compare his picture of success with theirs.

ACTIVITY 2: IN THE EYES OF THE BYSTANDER

Purpose

Give staff time to reflect on their own experiences as bystanders. There will be some people who will have similar stories and some whose stories will differ greatly. Sharing memories and the feelings behind them should help sensitize staff to why bystanders are reluctant to intervene and to report bullying.

Content

Tapping into personal experiences can sensitize staff to what students are facing. The research on bystander reluctance should resonate with personal experience.

Procedure

Ask staff to brainstorm reasons why students are often reluctant to intervene or report bullying. Facilitate a whole-group discussion and write on chart paper the reasons that staff have generated. Give a brief overview of the research on some of the reasons why student bystanders are reluctant to either intervene or report bullying. Compare the staff's answers to the research. Distribute copies of the Rigby and Johnson article titled "Playground Heroes" (2006/2007) in *Greater Good* online magazine (http://greatergood.berkeley.edu/article/item/playground_heroes?). The article summarizes the research in a concise way.

Have each staff member find a partner and share a personal experience he or she had in the role of bystander. Ask staff to explore the similarities and differences with their stories.

Follow-Up (optional)

See who from the staff is willing to take some time in the classroom to share his or her bystander story with the students. Ask those individuals to share the student response to the story at the next staff meeting.

Activity 3: Helpful Bystander

Purpose

Show staff an example of a bystander who helps someone in need. This can present a positive image of an empowered bystander. Too often bullying prevention is approached in a negative way with the goal of stopping something. This video clip shows a positive way of approaching bullying prevention.

Content

Show the video clip of the National Anthem being sung at the start of an NBA playoff game (Shapiro, 2003). It is available on YouTube at www.youtube.com/watch?v=q4880PJnO2E and titled "Mo Cheeks National Anthem" or "Mo Cheeks Leadership in Action." The clip is of a young girl who has won a contest to sing the national anthem at the start of a NBA basketball game. She starts singing it and makes a mistake with the lyrics, stops singing, and appears lost and unable to continue. Mo Cheeks, a coach of one of the teams, comes to her aid and helps her continue the song by softly singing it into her ear. She starts singing again, and within seconds, everyone in the arena starts singing along with her.

Procedure

Have the participants sit in small groups and watch the video clip together. After viewing it, have them each share their reaction to it.

Following this sharing, ask the groups to respond to the following questions:

> Have you ever been stuck like the young girl?
>
> How did you think she felt?
>
> How did the audience feel when she got stuck?
>
> Why do you think Mo Cheeks came to help her?
>
> How do you feel about what he did?
>
> What qualities or characteristics did he have?
>
> What was the effect his actions on others?
>
> Is everyone capable of doing what he did?
>
> What can be done to help all students do the type of helping that Mo Cheeks did?

After the small groups have responded to these questions in their discussion, ask for a representative from each group to summarize the key points of the discussion with the whole group. Ask the participants what they could do in the school to promote this type of empowered bystander behavior.

OUTCOMES

1. Staff can reflect on how effective bullying prevention and promoting 21st century learning mutually support each other.

2. Staff will redirect efforts toward understanding the role of bystanders and how to influence their response to bullying.

3. Provides a positive way of addressing the problem of bullying by promoting prosocial/altruistic behavior in students.

10

"Of the Students, By the Students, For the Students"

What School Leaders Need to Do

"As an essential part of the school curriculum, we have to teach children how to be good to one another, how to cooperate, how to defend someone who is being picked on and how to stand up for what is right."

—Engel and Sandstrom (2010)

At the first bullying prevention conference I attended, there was a panel of high school students who shared their experiences with bullying. At the end of the discussion, someone from the audience asked the students what they thought could be done about the problem. The students were unanimous in their opinion that nothing could be done—that high schools were the type of places where bullying would always go unchecked.

Those statements were as troubling to me as, if not more, their stories about bullying. Those students wanted to solve the problem of bullying.

Why couldn't they? Schools need to become places where students learn that problems can be solved and that they can solve them. If schools do that, they will also be preventing and reducing bullying.

IMPLICATIONS FOR PRACTICE: ABC

There are three main (ABC) categories of practices that support effective bullying prevention while also promoting leadership and 21st century skills:

A = Autonomy/Agency: Practices that involve students in solving problems, making decisions and choices in a responsible way, and balancing personal needs and goals with those of other members of the community. Autonomy is similar to self-governance; students feel that they are in control of their lives. Deci and Flaste (1996) say that being "autonomous means to act in accord with one's self" (p. 2). Johnston (2004) refers to this as "agency": "If nothing else, children should leave school with a sense that if they act, and act strategically, they can accomplish their goals" (p. 29).

B = Belonging: Practices that build a strong sense of community on a classroom, school, and district level, along with a sense of ownership and connectedness to *our* school. This includes feeling accepted unconditionally as a person even if one's behavior is not acceptable. Students feel at home in school; they can be themselves not just who others want them to be.

C = Competency: Practices that help students develop skills and competencies to successfully navigate the social world (including the bullying) in a responsible way. This also includes a sense of making progress and learning from mistakes. Effort in learning is emphasized more than the finished product of learning.

These categories of educational practice are interrelated and support each other. Students who have opportunities to make meaningful choices feel more engaged and connected to school. Being connected to school means being a member of a community of students. When students feel like they are in control of their learning and connected to a social community, they learn more. Students in this type of learning environment are less likely to bully and less likely to be bullied. All students are more likely to take some type of action to prevent or stop bullying when they see it happening to others.

AUTONOMY PRACTICES

Provide "learning menus" in the classroom.

One of the things that people most enjoy about dining out is choosing from a menu. Provided that the choices are not too overwhelming, the simple act of choosing what to eat feels good to most people.

There are ways to provide "learning menus" to students in the classroom. Research has indicated that when students have more choice in picking a task or assignment their motivation and persistence increases. Even apparently trivial choices can have similar positive effects on student performance. The concept of a menu as a range of reasonable choices is a more effective option than providing open-ended and unlimited choices to students (Patall, Cooper, & Robinson, 2008).

Grade level or department staff could meet and brainstorm a list of choices that could be given to students without lessening the expectations for them. For example, students could be asked if they wanted to do the odd-numbered examples or the even-numbered ones. They could be given a choice of how they want to demonstrate what they learned. They could choose from a list the free-time activities available to them. There are many ways to give meaningful choices on every grade level.

Develop a classroom mission statement and guidelines for achieving it.

Many teachers involve their classroom in developing classroom rules for the school year. This is positive way to promote group autonomy and preferable to just imposing the rules. Many teachers in my school added the preliminary step of having the class decide what type of class they wanted to be and what they would like to achieve—a mission statement. Operating principles, guidelines, agreements, promises, rules, and using whatever term the teacher (or the class) thinks is appropriate are developed as a way to achieve the mission. With this approach, the process of sharing ideas and reaching consensus on the right concepts and ideas is as valuable as the finished product. This is a way of making bullying prevention an integral part of the class's identity and students' responsibility toward each other.

Clarify for students what their choices are.

At our school, teachers devoted time to discussing with students where they had choices and where they didn't have choices. This type of discussion helped students see the reasons behind the decisions that adults make for them. Many students get into trouble because they haven't stopped and thought about what they are doing. Our teachers agreed to consistently use this vocabulary as they spoke to students. If the students internalize the phrase "Is this a choice or no choice?" they are more likely to avoid making inappropriate choices. We would post a list of the things that could be choices and things that were not to serve as a visual cue to the students. The teacher could point to the choice/no choice list prior to an activity as a helpful reminder to the students. We also discussed and summarized other concepts like ready/not ready; big deal/little deal.

Let problems be opportunities for learning.

A high school teacher once asked me how he could reconcile the need to get higher test scores with the need to promote creative thinking in his students. I responded that it was quite a difficult problem with no easy answer, but I also suggested that he share this problem with his students since it pertained to them. He could work with them to generate some solutions. They could then select some things to try and then evaluate how they worked.

When classes work together at solving problems that affect every individual in the class, they learn the value of having everyone contribute to the effort. They can discover something positive in students they might not otherwise know or like. They can see that individual learning is enhanced by social interaction.

If autonomy (agency) is being able to act in accord with one's needs and to achieve goals, then problems are opportunities for doing both. As opposed to just letting students solve problems on their own, adults can provide the structure for helping them understand the problem, see what their options are for solving it, and coach them in the process of solving it.

There is a natural motivation to solve one's own problem, and being able to solve it is a rewarding experience that builds confidence for solving ones in the future. Schools are full of real and meaningful problems that personally impact students. These problems are often pushed aside to work on problems stemming from academic curriculum. The most effective teachers are able to take the real problems of a student's life and connect them to academic content.

Example

Our school community valued recess time for students. Fortunately, our teachers accepted responsibility for supervising recess time and they could choose any time of the day. (This is an excellent strategy for decreasing the likelihood of bullying during recess—one teacher supervising twenty to twenty-five students works better than 200 supervised by a few monitors.) An experienced teacher from another building was transferred to our school. His practice was to use recess as leverage for getting students to complete their work. Students who didn't do their homework or work in school would have to do it during recess while the other students played. In the school year, he received a challenge from a parent in the class who didn't feel that recess should be withheld from students. He came to me for advice about how to solve his dilemma: his prior practice worked for him, yet he didn't want to start the school year at odds with a parent. I suggested that he share his dilemma with his students in a class meeting.

He came back to me in few days to report that the problem was resolved. He shared the problem with the students and presented the two valid perspectives on the problem: the need to make sure students got their work done and the need for students to have recess. He facilitated a problem-solving session, and the class reached consensus that each student should get a certain amount of time every day for recess no matter what. There should be an extra amount of time at recess for students who completed their work. Those students that didn't would miss the extra time to make up the work. Not only was this good solution, but he could be almost guaranteed that he would not have to enforce this practice; the students owned it and abided by it.

Be open to exploring many possibilities.

There are many more ways to incorporate opportunities for choice and autonomy for students into the classroom and the school. This is an example of a simple practice that takes little, if any, extra time, costs nothing, and is an *evidence-based* practice. It requires little, if any, professional development for staff. It does require the *will* to do it. A school leader needs to find ways to give *staff* more choices and share the reasons and benefits of the practice with staff. Staff who are given more choices give their students more choices.

BELONGING PRACTICES

Ask "Whose school is it? or "Are we a group or a community?"

School would not exist without students. Students are not just visiting a place owned by the school staff: students are the school. When guests leave a house, the owners continue to live there. This is not true of schools. Schools are not just buildings. How the students live in their house, however, is dependent on how they are viewed and treated by those who work in the school and have authority over them. Schools can be places where students feel at home, and when they feel at home, they are more likely to take care of their home and everyone in it.

Just having a group a people together does not make a community. Spending time talking about what a community is and why it is important sends an important message—a message that the students want and need to hear. A simple definition that I used with students is the following: "A group is just some people who happen to be together; a community is a group of people who care about what happens to each person in the group."

Chart 10.1 is comparison chart that could be expanded, modified, or left blank for staff or students to fill in.

Learning what a community is and working together to become one is the best (only) way to become a community.

Bullying has learned to hide and thrive in a school that hosts groups. Communities, however, have an immune system that doesn't necessarily prevent all bullying but recognizes it, identifies it when it happens, and sends antibodies (bystanders) to fight it off. A true community is *no place for bullying*.

Chart 10.1 Comparison of Group and Community

Group	Community
Set of individuals who happen to be together	Set of individuals with ties and commitments to one another
No common identity	Has a shared/common identity
Appropriate behavior is following the rules on an individual level to get or avoid something for self.	Behavior is governed by being responsible to community members.
Compliance with rules is dependent on the presence of authority.	Accountability to community members governs behavior.
Behavior toward others is determined by liking or not liking someone.	All members are valuable and deserve respect regardless of whether they are liked or not.
It exists without rituals or traditions.	Rituals and traditions enrich common identity and strengthen community.
Learning is not necessarily a result of membership.	Learning happens from working together and solving problems together.

Have the students' "fingerprints" all over the school.

People who own things have their fingerprints on them. Where are the students' fingerprints on the school? If student work decorates the halls and bulletin boards, students are more likely to feel a sense of ownership and connection. If their work is not up and displayed prominently, the opposite message is conveyed. Student-made antibullying posters convey a much stronger message to the students than any commercially made materials. Student plays, public service announcements, newspaper articles, etc., send a strong antibullying message in two ways: via the message and via the *messengers*.

Have *full employment* policies.

People who own things take responsibility for caring for them. There is enough to do within the school building to ensure that every student has some type of job or responsibility. There are many tasks that staff do not like to do that students would relish doing. If students cannot do the job alone, they can do it with support and guidance. With supervision, students who might be at risk for bullying can work on a team with some popular students in doing a job that the school needs. With full employment, the message is that all students are leaders. Be wary of any practice that even subtly suggests that some students are leaders and some are not.

Schools are full of Big Brothers and Big Sisters. When older students help younger students, everybody benefits. Fifth-grade students can help kindergarten students get settled in the morning and ready to go home. Older students can be reading partners with younger beginning readers.

Use student governments on every level. Students know how to make the school a better place. Ask them and support their efforts.

Everyone can join the (a) club. Depending on their skills and previous experiences, it might be difficult for some students to feel like they belong in the classroom. It is easier to belong when students find common interests and pursue them together. *(My wife, who is an elementary school social worker, runs an afterschool builders club for students who like to build with Legos. Even if they build separately with a minimum amount of talking, they still feel connected to each other.)* There should be a club appropriate and available for every student.

Tell students their help is needed in bullying prevention. Staff cannot do it alone.

If a school wants to find out what needs to done about bullying, it should ask the students. This might sound too simple, but they really are the experts since they see, hear, and feel bullying. They also know how their peers think and act. These two sources of knowledge are too often an untapped resource. This is why focus groups of students are an effective assessment strategy; however, all staff need to develop the habit of listening to students every day. Listening to students doesn't just provide the right information about bullying prevention; it sends the right message about who *owns* the problem.

If they don't enlist, draft them.

Some students might be reluctant to join anything. They might have found it safer to be alone and separate from others. Forcing them into situations where they don't feel comfortable with will only exacerbate their negative feelings toward school. Sometimes staff can skillfully get them involved without students even knowing it. This could be a simple request to help carry something down the hallway. A teacher can incidentally ask a student to help with a simple task on a one-time basis. These unspoken invitations can sneak reluctant students into becoming more involved in the life of the school.

Example

After about twelve years of meeting and greeting the students every day and giving them reminders to "walk, don't run" into school (I was glad they were eager to enter the building), I decided to try something different. I thought that I would enlist the help of students to do what I was doing every day. I would create a safety patrol of students who would wear a red vest with SAFETY PATROL on the front. They would hold up signs saying "THANK YOU FOR NOT RUNNING" or "WALK, DON'T RUN PLEASE." They would not be enforcers (although some tried to be) but would be helpers and reminders to the students who might forget.

I still hadn't thought how I would recruit the patrol as I stood out in front of the school on the first day of the new school year. Then, the first bus arrived. Two students had worked their way to the front of the bus and were determined to be the first into the school—they were ready to "run" off the bus. As they dashed out of the bus, I called and gestured to them, "Come here, guys," so they ran over to me. Not mentioning the running at all, I said, "I need your help this year. I am glad kids like to get into school fast, but I am afraid they could get hurt. I figure that, if I could get some kids to help me remind them to walk, we would keep the students safer this year." I asked if they would be interested in being on the safety patrol. They could not say yes fast enough. They ended up becoming very responsible leaders who helped the safety patrol become an established part of our school.

Link bullying prevention to citizenship: "For the common good."

This phrase, *for the common good*, is often forgotten in our culture today, yet it was at the heart of the founding of our country. One of the original purposes of public schools was to create responsible citizens who could come together as individuals to act for the common good. Bullying prevention is promoting the common good, so being an empowered bystander is the same as being a responsible citizen.

In a fascinating article titled "Silenced by Fear: The Nature, Sources, and Consequences of Fear at Work" (Kish-Gephart, Detert, Trevino, & Edmondson, 2009), the fear of speaking up is the default mode of responding to even the slightest threatening situation for most people. They explain that this is a biological and evolutionary protective response to even the slightest hint of risk. For this reason, the ability to speak up or develop *voice efficiency* is very difficult for anyone to achieve. The authors offer one possible way of overcoming this strong reluctance:

> Some organizations have learned to harness the power of organizational identity, such that employees actually care enough about the organization to feel angry about and personally responsible for doing something about perceived threats to the organizational well

being . . . individuals have been shown to develop a sense of ownership of an organization (reportedly "loving this place") that led to norms of accountability including "saying your piece." (p. 187)

Perhaps the best way to motivate reluctant or fearful bystanders is to make school a place for them to love and community to care about. Even research is showing that courage comes from being connected to something greater than oneself.

Community, connectedness, belonging, and *ownership* should be words that a school leader says and talks about on a consistent basis. It is difficult to turn a school into a community, and it can take a long time, but that should not deter the school leader from articulating it as a basic goal. An effective leader also knows that people cannot be told or forced to be a community, so time and effort will have to be invested in at least moving in that direction.

COMPETENCY PRACTICES

"Regrettably, educators too often believe that time and energy devoted to the social aspects of schooling detracts from academic learning."

–J. David Smith (2007)

Navigating the social world is hard and necessary.

Empathy without a set of skills can unfortunately fade away in students. This is another sad and tragic result of persistent and unchecked bullying in a school environment. Many schools are still depending on someone else to teach students not to bully and give them the skills to navigate the social world. Some students do learn more social skills at home than other students do, but all students need to learn to get along.

A principal once said to me that it was almost useless to teach students these social skills because, not only are they not getting them at home, they are learning the wrong skills at home—they are learning to bully. I asked her, if student's family didn't have a book in their house and all they did was watch TV so that the student was learning not to be literate, would we say it was useless to teach that child to read and write when he or she came to school. All it would mean is that our job would be harder and more important. The same can be said for learning to navigate the social world.

Common Sense on Social Skills

What's wrong with the following scenario?

A teacher is giving his students a math test as a way to review what they just learned. As he walks down the aisle, he notices that a student made a mistake in solving one of the problems. He taps the student on the shoulder and with a stern look and disapproving tone of voice tells that student to go to time-out on the other side of the room. After ten minutes or so, he tells the student to return to his desk and do the same problem again.

Common sense tells us that only giving a consequence with no instruction or explanation would not help the student learn the skills needed to solve the math problem. With academic learning, students are expected to make mistakes while learning. Not so with social and emotional learning: In that domain, the interaction in the scenario is unfortunately typical of what happens in most schools.

A strong and convincing case could be made that the level of difficulty and complexity in navigating the social world exceeds any academic challenge a student faces. In most cases, once an academic skill or concept is learned, it remains pretty stable in the student's knowledge and repertoire of responses, e.g., $2 + 2 = 4$ doesn't ever change. In contrast, how does a student respond to a positive and smiling face from a peer one day and a put-down from the same person the next day without any apparent reason for the change?

Students live in a complex social world that is not easy to navigate. Mistakes are an inherent and necessary way of learning those skills and acquiring judgment. Students need guidance, understanding, and direction from the adults in their lives. Unfortunately, when we primarily rely on rules and the consequences attached to them, we are not giving students what they need to be successful in this social world.

If we just reiterate rules and consequences to children who make mistakes in the social world, it's like giving a driver who is lost and asks for directions only the traffic rules along with feedback on how he or she was driving. *Students face an even greater challenge than a driver who is lost. They are not sure of where they want to go and need help in finding that out. They also don't know that they can ask for help, and they are not certain that there will be someone available to help them.* Rules are necessary and serve an important purpose, but they don't tell you how to get to where you want to go.

"Life needs a slow-motion replay": Take time in the classroom to talk and process events.

Life in the social world happens quickly and disappears out of sight. This is especially true with a new and unexpected experience where people have less background knowledge to use as a way of making sense of that experience. Since so much learning is by trial and error, remembering and reflecting on those past experiences is what helps us make the changes necessary to live better.

Life, however, doesn't have a slow-motion instant replay that can be used for that essential reflection. It would help if it did, but even that replay couldn't show the invisible social forces within and around students that determine so much of what they say and do. It is easy for students to get lost or stay stuck in patterns of behavior that perpetuate bullying. They need the adults in their lives to help learn from their mistakes or learn new and different ways of responding the world. Teachers need to think out loud for their students. They share their own thinking in how they responded in problems in their lives. Students want to hear these stories.

Coaching students: If it works for sports, why not life?

Perhaps the greatest and most essential challenge for a school leader is expanding the school community's concept of learning beyond just the academic domain. This does not mean that teachers need to become social workers or psychologists, but it does mean that they need to talk to students about how to live and work in the social world. It does mean sharing experiences, stories, and advice. It also means listening and letting students know that the teachers want to hear what the students have to share. For some teachers, it could be just knowing students' names and asking them how they are doing. It can be any action that acknowledges the social world that is so important to the students and that often appears so remote from teachers. Bystanders may be reluctant to tell adults about bullying, but if they see adults as resources or coaches, they may at least seek out advice about how to handle a bullying situation.

An analogy that teachers find relevant and that makes common sense to them is to compare the challenge a student faces with bullying with that of an athlete going into a game. Coaches call time-outs to diagram plays that the players have practiced. They do this to prepare them to deal with the many situations that could occur within a game. It increases their confidence and decreases the likelihood of them just responding impulsively or erratically to the evolving game situation.

Coaching bystanders for responding to bullying by showing them the different types of roles they play can be a very effective way of diagramming the "play" the way a coach would during a time-out. Teachers can use dry-erase boards to visually show what is happening in a problem situation in advance of one happening or in review after it happens (Figure 10.1). If bystanders are better prepared for bullying situations and are coached for what to say and do in them, they will be better able to put their empathy into action.

Figure 10.1 Circle of Bullying

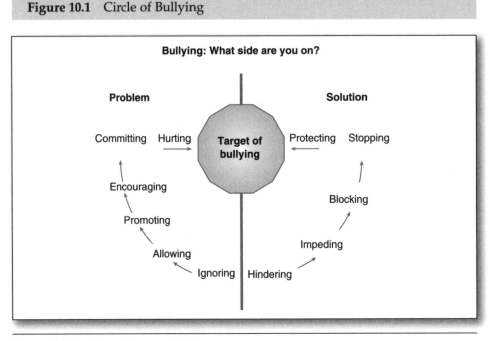

Source: Adapted from Olweus (1993).

COACHING IN THE SOCIAL WORLD OF BULLYING

The challenges students face in the social world, especially when bullying is present, are greater than any situation in a sporting event. Students often find themselves in situations where they might want to help a victim and intervene, but they don't know what to do or what might be effective. The difficulty of the situation is compounded by the emotions they experience. Even if students might know what to do, the fear and uncertainty of the situation can suppress the availability of that knowledge to the forefront of the student's mind.

If we prepare students with the knowledge and skills they need to face these social situations, they will view us as more trustworthy and caring. This also increases the chances of them sharing a problem or dilemma they are facing. In bullying prevention, the *readiness* can be the difference between success and failure.

Students should be coached for the developing the following skills:

- How to prevent being caught in bullying situations, e.g., choosing where to sit, avoiding certain areas, and finding a friend to walk with
- How to respond to verbal bullying, by developing and practicing comeback lines.

- Developing covert ways of supporting students who are bullied, e.g., talking to the students who bully after the situation, talking to the student who was bullied after the situation, and going with the bullied student to report the bullying
- Developing overt ways of supporting students who are bullied, e.g., how to use humor to defuse situations and how to distract the student who is bullied
- Developing strategies for moving several positions in the bullying circle away from the students who bully and more to the student being bullied
- Developing strategies for preventive protection to students at risk of being bullied

Students can also brainstorm their own strategies and discuss how they could be used.

Give them a bag of tricks and coach them on when and how to use them.

Very Important!
*It should be made very clear to students that these strategies are worth trying, but if they don't work, it is not because **they** have failed. Some students will persist at bullying regardless of what anyone says or does. Students must know that their fallback response is to enlist adult help, and if the first adult doesn't help, then they need to go to another until someone does help.*

Build background knowledge on bullying.

All students should have a basic understanding of the definition of bullying, its key concepts and vocabulary, and its forms. They can also read the research and statistics related to bullying. Student can be aware of the social dynamics of bullying, as well as the school policies and procedures pertaining to bullying. This should be considered a part of the basic school curriculum for all students and can be mapped across all the grade levels.

Teach simple definitions and have them posted around the school, for example:

Tattling is when you want to get someone in trouble.

Reporting is when you want to get someone out of trouble.
(Morrison & Marachi, 2011)

Know the difference between *controlling* and *influencing*.

School leaders and school staff are right to feel that they are effective in controlling student behavior in schools. To get hundreds, if not thousands, of students to move through a school building and follow a schedule is a difficult task that schools routinely do well. For teachers, the ability to control a class is considered a basic and essential skill. A teacher who is not in control of the class is usually considered ineffective and not competent. This type of control, however, does not control bullying in school; believing it does only forestalls moving toward more effective approaches.

The social dynamics of bullying occurs in the blind spot of those who have the power and authority. Students who bully do so for various reasons and learn how to use the blind spot to their advantage. Bystanders often think that it is not their responsibility to do anything about bullying. They are used to deferring to adults when it comes to controlling students. Who could blame them for thinking "If the adults can't control a bully, who am I to think that I can?"

Admitting the limits of control does not mean giving up or ignoring the problem of bullying. With an educational mindset, control should be redefined as influence. Influence is more effective because it acknowledges the social dynamics that determine so much of what students do and say. Salmivalli (2010) summarizes how influence can work:

> Bystanders might even be easier to influence by interventions than the active, initiative-taking bullies. Bystanders often think that bullying is wrong, they feel bad for the victim, and they would like to do something to help. Converting their already existing attitudes into behavior is a challenging task, but it might be a more realistic goal than influencing an individual bully by adult sanctions alone. (p. 117)

Teachers can have students state their feelings about bullying in a class meeting. The students who bully others in the class might be surprised to hear that most students disapprove of bullying. Without this type of opportunity, the students who bully might inadvertently think that most students approve of it. Some students who bully interpret the silence of bystanders as tacit approval or support for their bullying. By removing this silence, some of the motivation for bullying could be decreased. Teachers who provide these opportunities are influencing how students think and act without having to control them.

The best example differentiating control and influence concerns substitute teachers. I have often said that, if I wanted to know who the best teacher in a school was, I would go observe the class when the teacher was out and a substitute was there. If the students in that class were learning as they would on any day and were actively supporting the substitute, it was a clear indication that the teacher had invested time and energy in empowering the students to take ownership and responsibility for their own learning. The students' control came from internalizing the social values and norms of that classroom environment. It did not happen by chance; that teacher had many discussions with the students, communicated and practiced respect, and gradually released responsibility for the functioning of the room to the students. This is the type of influence that can also work in bullying prevention.

Chart 10.2 illustrates the difference between control and influence.

Competency practices on the secondary level: Learn about bullying academically.

Most of the content information generally available on bullying prevention is appropriate for secondary school students. Although all activities and materials need to be screened by staff, much of what is used in training staff can be used and adapted for students either in a classroom or with a small group of students. Most of the activities I have provided in this book along with the recommended video clips and links can be modified for students. Getting them to think differently about the problem can be the catalyst in mobilizing their energy to help solve the problem. Preventing and reducing bullying ultimately is in the students' own best interests. It is not just another thing that adults are trying to get them to do.

Some examples could include the following:

- Math classes analyzing and interpreting bullying survey data
- Social studies classes studying the latest research on bullying
- English language arts classes reading fiction related to bullying and social dynamics

Chart 10.2   Comparison of Control and Influence on Student Behavior

Control	Influence
External: Requires adult presence	Internal: Does not require adult presence
Rule focused: Right is following rules, wrong is not following.	Relationship focused: Based on how others are treated
Dependent on rewards and punishments	Dependent on values, relationships with peers and adults
Primary goal is compliance.	Primary goal is responsibility.
Adults seen in policing role	Adults seen in a modeling, leadership role
No room for error	Children are works in progress.
Doesn't require trust in students	Relies on viewing students as capable but needing education
Short-term, situational effects	Has lasting effect beyond current situation

Integrating 21st Century Learning and Bullying Prevention

Entrepreneurship requires creative and integrative thinking to solve a problem or meet a perceived need in a community. It can involve groups of people working together and pooling their collective skills and abilities to create new ways to solve a problem.

A creative way of addressing bullying in a high school would be to have an interdisciplinary course where the students in the course could be considered a marketing company assigned the task of creating an effective ad campaign to prevent bullying in the school. This course would mix a diverse group of students who might not otherwise work together on a common goal of raising awareness about the problem of bullying in the school and greater community. This would be an authentic learning experience where appropriate business practices would have to be researched and applied. An interdisciplinary group of teachers could teach the class and supervise the activities of the students.

Provide specialized support and training for children who are bullying victims.

There are students who are sometimes victims of bullying and sometimes bully others. They have also been called provocative victims. These students often have poor impulse control, lack social skills, and have problems attending and regulating their behavior. They are often not liked by their peers. They can often "reward" students who bully by easily getting upset and angry. Students who bully can more easily gain bystander support by targeting these students. These students, in order to have some sense of control, can find younger or other vulnerable students to bully.

School leaders should be aware of these students and be proactive in giving them support. Teachers need to understand the needs of these students and how they are at great risk for being targets of bullying and for school failure. Parents of these students also need support and should work cooperatively with the school rather than becoming antagonistic and hostile to the school's efforts. School counselors, social workers, or school psychologists need to be involved with these students and with their teachers.

HIGH LEVERAGE (ABC) PRACTICES NOT SPECIFICALLY DESIGNED FOR BULLYING PREVENTION (BUT WORTH THE INVESTMENT)

These are just a few approaches that can promote the three key areas of classroom practice (autonomy, belonging, and competence) that will also foster effective and comprehensive bullying prevention.

- *Cooperative learning*: This is one of the most researched and proven instructional strategies. It is designed to integrate social and emotional skills into academic instruction. The teacher skillfully chooses a variety of cooperative strategies to meet academic goals. The students learn to learn from each other. This is not just putting students into groups. It is a highly structured approach where teachers are trained in theory and practice using specific skills and strategies. It must include key components of individual accountability, social skills instruction, positive interdependence, and group processing.
- *Social and emotional educational programs*: There are many programs and resources specifically designed to help students learn to manage their emotions; self-regulate their responses to situations, resolve conflicts peacefully, and solve a variety of problems. Although these programs are not specifically aimed at reducing bullying, they certainly can support and strengthen bully prevention efforts.
- *The Responsive Classroom:* Responsive Classroom is a widely used, research-backed approach to elementary education that increases academic achievement, decreases problem behaviors, improves social skills, and leads to more high-quality instruction. This approach offers resources and training on conducting class meetings, positive discipline strategies, and communicating effectively with students.

SUMMARY

- There are three categories of educational practice that can empower bystanders and build 21st century leadership skills in students: Autonomy/Agency, Belonging, and Competency (ABC).
- These areas are interrelated and support each other. Students who are given the support and opportunity to make meaningful choices feel connected to their school. When students feel connected and supported, they learn more.
- An effective school leader needs to help staff to see and understand their responsibility to support all learning, including the skills and knowledge needed to be successful in the social world.
- The culture and climate of a school have a greater influence on student behavior than rules and consequences. Staff should direct their efforts toward coaching, modeling, and connecting with for students as a way to influence them rather than just trying to control them.
- School leaders need to invest in professional development practices that can meet several needs at once. Cooperative learning and social and emotional learning are examples of such practices.

ACTIVITIES TO SUPPORT STUDENTS' RESPONSE TO BULLYING

ACTIVITY 1: "MY KID WOULD NEVER BULLY"

Purpose

Being a bystander when bullying is occurring is a challenging and emotional situation for students. Each situation is different and involves social dynamics that are complex and often confusing. If is often hard for adults to understand why students fail to intervene in bullying situations. This activity provides an opportunity for gaining more insight and understanding about the challenges that bystanders face.

Content

NBC's *Dateline* program devoted to bullying, available from YouTube as *My Kid Would Never Bully* (Keller, 2011a), shows students confronted with bullying situations. There are two scenarios: one showing a group of girls selecting fashionable clothes (www.youtube.com/watch?v=MDa9jTgRa0k) and another (Keller, 2011b) showing a group of boys in a gym (www.youtube.com/watch?v=yPKqpn3O6NQ). Each situation is staged with the students who bully and the students who are bullied being actors. The bystanders in both situations do not know that the situation is staged. The parents of the bystanders are in a nearby room observing the situations via closed circuit camera. In each clip, the parents are asked to predict how their child will respond. After the staged situation is revealed to them, the students are asked to share their own reactions.

Procedure

Have people sit in small groups of four to five to view the video clips (each clip is seven to eight minutes long). Ask people to privately reflect on the clip and briefly write down their thoughts before discussing them. Assign the roles of facilitator, recorder, timekeeper, and reporter to each group. After writing down their initial reflection, the participants should take turns briefly summarizing their thoughts with the group.

Following this sharing, the facilitator should lead a discussion using the following guide questions:

Why do you think the students responded the way that they did?

How did their response match what their parents predicted?

How did the students vary in their responses to the bullying?

Why do you think some students didn't help the bullied student?

In the situation with the girls, one student did actively confront the girls who were bullying. What do you think of how she intervened?

There are two scenarios involving boys in a gym. The coach responded differently to bullying in each scenario. How did his response affect bystander behavior?

What can be done to help bystanders be more effective in bullying situations?

What influence can adults have with bystander behavior?

Compare and contrast the boy and girl scenarios.

What can our staff do differently based on what we just viewed?

ACTIVITY 2: OCTOBER SKY

Purpose

This activity will give staff an opportunity to reflect on how having students work together on academic tasks can also prevent and reduce bullying.

Content

The movie *October Sky* (Johnston, 1999) shows how a small group of students worked together on building rockets to win a science fair. It is based on the true story of Homer Hickham who became a rocket engineer for NASA. There is a sequence in the movie that shows how the small group formed and how they worked together. In particular, there was a student who was isolated socially but was very knowledgeable about science. The movie shows how this student was welcomed into the group and became a key contributor to the group's ultimate success. The clip occurs approximately at the ten-minute mark of the film (available on You-Tube at www.youtube.com/watch?v=uMREOwMS4Ys&feature=youtu. be).The sequence begins at Homer's breakfast table with his family and extends to the group sitting at the lunch table showing the small rocket they built. The scene ends when the suspicious principal says to them that he "has his eye" on them.

Procedure

Have people sit in small groups to view the video. Assign the roles of facilitator, recorder, materials manager, reporter, and timekeeper (for groups of five). After they have viewed the video, have each person write down his or her initial response to the video. They can take turns sharing their response with each other.

The facilitator can use the following discussion questions:

What happened when Homer decided to approach the socially isolated student?

How did this student respond to the Homer's invitation?

How well did the group work together?

Where was the real learning taking place: in school or out of school?

What was the principal's response to their work on rockets?

Did his response help or hurt the work?

Compare and contrast Homer's qualities/characteristics for success with the Richard St. John's summary on eight secrets of success (TED2005, 2005).

How does what happened in the movie relate to bullying prevention?

OUTCOMES

1. Staff should be able to see how empathy in bullying situations is not enough. Students need to develop a variety of skills and strategies to confront bullying when they see it happening.

2. Staff can see how cooperative learning on tasks that require interdependence can be a valuable tool that can get a diverse group of students working together. Staff should reflect on how to incorporate it into their teaching.

Section Three

The Follow Through (Infrastructure)

11

Leadership for a Change

"If we are facing in the right direction, all we have to do is keep on walking."

—Buddhist saying

"You can't connect the dots by looking forward; you can only connect them looking backwards. You have to trust that the dots will connect in your future."

—Steve Jobs

GETTING STARTED

I was fortunate to start my career as principal at a well-established, excellent school with very competent and professional teachers. Since I had been a special education teacher and never had my own elementary classroom, I was a little apprehensive about how I could help these teachers, who probably didn't need my help. I decided that, for my first year, I needed to listen, establish trusting relationships, and learn as much as I could from these expert teachers. I reminded myself that I was skilled in collaborating with others in solving problems.

When I looked ahead to the school year, I could be certain that teachers would have problems. When they did, I would be supporting them, not by solving the problem for them, but working with them on solving the problem. Some problems would not be easy to solve, but we would learn more from these problems. As we worked together, we would learn each other's perspective on education and students; we would also reveal our values to each other. I didn't have a master plan or grand vision to follow, but I was confident that, by learning and working together, we would forge trusting relationships that would be the foundation for improving our school. I knew that we would be going in the right direction. Looking back seventeen years later, I can see now that we were creating a school culture that was incompatible with bullying: "bullying prevention" started long before we called it bullying prevention. (Dillon, 2010)

STUMBLING AND STRUGGLING: THE RULE, NOT THE EXCEPTION

I do not like to stumble or struggle. Like most people, I like smooth sailing when things are going well. I do not like to get lost and feel lost. Those feelings never left me during my time as principal; however, I learned not to waste my time and energy wishing the struggling and stumbling would just go away. I did not spend time looking for the solutions that would quickly make it all smooth again. I accepted and embraced the struggle and learned what I could from it. School leaders shouldn't promise a straight and clear journey but should show confidence in the community's ability to move forward through difficulty and adversity.

Leadership is like driving a car in the dead of night and seeing only as far as the headlights. It is important to go in the right direction and stay on the road. Roadside reflectors don't light the road, but they work with the headlights to guide the way until there is more light and the destination becomes clearer.

This chapter will not tell school leaders what to do to solve the problem of bullying. Each school has a different set of assets and needs and must find solutions that fit. There are, however, some guiding principles that can serve as road reflectors that school leaders can provide to help the school-community head in the right direction and stay on the right course.

GUIDING PRINCIPLES

Bullying prevention has to be a schoolwide and comprehensive approach that should improve the culture and climate of a school. Schools that ultimately succeed in preventing and reducing bullying reflect the type of environment for students described in Chapter 10. Culture and climate change happens in super slow motion and can only be seen looking backward at a distance. School leaders cannot tell the school community that it should change its culture/climate and expect to get enthusiastic support.

School leaders can and should get started. Change is a process, not an event, so it can start without a clear plan or having all staff committed and on board. Getting a small group of people to look in the right direction and take few steps together is a modest but sensible way to start. The vision, the commitment, and the plan will grow as you go.

Here are guiding principles, the first four statements being from Morrison and Marachi (2011), that point the school community in the right direction for effective bullying prevention and a positive change in school culture and climate:

1. Reflect on your own use of power in relationships.

2. Treat students the way you want them to treat each other.

3. Help all students look valuable in the eyes of their classmates.

4. Take action when bullying is observed or reported by a student.

5. Accept the person, but don't accept the person's bullying.

6. There is never an excuse or justification for disrespecting any person.

These six guiding principles that point in the right direction are deliberately not specific or designed to tell people what to do or how to do things. They are a springboard for thought, reflection, and conversation. They can be used to make decisions or evaluate decisions. The overall purpose of using principles rather than rules is for the school community to develop a collective wisdom and ability to do the right thing even in ambiguous situations not covered by the rules. They are also not meant to be goals, since they cannot be checked off a list. Principles should be a constant reminder of the school's values and moral commitment.

School leaders' main responsibility is to keep the school community guided by these principles. As the members of the entire school community act consistently in accord with these principles, the school will change for the better, and bullying prevention will be integrated into the daily interactions of the school day. This does not mean that a school leader has to enforce these principles on others, for to do so would contradict their meaning. When these principles become more and more reflective of all interactions in the school, every member of the school community exercises leadership and accepts responsibility for governing him- or herself. They will eventually form the cultural norms of the school.

Set the bar high with cushions underneath it.

Those six guiding principles set high expectations for all members of the community. Having high positive expectations for how people treat each other is a positive way of reframing antibullying behaviors. These principles represent behaviors and attitudes that are incompatible with bullying. When more and more people act in alignment with these principles, bullying loses its grip on a school because it is so clearly in conflict with the cultural norms of the school.

Amy Edmondson (2008), a Harvard researcher in the field of leadership and management, has studied leadership and how it affects the learning of an organization. She has looked at the interaction of two key factors: psychological support/safety and high accountability in creating a positive and productive learning environment. Fullan (2011a) describes leaders who balance high accountability and high psychological safety as having a moral resolve and impressive empathy. Organizations that combine high accountability (moral resolve) and psychological safety (impressive empathy) provide the optimal conditions for learning and creativity.

Leader's Dilemma: Case Study of "Setting the Bar High With Cushions"

Combining these two factors in words and actions is quite a challenge for school leaders. Here is a case study to illustrate how a school leader maintains the high expectations of all the guiding principles. An experienced teacher who bullies students can undermine all bullying prevention efforts. A principal who looks the other way also undermines these efforts because his or her actions have not been consistent with the principle of taking action when bullying is reported. I have provided some recommendations on how to skillfully approach and address this problem in a way that is consistent with the guiding principles. It is an example of how to have high accountability combined with psychological support (*setting the bar high with cushions underneath*). (See figure 11.1 on page 166.)

> *A principal supervises a veteran teacher who rules her class with an iron hand or runs a tight ship. She has been successful in getting students to achieve academically. Her peers respect her, although she is perceived by some as being too tough on students. She has a great deal of pride in how she does her job and the results she gets. She does, however, use shame and ridicule in the classroom as a way to control uncooperative or misbehaving students. Some parents have reported this to the principal and said that their child is afraid of her. What can the principal do about this situation and teacher? Using the six direction principles as a guide for acting, what should the principal do?*

Key Points to Consider

- The teacher is misusing her power with that student and inviting other students to bully that shamed student.

• This is a tenured teacher who has had high performance reviews in her past. She is not protected from disciplinary action, but such action is not a guaranteed solution to the problem.

• The guiding principles can constrain each other. A principal should take action since this could be a case of teacher bullying a student, yet he or she needs to carefully consider how to use power.

• A principal can use the power of his or her position to tell the teacher to stop and threaten the teacher with consequences for not stopping. That approach might work (stop the teacher from bullying) but could undermine that principal's own message about how to use power.

• The teacher might comply with that directive but could find other ways of controlling students though not as severe but still inconsistent with the other guiding principles.

• The teacher could also undermine the principal's leadership on other issues. Her colleagues might take her side, because the principal treated her too severely.

THE BALANCING ACT OF LEADERSHIP: HOW TO RESPOND TO TEACHER BULLYING

Before the Meeting: What to Consider

• *The prior relationship with teacher*: If the principal has a trusting and respectful relationship with the teacher, there is a greater chance that the teacher will listen to what the principal has to say. If the relationship is antagonistic and mistrustful, it will be a much harder situation to resolve on all levels.

• *The teacher's view of the principal and his or her leadership*: Is the principal seen as someone who helps and supports others or someone who likes to control others? The principal's track record has a significant influence on how the conversation is perceived by the teacher. People respond positively to someone who respects them and values them more than someone who bosses or controls them.

• *Understand the teacher without accepting the behavior*. This teacher has a method of controlling students that works for her. In her mind, the end justifies the means since the avoidance of shame has motivated students to perform and achieve academically. She has gotten good results, so she will see no reason to stop. Most likely in the past, other principals, colleagues, and some parents have approved of her style and methods. This teacher would profess love for her students and wants the very best for them. This is hard to contradict or invalidate.

• *Consider what can replace the strategy that worked for her.* Even if the teacher decided to stop her shaming as a strategy of control, she still has to teach her class. She will not have the strategy that worked for her and will feel vulnerable and less competent. This teacher will need another strategy to replace the one that worked for her.

• *Decide on what to offer her to support the change she needs to make.* The principal will need to offer his or her help in a concrete way to support the change the teacher needs to make. Any personal gesture to support the change will be more effective than just a referral to another resource.

• *Know what has worked in the class that is compatible with the guiding principles.* This teacher probably uses strategies that are consistent with the guiding principles. Sharing specific examples of how she has been consistent with the principles will give the teacher something to build on and demonstrate recognition of her commitment to helping students.

• *Prepare a few key points for discussion and avoid appearing scripted.* The conversation should be genuine and not just an opportunity to tell her what to do. Since these conversations are stressful, it helps to have a game plan outlining the key points that need to be made.

In the Meeting: At the Start

• *Move from behind a desk and sit facing her as a colleague.* The physical environment and body language send a stronger message than the words of the meeting. This should be a conversation, not a power play. The principal needs to model the behavior that he or she wants the teacher to try.

• *Thank her for coming and giving up her time to meet.* Recognize that her time is valuable and that she is helping just by coming to the meeting.

• *Make sure the prefacing statements set the right tone and context for the meeting.* Let the teacher know the reason and purpose for the meeting. Statements like "I need your help in understanding what's happening," "Although it's not easy to have these conversations, talking about them honestly as colleagues is the best way to deal with them," "My goal is to support you and find a way to address the problem in a positive way" can set the tone and relieve some of the uncertainty and anxiety for the teacher.

Addressing the Issue

• *Be candid and matter of fact about the problem.* Simply state what the issue is and why it warrants a conversation.

• *Avoid putting her on the defensive.* The meeting shouldn't be about her defending her actions or explaining them, although she probably will. The principal should make her aware of the problem, express concern about it, and clearly state expectations for future behavior.

• *Make it clear that it is ultimately in her best interests to change her methods.* On some level, she probably realizes that her approach is causing her problems. Act on the assumption the problem is a lack of skill rather than intent. If she improves her skills, she will ultimately feel better about what she is doing.

• *Make it clear that your goal is to help her but also let her know that she can help you.* The principal should give her the support she needs to resolve the problem. The principal should reiterate the guiding principles and state why they are important. The principal should also acknowledge that it is hard to consistently act in accord with them. Since she is so respected by her colleagues, if she tried a different way, she would be leading others in the right direction.

• *Empathize with her situation.* The principal should share his or her reflections made prior to the meeting. She is an effective teacher but needs to change some of her strategies. She is doing what she thinks is right and was supported for doing so. The principal should help her understand how her strategy *might have worked for her but how it doesn't work for the student.* The principal should acknowledge and articulate the positive things she is doing that are consistent with the guiding principles, so she can change without losing "face."

• *Share an experience about having to relearn something.* The principal can share an experience of how he or she needed to relearn something. This will demonstrate empathy for her experience.

• *Involve her in her own support plan and have a menu of choices for her.* Asking the teacher to share what she needs to make the necessary changes in her strategies demonstrates respect to her and helps her take ownership for the problem. If she has difficulty coming up with some ideas, the principal should offer her appropriate options.

• *Acknowledge that change is hard and clarify your expectations.* Recognize that habits are hard to change. Make it clear that you are not asking for perfection or a radical change, but rather her commitment to try to step in a different direction.

• *Provide a definite, scripted response she could use instead of the shaming.* The principal should provide a very concrete and specific alternative to use in lieu of the shaming. She might have to call the office for situations that she previously addressed inappropriately. The principal or a designated staff person could intervene as a temporary way of at least preventing the shaming.

- *Provide opportunities for professional development in behavior management.*

- *Enlist the support of school counselors or social workers.*

- *Recommend an article to read related to the problem and the solution.* Realize that this crisis could be an opportunity for this person to rethink many of her ideas. She might read such an article very differently than she did before this became a problem for her.

- *Let her know the bottom line and why it is the bottom line: shaming and ridiculing students is not acceptable.* Allowing for all that was discussed, she has to know that shaming students is not an acceptable strategy for motivating or controlling students. She needs to stop that behavior immediately. Make it clear that the expectation for how to treat students is a common value and part of the larger mission of the school—it applies to everyone.

- *Thank her for listening and sharing.* Let her know that you pledge ongoing support and you will be checking in to see how things are going.

- *Confirm one specific resource or strategy for supporting her in making the change.*

After the Meeting

- Summarize in writing what was discussed and the plans that were made.

- Include in the notes the explicit expectation given to her.

- Drop her an informal note thanking her for listening.

- As soon as possible, find an opportunity to notice something that she did that is consistent with the guiding principles. Give feedback on how it worked effectively and show appreciation for her efforts.

- Enlist her support for bullying prevention efforts in the school.

A Helpful Conceptual Model

Edmondson's (2008) model, presented in Figure 11.1, illustrates the type of environments that emerge from the various combinations of high accountability and psychological support. Balancing these two factors for staff is a prerequisite for the staff balancing it for students. A psychologically safer environment promotes the collaboration and creativity that will produce a variety of effective strategies to prevent and reduce bullying. A school environment where bullying prevention is a collective responsibility of the school community ends up being psychologically safe and a place of optimal learning.

Figure 11.1   Psychological Safety and Accountability

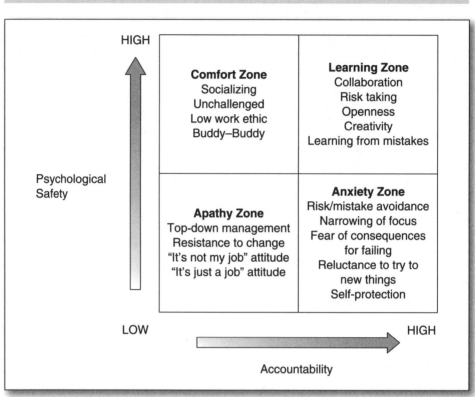

Source: Adapted from Edmondson (2008).

LEADERSHIP PRACTICES THAT PROMOTE LEADERSHIP AND LEARNING (AND PREVENT AND REDUCE BULLYING)

School leaders who can balance support and accountability are promoting the leadership of everyone in the school community. School leaders can start the process of changing the culture and climate and point it in the right direction, but if they are the only ones who are working on the problem, the problem will persist. The best way to get staff to promote autonomy, belonging, and competency for their students is for school leaders to promote them for staff. Schools that promote autonomy, belonging, and competency inevitably grow leaders: people who care about others and have the knowledge and skills to effectively do the right things. Shared leadership is a team of leaders working together and influencing each other. Garvin, Edmondson, and Gino (2008) give this description of such an organization: "A learning organization is a place where employees excel at creating, acquiring and transferring knowledge. There are three building blocks of such institutions: (1) a supportive learning environment, (2) concrete learning processes, and (3) leadership behavior that reinforces learning" (p. 110).

It shouldn't be a radical idea to assert that schools become learning organizations. Schools should be places where the daily interactions in facing challenges, solving problems, and learning to get along does the teaching, or as Dewey (1985) said, "the very process of living together educates" (p. 25).

Although a leader alone cannot change a school, what a leader does or doesn't do influences whether the school starts to move in the right direction or stays stuck in traditional patterns and practices. The words and actions of a school leader can plant the seed for change in a school, but it takes the shared leadership of everyone to ensure that it grows.

Keep It Simple (and Meaningful)

Sometimes stepping into a school is like stepping into a whirlwind. Many things fly by, some stick, some hit you in the head, and some disappear quickly. School leaders need some easy to remember sayings for the times that require wise decisions with little time to think. To practice what I preach, I have tried to condense some of the leadership practices into simple phrases that might stick even in the windstorm of a school environment.

In the book *Made to Stick*, Heath and Heath (2008) recommend that leaders use proverbs to communicate: "Proverbs are helpful in guiding individual decisions in environments with shared standards. Those shared standards are often ethical or moral norms. Proverbs offer rules of thumb for the behavior of individuals" (p. 47). Given all the complexity related to the problem of bullying, proverb-like phrases can be the subtle but critical difference between staying on and going off course.

Here are specific leadership practices that can point the school in the right direction. These are leadership practices that embody the six direction principles. For these principles to have any influence on the school, the school leader must translate them into words and actions.

Space Practices

Don't Be Hard to Find

School leaders should be *visible and accessible* to students and staff. Where leaders put themselves sends a message about what they care about and value. Students and staff are busy and under time constraints; they can't spend too much time looking for anyone. If school leaders are hard to find, eventually staff and students will give up even looking for them.

Play Catch With Your Staff

Most people don't like frequent meetings for very good reasons. If meetings are the preferred way of communicating, there will be less communicating in a school. School leaders should be willing to talk with a staff person on the go, i.e., walking down the hall together. They should make it easy for teachers to *catch* them. It is good to hear them say: "I am glad I caught you." The best opportunity for learning can be when a problem has just happened and somebody catches the principal. A quick conversation can be a very productive and useful way for solving that problem and strengthening that relationship.

It Begins With the Kids

In a school, familiarity does not breed contempt; it breeds trust. The foundation for being a successful principal is having positive and trusting relationships with the students. School leaders should convey to students that their main job is to help them, not police them. When a student goes home and even casually mentions the principal in a positive way, the relationship between the parents and principal has improved. If staff see that principals can engage students and gain their respect, they will be more likely to ask for help and be candid about problems with students.

Make Friends With Trouble

I usually had a pretty good sense of what students were at risk of getting into trouble in school. I made it a priority to establish a positive relationship with those students *before* they got in trouble. These students were not the only students I had positive relationships with, so knowing the principal didn't single them out. My relationship with them gave those at-risk students support and reassurance. It removed the anxiety and uncertainty of whom they had to confront when they got into trouble. This did not diminish my authority with them; it increased it. As a result, they were honest about accepting responsibility for what they did and open to hearing my response to the problem. It also conveyed to the rest of the students that these students were full members of the community who needed some extra support; they were not bad kids. I also found that these at-risk students needed to know that they had "support from above."

Show and Tell Practices

Show Your Heart and Mind

If the real task of leadership is getting people to change their hearts and minds, school leaders need to reveal and share what is in their hearts and minds. Staff and students should know what the school leader values, believes, and wants for the school. They also need to know how they view and think about issues.

Learn in Public

School leaders who make a mistake should admit it and talk about it. They should also talk about what they learned from their mistakes. School leaders who are fallible say it's okay to make mistakes. Edmondson, Bohmer, and Pisano (2001) say that admitting fallibility "signaled to others on the team that errors and concerns could be discussed without fear of punishment" (p. 132).

Spend Time Wisely

School leaders reveal what is in their hearts and minds by how they spend their time and other people's time. An agenda for a faculty meeting is a good reflection of what is important to a school leader. How much time is devoted to issues related to learning as opposed to more managerial or logistical issues?

Practice Talking About Practice

It is hard to get teachers to talk about their practice (how they do their jobs). They are tremendous resources to each other. If teachers could talk to each other and learn from each other, they could share and develop the best practices together. Staff working together can develop effective bullying prevention strategies that fit the particular needs of a school.

How You Frame It Is How They See It

School leaders have the opportunity to frame an issue or a problem for the school community. The frame they provide will govern how people respond to that problem. This is especially true of bullying prevention. If a school leader frames bullying prevention as part of a school's core mission and as a continuation of the positive work already done, the staff's will be more receptive to working on it.

Communication: More Is Better Than Less

Communicating is time consuming. Schools leaders are responsible for communicating with many people. It can be tempting to decide not to call a parent about what could be perceived as a minor issue. In bullying cases, calling the parents of the perpetrator and victim should be mandatory; it could be tempting not to call the parents of students who were bystanders. Taking time to make those extra phone calls, however, is a very worthwhile investment, because it enlists parents to give the right message to their child about responsible action. It also conveys to the school community that bullying prevention is about how people care for and treat each other.

Learn How to Make Things Stick

Schools are hard places to change for many reasons. Building a case for bullying prevention with facts, figures, and research will not change hearts and minds. A school leader needs to be crafty in getting people's attention. This book has provided activities designed to connect to people's hearts and minds. Other books like *The Tipping Point* (Gladwell, 2002) and *Made to Stick* (Heath & Heath, 2008) can be useful resources for change strategies.

Practical Practices

Manage to Lead

Management was not the part of my job that I liked, but I knew that I needed to do it well enough to make it invisible and automatic. I relied on my support staff with strong skills in those areas to take a leading role on management issues. This allowed me to focus on building relationships with people and focusing on learning.

Don't Become the Problem

If bullying prevention becomes something that administration wants and then tries to impose on a staff, the focus becomes the power struggle and not the real issue. As discussed earlier in this book, there are many reasons for staff to balk at supporting another initiative or program. School leaders need to work with staff, students, and parents to understand the problem and plan some initial achievable goals. This approach succeeds better than quick fixes or elaborate programs and plans.

Let Go and Check In: Don't Sign Off

Schools leaders who delegate both authority and responsibility to others demonstrate their trust and confidence in them. This shared leadership and collective responsibility, so essential for effective bullying prevention, grows out the trust and confidence from the school leader. Unless school leaders stay involved by checking in with people and being available to support them, this delegating can be seen as checking out from the less desirable duties, i.e., cafeteria, bus, or hallway supervision. Some principals make the mistake of assigning all the bus or cafeteria problems to an assistant principal and thereby cut themselves off from what is going on in those environments. Effective school leaders stay involved and in touch with all that is going on in a school without micromanaging it.

Baby Steps Will Take You Far

It is important to act on the problem of bullying even before everyone is on board with bullying prevention. School leaders should be wary of large-scale changes that more likely will backfire and create more resistance later on. School leaders should work with the bullying prevention team to calibrate the first steps in bullying prevention. Many small acts, done by many, not apparently related to bullying prevention, can contribute to substantive progress on the problem. School cultures and climates don't change dramatically overnight. Those in the culture are the last to see the change, but baby steps in the right direction do eventually change the culture and prevent and reduce bullying.

Always a Teacher

School leaders are most successful when they continue to educate and not switch exclusively to policing, adjudicating, and managing problems. Effective leaders lead the learning for the organization. They find teachable moments for the whole community. I had a dry-erase board in my office, so when I was working with students who got into trouble, I could draw or have them draw a picture of what went wrong. I knew that *discipline*, like the word *disciple*, is about learning. I accepted the responsibility for educating students when they didn't handle their problems the right way and got in trouble.

Heart Practices

People Are Works in Progress

As much as possible, give people the benefit of the doubt. Their words and behavior often are the result of stress or influences that cannot be seen. This type of attitude won't change the issues but should help school leaders stay calmer and help them avoid reacting to people in a way that will exacerbate the problem at hand. When school leaders manage their emotions and respond to people with understanding, it will set the right tone for how all people should treat each other.

Integrity Has No Need for Rules (Albert Camus)

This does not mean that a school should have no rules. School leaders, however, need to convey a belief and trust that people are *not* one step away from doing the wrong thing unless they are tightly watched and controlled. The desire to eliminate the exceptional case of someone breaking the rules should not create situations where *everyone* is treated as a potential rule breaker. It is always better to communicate about problems or conflicts than to always rely on a rule to settle the matter.

Give Respect Even Before People Deserve It

Michael Fullan (2011a) states that this is a key practice fostering positive change:

> If you want to have any chance of changing a negative relationship, you have to give other people respect before they have earned

it . . . If a leader enters a negative culture . . . he will encounter a situation in which people have, so to speak, learned to be disrespectful. Thus they will not give you respect on day one. You have to model and demonstrate respect . . . even when it is not being reciprocated. This is hard to do, but confident change leaders are able to pull it off. (p. 32)

"You get what you expect": if leaders want everyone to be responsible and empowered bystanders, they need to treat everyone as being responsible and empowered.

Don't Let Them Guess; Let Them Know

The best compliments I received were from staff telling me that they believed in themselves as teachers because I believed in them and told them that. People don't need school leaders to constantly reward them for what they do; they do need school leaders to respect them, believe in them, and need them for their shared mission. I also learned that telling parents that I like their child and shared what I appreciated about the child made a significant difference in how they perceived everything else I said. School leaders who feel positively about the people they serve should remove any doubt from those people's minds.

It's Not a Test; Just Do Your Best

This saying is for school leaders to repeat to themselves. It should also be said to all members of the community. There is a very strong emphasis in education on evaluation, testing, and accountability. Teachers can view every expectation as just another opportunity to be judged and evaluated. Creating the type of culture and climate that allows bullying prevention to work requires the psychological safety for all members of the school community to try new things, offer feedback, and raise issues or concerns. School leaders often need to remind people that their effort is important, not just their results.

"If you think you can or think you can't, you're right."

—Henry Ford

"The best way out is always through."

—Robert Frost

These two sayings often kept me headed in the right direction and on track. They not only helped me with my struggles, but they helped me realize and accept that struggling was part of the process and that there were no quick fixes or shortcuts in education. It is easy to have doubts as part of the struggle, but it is more important to remember that persisting through doubts and maintaining the effort is really what is essential for success.

SUMMARY

- Successful bullying prevention consists of many words and actions not apparently related to bullying prevention.
- School leaders' primary responsibility is to set the right direction for bullying prevention efforts. A set of guiding principles that is shared and articulated can point bullying prevention in the right direction and help keep those efforts on track.
- These guiding principles focus on how people treat each other. They set high standards and expectations for all members of the school community.
- School leaders need to follow those principles knowing that they often seem to contradict each other. A school leader often faces a difficult challenge in being consistent with those principles when confronting a teacher who bullies students.
- High accountability for meeting important goals is one essential element for high levels of learning, but it must be balanced with a high level of psychological safety and support.
- Effective bullying prevention requires a shared ownership and leadership for the problem by the entire school community.
- There are leadership practices that promote the leadership and learning of members of the school community. The words and actions of the school leader is a key determinant for getting all members of the community moving in the right direction even if the progress is slow.
- Since so many things are happening all at once in a school environment, helpful reminders in the form of proverb-like sayings are more likely to be remembered and used in the daily interactions between the school leader and the members of the school community.

ACTIVITIES FOR "LEADERSHIP FOR A CHANGE"

ACTIVITY 1: GUIDING PRINCIPLES—Y'S

Purpose

Although the guiding principles are not specific or shouldn't dictate a definite course of action, the school community needs to talk about them and share its interpretations of them. Members of the school community need the opportunity to talk about the guiding principles to develop a shared meaning and common language for how they manifest themselves in the school.

Content

The principles can be presented one at a time to any school community group. A shared meaning can be developed when members of the group translate their understanding of them into specific words and actions. Members of that group may have similar interpretations or may differ significantly from one another. The more opportunity that members of the community have to discuss their similarities and differences in their understanding of them, the better they will be in supporting each other's efforts to be act in accord with the principles. Participants at the meeting will have to work individually and then in groups to translate the principle into what it would look like, sound like, and feel like in action.

Procedure

Participants will use a Y-chart for translating a principle into words, actions, and feelings.

A Y-chart has three components for each principle (e.g., treat students the way you would want them to treat each other.)

Looks like: People picking up something someone dropped, holding the door open for someone, smiling, nodding to someone.

Sounds like: "How are you doing?" "Let me help you out." "How do you feel?"

Feels like: Safe, calm, happy.

Each participant can be given his or her own sheet of paper with a Y-chart on it and instructed on how to fill it out. There can be a sample one on a sheet of chart paper or displayed on a screen.

After each participant has worked on an individual sheet, they can form either pairs or groups of four to five to share their Y-charts. They should work cooperatively to create a large chart on a sheet of chart paper. When each group is finished, the group can tape the large Y-chart to the wall. When all the Y-charts are on the wall, the entire group can walk around and view all of the charts.

After all the participants have viewed all the charts, they can return to their small-group table and discuss similarities and differences between their chart and the other ones.

The large (whole) group can discuss these similarities and differences. Ask the group to nominate two to three "looks like" behaviors and two to three "sounds like" words that they recommend for everyone to use. See if the whole the group can come to some consensus on a set for the school.

ACTIVITY 2: BUILDING THE MATRIX

Purpose

The matrix developed by Amy Edmondson, with the variables of high accountability and psychological safety and support, visually shows the effect on learning. This activity will have the participants discuss how those variables are manifested in a school.

Content

There are two parts to the activity: identifying examples of each of the variables and then predicting the type of learning environments that occur as a result of the combinations of them. The participants will be shown the empty matrix and work together to fill in the quadrants. They can then compare their descriptions with the ones from the original article by Edmondson.

Procedure

Present the matrix (with the quadrants empty) to the entire group. This should also include having Accountability for Meeting Goals along the horizontal axis and Psychological Safety along the vertical axis. Also have *high* at the top of the four quadrants, *low* at the bottom, and *high* along the horizontal axis to the far right. (See Figure 11.1.)

Have staff sit in small groups of four or five and assign the roles of facilitator, recorder, materials manager, and reporter (and timekeeper if there are five people). Each group needs to brainstorm actions or attitudes that would constitute psychological safety and high accountability. Examples of psychological safety could include voicing disagreements without fear of negative consequences and experimenting with new teaching strategies without fear of criticism. Examples of high accountability could include having high standards for professional behavior and having individual and collective goals for professional development.

Each group would list the actions and attitudes for each variable on a piece of chart paper and post on the wall. Participants would walk around the room to view each chart.

When they have returned to their group, they should take another piece of chart paper and draw a square with four quadrants (large enough to write several phrases in each of them). They are to work as a team in filling in the quadrant describing the type of environment that the different combinations would produce. For example, low psychological safety and low accountability would produce an environment characterized by apathy, low effort, and resistance to new ideas.

Each group would put their completed square on the wall next to the descriptions of the two variables. Each group should have the opportunity to review each chart on the wall.

Show the chart with the quadrants filled in representing the Edmondson's research.

Facilitate a large-group discussion about how the staff answers compared with the original chart. Have staff share any ideas they have for improving the learning environment or everyone. Try to get consensus on one to two changes that could be made to improve the learning environment.

ACTIVITY 3: "BABY STEPS" FOR CULTURE CHANGE

Purpose

Positive changes in school culture are a result of many actions done by many people over time. This activity will give staff an opportunity to reflect on positive things they are already doing to make the school a better place and on what other things could be done in the future. It is also an opportunity to reflect on the inherent fears people have about change and how moving slowly in the right direction can lessen the fear while still ensuring progress.

Content

Show a brief clip from the movie *What About Bob?* (Oz, 1991) available on YouTube at www.youtube.com/watch?v=1dWk0eHBOvk&feature=youtu .be. The scene is called "Baby Steps" or "Therapy" and occurs approximately at the ten-minute mark of the movie. It is the scene in the psychiatrist's (played by Richard Dreyfuss) office when he gives his new highly phobic client (played by Bill Murray) his book titled *Baby Steps*. Continue the clip until Bill Murray finally makes it out of the office and onto the elevator and after the elevator's door closes, you hear his screaming.

Present the idea that change does create anxiety but that having some control over the situation and taking it slow can lessen the fear and get unstuck from not acting at all.

Procedure

Following the clip, have participants find a partner and share a time in their life when they had to deal with an anxious situation and how they managed it. Ask for volunteers to share their story with the group. If no one volunteers, the school leader should be prepared to share.

Distribute a slip of paper or ask participants to use their piece of scrap paper and jot down their answer to the following questions:

What is one thing I do now and/or have done to make this school a better place?

What is one thing I could do in the future to make the school a better place?

What is one thing that if everyone agreed to do on a consistent basis would make the school a better place?

Ask people to share their answers with a partner. Ask for volunteers to share their answers. Try to make sure that everyone does his or her share.

The school leader could facilitate a large-group discussion to see if there were one to two actions from the suggestions to the third question that staff would agree to try.

Another option would be to collect the slips from everyone and have the bullying prevention team review and organize them. At the next meeting, the participants could be given a menu of actions from the larger list, and staff could discuss and decide on one to two they would like to try for a month.

OUTCOME

1. Participants would have opportunity to reflect on key concepts related to leadership and change and then translate those concepts into specific but relatively simple actions that would improve the climate and culture of the school.

12

Policies, Programs, and Practices

"Prevention programs in schools need active leaders and careful planning. They need to begin in the early grades and extend over time, involving the entire school community."

—Gayle Macklem (2003, p. 123)

WHAT'S THE POLICY?

When people had strong feelings about a problem, they would ask me, "What's the policy on that issue?" There might have been a practice, procedure, or protocol that pertained to the problem, but in most cases, there wasn't a policy. I learned to interpret that question, however, as an expression of their strong desire to find a higher source of authority to fix the problem in their favor. I would listen and ask questions and reassure them that I would help. When we realized that we were not automatically at odds with each other, we could then talk about the problem constructively.

I value good policies. They are necessary and provide the basis for action on critical issues. Some people think that policies, programs, and practices alone solve problems—they don't and never will. Good policies, programs, and practices in the hands of skilled, knowledgeable, and wise professionals are the critical elements for effective bullying prevention.

This chapter will provide some basic information on policies, programs, and practices for bullying prevention. I will focus my discussion on how leaders can wisely use them as tools to solve problems and take positive action. School leaders will need to help members of the community understand the role that policies and programs play in bullying prevention.

Policies

School leaders should know how extensively both state laws and district policies articulate what schools must do in addressing the problem of bullying. There is great variation among state laws, and consequently, even greater variation among the policies of local educational agencies.

Almost every state has a law specifically related to bullying in schools. Most state laws mandate that school districts adopt an antibullying policy. Some states require more comprehensive policies than others. School leaders should know the state law and what it requires of school districts. Obviously, they need to be very familiar with their own district's policy. Some policies require administrators to respond to school bullying in a certain way; others are much less specific.

Many states require annual reporting of bullying incidences to their state education departments. In these situations, school leaders need to have a thorough understanding of the definition of bullying used in the policy and ensure that all members of the school community know that definition. Staff should know the definition of bullying so they can intervene when they see it or hear of it. All members of the community must know that same definition in order to report it accurately.

Ironically, districts with a serious bullying problem could have fewer reported incidences than districts that have been successful in addressing bullying. When people trust that something will be done about bullying, they are more likely to make a complaint to that school. Conversely, bullying could be underreported in schools where bullying prevention is not a priority. People are less likely to report if they are unclear about what constitutes bullying and are unsure of how the school will respond to a complaint. School leaders need to be acutely aware of this possible problem. This is also why it is very difficult to compare schools or districts. No school therefore can rely solely on the number of complaints of bullying and/or incidents as any reliable measure of how the school is actually doing.

A REVIEW BY THE U.S. DEPARTMENT OF EDUCATION/CENTER FOR SAFE AND SUPPORTIVE SCHOOLS OF PROVISIONS IN STATE LAWS

By reviewing the laws of over forty states, the U.S. Department of Education (2011) has organized the components of bullying prevention into eleven categories:

1. *Purpose statement*: Some laws clearly state the negative impact that bullying has on student learning and the school environment. The benefits of preventing bullying are outlined in some laws.

2. *Statement of scope*: This delineates what areas or events should be covered by the law or policy. Some laws include protection of school personnel in addition to students. This would include protection within the school building but also at school-sponsored events whether on or off the school campus and on school transportation. Some laws indicated that any bullying behavior that disrupts the school environment is included. Cyberbullying would be covered under those type statements.

3. *Specification of prohibited behavior*: A clear definition of bullying should be part of this component along with a nonexclusive list of examples or forms of bullying. Laws vary in how they distinguish bullying from harassment. Retaliation against those who report bulling is expressly prohibited in some laws and policies, but not all. Cyberbullying is specified in some states but not all.

4. *Enumeration of specific characteristics*: Some laws mention certain characteristics of students who have been traditionally targets, but bullying should not be limited to people with these characteristics.

5. *Development and implementation of policies for all districts:* Some states mandate that all districts have antibullying policies and provide a model for them to use.

6. *Components for policies to cover* are the following:
    a. *Definition of bullying*
    b. *Reporting bullying*: Recommendations for specific requirements for reporting bullying incidents.
    c. *Investigating and responding to bullying*: This usually includes recommendations for how to respond to complaints, protect the victim, and communicate with parents and staff.
    d. *Written records*: Requires written documentation and record keeping for complaints and investigations.

e. *Sanctions/consequence*: Some states require a clearly articulated and progressive approach to discipline.

f. *Referrals*: Recommendations for the type of referrals to make to other services that could help students and families. This could include specific recommendations for students who bully, are bullied, or witness bullying.

7. *Review and evaluation of how laws and policies are implemented*: Some laws and policies require an annual review and evaluation of bullying prevention efforts.

8. *Communication to school community*: This requires that all districts and schools communicate some information about bullying prevention and the law and policy to the public.

9. *Training and prevention professional development*: Some laws and policies require specific professional development activities for staff and parents. Some laws mandate that states use evidence-based programs.

10. *Requirement for reporting data/progress and any actions taken to address bullying*

11. *Statement that indicates that those victimized can seek other legal recourse*

This list of components should be shared with the bullying prevention team. If a district policy does not specify or require one of these components, the team could decide if a component should be instituted in their own school. Each team should use both state law and district policy as a guide for their work.

MEMO TO THE FIELD: ISSUES OF CIVIL RIGHTS VIOLATION

In October 2010, the Civil Rights Division of the U.S. Department of Education sent a field memo describing the responsibilities of local educational agencies for addressing student misconduct covered by the antibullying policy and that could also be a violation of federal antidiscrimination laws. When a certain protective class of students is the target of bullying, various civil rights laws come into play. Harassment of students based on their race, color, or national origin; gender; or disability can be considered a violation of their civil rights. In these situations, district have obligations not just to protect the individuals involved in particular instances but also to take prompt and effective action to protect all students in that protected class. This information is critical for school leaders to know, understand, and communicate to the school community.

This memo highlights the responsibility that schools have to address possible hostile environments that interfere with students' ability to learn and participate in the full range of school activities. It makes it very clear that districts cannot wait for an incident to occur and then merely use disciplinary procedures toward only those students determined to be the perpetrators.

The memo indicates that schools need to do the following:

• Address harassment even if it is determined to be unintentional. This also includes harassment that is not directed toward a specific person but rather represents a pervasive way of acting or speaking.

• Address incidents that they reasonably should have known about based on physical signs of harassment in the environment. They also should be aware of any ongoing harassment that the general population has knowledge of.

• Publicize its policies and procedures regarding bullying and harassment.

• Take steps to prevent harassment from happening again. These steps could include providing training for the perpetrators to prevent incidents and services to support the targeted student(s). In addition, training might be required for all members of the school community.

The memo summarizes the responsibility of schools this way:

School administrators should look beyond simply disciplining the perpetrators. While disciplining the perpetrators is likely a necessary step, it often is insufficient. A school's responsibility is to eliminate the hostile environment created by the harassment, address its effects, and take steps to ensure that harassment does not recur. Put differently, the unique effects of discriminatory harassment may demand a different response than would other types of bullying. (U.S. Department of Education, 2010)

Earlier in this book, I advocated for an approach to bullying prevention that went beyond the default response of addressing bullying primarily as a discipline problem. Schools that are unable to see the problem differently and adopt a more comprehensive approach are not just failing to help their students but also risk failing to meet the requirements of the law. It certainly makes sense to change before being forced to change.

(*Point of clarification*: Although related, bullying should not be equated with harassment. Harassment can sometimes occur without the power imbalance that is a critical attribute of the definition of bullying, e.g., an off color joke could be made by a peer and be offensive to people who overheard it. Bullying is also usually dependent on bystander's response, while harassment can often just occur between two individuals even if they are of equal status.)

CAUTION: WORDS MATTER

Some law enforcement officials prefer to use the term harassment to include all bullying. Since harassment has legal implications, they feel that, if bullying is breaking a criminal law, students will be more reluctant to bully someone because of the legal sanctions involved.

This approach also implies that educators should turn over the policing of bullying to law enforcement. (Unfortunately, many educators would like to do that.) The public often supports this "get tough" approach, and school administrators can *appear* to be taking decisive action by involving law enforcement personnel. A very small number of bullying or harassment cases could be considered criminal offenses, but most are not. Bullying is a social problem involving how people interact with each other. Educators working with students and parents remain the most important and influential people in bullying prevention.

BULLYING PREVENTION PRACTICES AND PROGRAMS

A school's decision for how to approach bullying prevention is very dependent on the number of requirements in the state law and district policy. Many schools address bullying because of mandates and regulations. Most bullying prevention programs are designed to meet the requirements of even the most comprehensive state laws and the civil rights laws. Finding and implementing the right program can help schools meet these mandates and keep them in compliance with the law. *Schools primarily motivated to meet their legal requirements may find a program that will do that for them, but that will be no guarantee for success in preventing or reducing bullying or improving their culture and climate.*

WHAT RESEARCH SAYS ABOUT BEST PRACTICE

Educational research is a complex endeavor, since scientifically controlled studies are very difficult to do. It is difficult to identify the variable that is correlated to a specific outcome. Given the added complexity of a problem like school bullying, research to determine what's effective is ever more problematic.

In an article titled "What Can Be Done About School Bullying? Linking Research to Educational Practice" (Swearer, Espelage, Vaillancourt, &

Hymel, 2010), the authors make the following statements regarding bullying prevention efforts:

> *"Mixed results suggest that although school-based and schoolwide bully-
> ing prevention efforts can be effective, success in one school or context is
> no guarantee of success in another" (p. 42).*

> *"Before selecting a specific intervention, educators should investigate
> whether or not the intervention is based in research, if it promotes proso-
> cial behavior . . . one challenge has been to adopt such evidence-based
> programs" (p. 43).*

> *"Researchers are only beginning to understand the factors that contribute
> to this variation in outcomes across schools and countries" (p. 42).*

> *"Unfortunately, the research suggests that the majority of school-based
> bullying prevention programs have had little impact on reducing bullying
> behavior."*

> *"The linkage between research and practice is the answer to the question
> how to eradicate bullying among youth" (p. 42).*

This is an excellent article that school leaders should read and share.
Many schools leaders, who have very little time to read, could be confused
about its conclusions. The research is unclear, yet they need to use research
to guide their decisions. Given the laws and mandates they face along with
the pressure to raise student achievement, school leaders want to know
what to do and want experts to "cut to the chase" to give them answers
and solutions to their problems. How does a school leader choose the "best
practice that is evidence based" when there is no clear answer for what
that is?

In his book, *Children and Bullying: How Parents and Educators Can Reduce
Bullying at School* (2008), Ken Rigby aptly sums up this dilemma for school
leaders:

> There is more that needs to be done before we know precisely what
> "best practice" is . . . Meanwhile schools must act. We must do the
> best we can. It is best to see evidence-based, best practice as an
> ideal towards which we must strive, and not be taken in by ques-
> tionable or bogus claims. (p. 152)

THE TOP TEN PRACTICES: A RELIABLE SOURCE

As I stated in Chapter 6, schools leaders should know what *not to do* in
bullying prevention. They also should know what has emerged in the
field as recommended practices. There are so many resources available on

bullying prevention promoting programs and practices. Many of those are commercial products and services claiming to have the answer for school leaders who "have to" address bullying prevention. I highly recommend that schools leader rely on a neutral, noncommercial source of information.

The www.stopbullyingnow.gov website is a government resource with a wealth of information, resources, and support that is free and readily available to the public. They have published a fact sheet summarizing the ten best practices in bullying prevention. I have integrated these practices into the various chapters of this book. As sound as these practices are, each one of them presents a significant challenge for any school leader who has the responsibility of implementing them into the life of a school.

1. Focus on the social environment of the school.

2. Assess bullying/victimization.

3. Garner parent support for bullying prevention.

4. Form a group to coordinate the school's bullying prevention efforts.

5. Train staff in bullying prevention.

6. Establish and enforce school rules and policies related to bullying.

7. Increase adult supervision in hot spots where bullying occurs.

8. Intervene consistently and appropriately in bullying situations.

9. Focus some class time on bullying prevention.

10. Continue these efforts over time.

BEST PRACTICE FOR BEST PRACTICE

Just as there is a *qualified best practice* for bullying prevention, there is also a qualified best practice for leadership. This book has been an attempt to bring the two of these practices together to guide school leaders. As a principal, I know how difficult it is to get *any type* of change in a school. As discussed in this book, just telling a staff to do it doesn't get it done. Although there is no one grand strategy for change, school leaders need to be *strategic and skillful* in facilitating change.

Here is an example of a principal's *strategic leadership* in balancing "best practice" with the particular needs of a school.

A middle school principal contacted me and asked if I would come and speak to his faculty about bullying prevention. I typically refrain from speaking to any group if I am going to be the *only* "professional development" on bullying prevention. I only agree to speak if I can meet with the principal to explore how my efforts can support the school's ongoing bullying prevention efforts. If a principal is committed to ongoing bullying prevention and has a plan that looks like it is going in the right direction, I will work with that principal to support those ongoing efforts.

In this particular situation, after meeting with the principal, I was happy to help him. What I observed turned out to be a great example of how a principal used his knowledge of his staff and school culture to develop a plan that would gain support and start to move in the right direction using best practice.

Here are the particulars of his situation:

- The central office wanted him to implement a "brand name" bullying prevention program that they had selected. It was an excellent program with record of positive results.

- He was not opposed to the program but knew that his staff would view the imposition of it as a criticism of their current efforts to improve the school climate and support students.

- Although their school did not have a bullying prevention program (by name), they had done much to prevent bullying by building community and promoting social and emotional learning.

- He realized that more needed to be done specifically to assess bullying and to develop goals and plans based on that assessment.

- He wanted to build on what he thought was a good foundation— rather appear to start from scratch that would imply that *nothing* had been done previously about the problem.

- When I met with him, I reviewed the top ten practices, and he agreed those were essential for bullying prevention and would be part of the school's efforts.

I would gear my message to how difficult it is to see and hear bullying (sharing the example of the blind spot) and emphasize the need to continue to build community and trust with the students. I reviewed the information about bystanders and how they needed to be empowered. My message to his staff boiled down to this:

Bullying prevention is harder and more complex than we think. Faculty and staff of the school care for students and have done a lot to help them. Educators need more support and resources to "do the job that they want to do." Bullying prevention is one part, albeit important one, in their ongoing efforts to make their school a better place. More important than what one strategy or plan to use was the need for commitment and collaboration to address the problem in the way that would fit the unique needs of the school.

Following my talk, a teacher, who had an interest in bullying prevention, spoke to the staff to solicit additional volunteers for their standing committee on school climate. This committee would focus more of its effort on bullying prevention. The principal informed me later that there was a positive response to my message, and he was encouraged by what he was hearing from his staff.

In the following weeks, the principal worked with this committee to develop a plan to include the top ten practices. Central office wisely let this principal and the school community proceed with their homegrown customized bullying prevention plan.

PRACTICAL WISDOM: MAKING POLICIES, PROGRAMS, AND PRACTICES WORK

According to Schwartz and Sharpe (2010),

> Practical wisdom is akin to the kind of skill that a craftsman needs to build a boat or a house, or that a jazz musician needs to improvise. Except practical wisdom is not a technical skill or artistic skill. It is a moral skill—a skill that enables us to discern how to treat people in our everyday social activities. (p. 8)

The principal in this example knew what he was doing. He had *practical wisdom* and applied it to bullying prevention. Perhaps the missing element or variable in the research in bullying prevention is the practical wisdom of the people inside of the schools who implement bullying prevention programs.

Schwartz and Sharpe's analogy of building a house is a useful one for bullying prevention. A successfully built house is a result of architectural plans based on principles of engineering and artistic design. Those plans must meet the requirements of local building codes and other government regulations. A well-built house is the common goal of a team of skilled people working together to implement those plans using the best tools and materials available to them. There are leaders that help organize and coordinate the work and facilitate the many decisions needed to be made as the work proceeds. The stated goal is to build a house, but the ultimate outcome is a home for people to love and grow in.

Successful bullying prevention requires plans that meet government mandates and regulations. Those plans must reflect the best available knowledge of human development, social psychology, and education. A team of skillful and caring people using quality programs and practices implements the plans using judgment and creativity to fit the particular needs and assets of a school community. School leaders must know the importance of good plans, good practices, and programs but more importantly know how to get caring and skilled people to use the plans and tools to make the best school possible for everyone to live and learn in. The overall goal would be to create a school where every student is cared for and valued and can feel at home.

PRACTICAL WISDOM FOR USING PROGRAMS AND PRACTICES

- People, not programs, are what make the difference.

- Programs are tools, not game changers in and of themselves.

- Leadership is getting people to believe and accept that they can make the difference.

- Don't just equate success with instituting a bullying prevention program—it is about making the school a better place for learning and living.

- Bullying prevention can and should start any time and doesn't need extra funds or specialized training.

- Build on the positive things already happening—bullying prevention is a natural extension of them.

- Affirm what staff has done and attribute problems not to their shortcomings but to their need for more support and professional development.

- Know why the practices work and what they are designed to do.

- Bullying prevention should not replace other initiatives but can work with them.

- Programs are like full dinners, they are great for some people, but for others, à la carte is a viable option.

- The school community can set their own timetable and decide when to start and how to proceed.

- Decisions should be based on data (what is really happening in the school).

- Bullying prevention is an *ongoing process* of assessment, goal setting, implementing plans, evaluating progress, and making necessary changes based on that evaluation.

FINDING EFFECTIVE PROGRAMS/PRACTICES

A bullying prevention program implemented by committed and skilled members of school community can significantly improve school climate and reduce bullying. Effective school leaders work with their bullying prevention teams to find a program or practice that will meet the needs and the goals of the school. Part of the leader's role is to facilitate the process for deciding on the best tool for the school. This approach takes more time than simply selecting a program and presenting it to either the bullying prevention team or the school community. The extra time it takes to empower the team to make that decision will create a greater sense of ownership and commitment to bullying prevention—it is worth the investment.

After the bullying prevention team has decided on a plan of action that includes using a program, school leaders can refer them to reliable and neutral resources for viewing what is available. Here are some websites that can provide that type of information:

Substance Abuse and Mental Health Services Administration (SAMHSA): www.nrepp.samhsa.gov

Safe and Supportive Schools (U.S. Department of Education): safesupportiveschools.ed.gov

The Developmental Services Group: Model Programs Guide and Database: www.dsgonline.com

American Federation of Teachers: www.aft.org/yourwork/tools4teachers/bullying/resources.cfm

Center for the Study and Prevention of Violence, University of Colorado at Boulder: www.colorado.edu/cspv/blueprints/modelprograms.html

National Association of School Psychologists: www.nasponline.org/resources/principals/nassp_bullying.aspx

SUMMARY

- School leaders need to know their state laws and requirements regarding bullying prevention.
- Many state laws require districts to create policies on bullying and mandate what those policies should include.
- School leaders need to ensure that a particular school's bullying prevention efforts are in line with state and district requirements.
- School leaders need to make informed and knowledgeable decisions about what programs and practices to use.
- It is difficult to reconcile the inconsistent research on the effectiveness of bullying prevention programs with the need to be informed by best practice and research in the field of bullying prevention.

- There is a consensus in the field of bullying prevention on ten essential bullying prevention practices.
- School leaders need to be strategic in how they present programs and practices to the school community.

ACTIVITY FOR "POLICIES, PROGRAMS, AND PRACTICES": PRACTICAL WISDOM

ACTIVITY 1

Purpose

Here is another quotation from the book *Practical Wisdom* by Barry Schwartz and Ken Sharpe (2010):

> Rules are aids, allies, guides and checks. But too much reliance on rules can squeeze out the judgment to do our work well. When general principles morph into detailed instructions, formulas, unbending commands—wisdom substitutes for the important nuances. Better to minimize the number of rules, give up trying to cover every particular circumstance, and instead do more training to encourage reasoning and intuition. (p. 42)

There is no shortcut to wise leadership, especially wise shared leadership. It develops by confronting difficult and complex problems and struggling with them. When members of the school community accept the challenge of working together and sometimes struggling together, they can grow wise collectively. If some members, however, insist on quick fixes and an overreliance on rules and regulations to solve problems, it will be much more difficult for the community to grow together. Devoting some time to discussing the ideas presented in a book like *Practical Wisdom* is a *wise* investment.

Content

There is a talk given by Barry Schwartz on the topic of practical wisdom on the website (TED2011, 2011). It is also available on YouTube (www.youtube.com/watch?v=IDS-ieLCmS4) and on iTunes podcasts. It is free and easy to download. Show this video to the participants in the meeting.

Procedure

Give staff an opportunity to write down their reaction to Schwartz's talk. Have the group break into groups of four to five and share their reaction with each other. Ask each group to share two to three ideas that they think are most relevant to their work in school. Ask each group to discuss the implications of these ideas on the school's bullying prevention efforts.

After each group has shared, the principal should facilitate a general discussion with the whole group.

Some staff might be interested in participating in a book study group.

OUTCOMES

1. Staff should realize that they are leaders who have the knowledge, skill, and wisdom to make a significant difference in bullying prevention.

2. Policies, program, and practices are useful tools but need to be in the hands of skillful and knowledgeable professionals.

13

Discipline in the Right Climate

Rules, Consequences, Supervision, and Intervention

"There are few things more powerful than the commitment of the group. Change leaders need the group to change the group: when it comes to socialization there is no better teacher than one's peers."

—Michael Fullan (2011a, p. 85)

THE BEST OF BOTH WORLDS

Following a presentation I made, a parent shared with me two very different and revealing experiences she had with the problem of school bullying. She had one child in a small, progressive private school and another child in a suburban middle-class public high school. Emphasizing how she liked both schools, she wistfully declared, "When it comes to bullying prevention, they could really learn something from each other."

In the high school, the administration took her complaint about bullying very seriously. They did a thorough investigation and promptly reported back to her about what they planned to do. In the small private school, the principal listened to her complaint and suggested that her daughter who had been bullied join a friendship club.

She thought that the high school needed to do more to build community and promote social and emotional skills as a way to prevent bullying. She thought that the private school needed to acknowledge that students bully and can hurt one another. She wished that the private school had addressed the problem more directly rather than just promote social and emotional skills.

She was right on both counts: schools should improve their climate and directly address the problem of bullying. I call this best of both worlds approach: *Discipline in the Right Climate*.

APPLYING THE THREE-TIER INTERVENTION MODEL TO BULLYING PREVENTION

Effective bullying prevention requires a comprehensive schoolwide approach. The three-tier model, often used in Response to Intervention (RTI), illustrates how this approach can be applied to bullying prevention. (See Figure 13.1.)

The bottom tier represents schoolwide universally applied practices that will improve school climate. These practices should promote autonomy, create a sense of belonging, and build competency in all students to empower them as bystanders and equip them for success in the 21st century. When

Figure 13.1   Response to Intervention Applied to Bullying Prevention

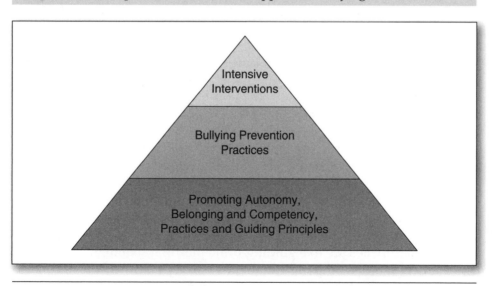

Source: Adapted from Fox et al. (2003).

adults' words and actions are guided by the six guiding principles listed earlier in this book, they will practice what they preach and provide the right model for students to follow.

The second tier represents the ten research-based practices described in the previous chapter. These practices specifically address bullying in the school. The practices provide specific information, a common vocabulary, and a skill set to all members of the community.

The top tier represents specific interventions to help students who have been victimized for long periods of time or students who persistently bully. The families of these students might need support and training. Very often these students also receive services related to learning and behavior needs or special education.

RULES: LOOK CLOSELY

One of the recommended practices is to establish a clear set of rules about bullying. Schools may develop their own set of rules. If they do, however, the verb *bully* should be specifically stated within the rules. There should also be a commonly understood definition of bullying for the school community.

These rules are from the Olweus Bullying Prevention Program (Olweus et al., 2007):

1. We will not bully others.

2. We will try to help students who are bullied.

3. We will make it a point to include students who are left out.

4. If we know someone is being bullied, we will tell an adult at school or an adult at home.

I highly recommend them. They are simple, clear, and straightforward, yet they need to be taught and discussed on a regular basis with all members of the school community.

Here are some important things to notice about these rules:

- The word *we* is prominent and emphasizes community.
- *We* means everyone, not just students. These are rules for everyone's benefit, and everyone benefits from following them.
- Only the first one is "not," the rest are positive actions.
- Following all four rules will build a stronger school community.
- The four rules define what a good citizen is and does.
- The four rules are like guiding principles that require interpretation and judgment. Students cannot just blindly follow them—they need to understand them and make them their own.
- If rules 2, 3, and 4 are practiced, it becomes easier for everyone to follow rule 1. This shows the impact on bystander behavior on bullying.

Rules for the Rules

Rules by themselves will not sufficiently address the problem of bullying. Some staff might be eager to have rules, believing that it's the enforcement of them that will solve the problem of bullying. Most students already know that bullying is wrong and know they would they get in trouble if they were caught bullying someone.

Rules, however, are important for another reason: they are a public statement of the values and priorities of the school community. Not having rules about bullying would inadvertently convey to students that bullying is not a problem and that preventing and reducing it is not a priority for the school community.

Students should know how these rules differ from other rules that are procedural and address more distinct behaviors, e.g., running in the halls, leaving the building without permission, etc. Since bullying is a relationship problem, the social nature of the rules should be emphasized and explained to them.

For these rules to work, the adults in the school need to follow some *rules* about them:

- Rules should be posted and prominent in every room.
- They should be a regular topic of discussion and a reference point for understanding social situations and problems.
- They need to be connected to the school's mission and core values.
- Students need to understand how following the rules helps everyone feel safe and how feeling safe helps everyone learn.
- When the rules work (people take care of each other), the school community should recognize and celebrate that success.
- Teachers should help students internalize the values that these rules represent, so students will do what is right even without adult supervision.
- Have high expectations for following them yet understand how people learn from breaking them.
- Rules will become meaningless and ignored even if just a few adults fail to follow them.
- Strong, positive, and trusting relationships help students learn the rules and what they mean.
- Make sure the students know how following rules 2, 3, and 4 affects rule 1.

SUPERVISION OF STUDENTS

The presence of adults in an environment has great influence on all students' behavior. Although bullying can occur under the direct supervision of adults, adult presence can lessen the frequency and intensity of bullying in any environment.

One of the key practices for effective bullying prevention is adjusting the supervision of students based on the data from bullying assessments. Supervision, however, is more than just putting an adult in the right place at the right time. Adults in supervisory positions can do more than just stop bullying; they can develop relationships with students that will improve the climate of the school.

Code of Conduct for Supervising Adults

As I have previously mentioned, adults in schools have less control but more influence over student behavior than they realize. Students want positive relationships with adults, even if their behavior sometimes indicates otherwise. They may posture or show defiance to those in authority, but that is a reaction to adults whom they think don't care or respect them.

School monitors, therefore, need training and support for how to interact with students and intervene with problems. They need guidelines and procedures to help them with their challenging job. This support will lessen their uncertainty and anxiety when interacting with students. When they are more relaxed, and confident of support from school leaders, they will make more thoughtful and effective decisions. Adults who form trusting relationships with students can be a source of safety for vulnerable students and bystanders.

Students are reluctant to report bullying to adults. Many students want to stop bullying but don't know how to do it. The right supervision can be the difference between bystanders being stuck in this uncertainty or having more options for doing what they think is right.

The article *Bullying and the Politics of Telling* by Oliver and Candappa (2007) describes how the quality of relationships affects bystanders' reporting of bullying:

> The quality of the relationship between teachers and pupils may be an important mediating factor in reducing the "risk" of telling . . . pupils need not rely solely on a positive relationship with one teacher, but on improved quality of relationships between pupils and teachers generally . . . Listening to students would form the fabric of everyday interactions in school life. (p. 84)

Students are more likely to report bullying to an adult they know, trust, and talk with on a regular basis, rather than someone who is just there to maintain order. Even if students are reluctant to report a specific incident, they could in a casual conversation convey some information to alert an adult to a bullying situation.

Adults in supervisory positions need to maintain four dispositions to create this fabric of everyday interactions:

- *Professional*: Adults should be friendly but not friends with students. Their language and demeanor need to be appropriate at all times.

- *Pleasant*: Students need to see that adults enjoy their job and being with them. A smiling face and welcoming tone sends that message to them.

- *Personable*: Adults can share appropriate stories and experiences with students. Students need to see adults as people who care and who are doing an important job. Supervisory staff should check in with students and inquire about how they are doing. This checking in with students needs to be a habit developed by all staff. A lonely, isolated student may need someone to check in twenty times before there is enough trust to respond. If an adult gives up after fifteen times, that student might never respond.

- *Positive*: Students need adults to find and share something positive about them. Asking a question and being curious in a friendly way about what a student thinks or feels conveys a respect for the student as a person.

Part of the training and preparation for those in a supervisory position should be translating the six guiding principles into specific words and actions to use with students. The ideas generated from that training could become the basis for developing a code of conduct for adults in supervisory positions.

Intervening in Bullying Situations

Even though adults do not witness most of the bullying that occurs in schools, it is essential that adults intervene when they observe any type of bullying. To intervene appropriately, staff should recognize and identify bullying behavior. All staff must accept responsibility of intervening in any bullying situation, not just ones involving students in their class. Staff should know how to intervene and have the assurance that they will be supported if they do.

Staff Reluctance to Intervene

Just as all students are bystanders to bullying, staff are also bystanders. Although they witness less bullying than students, they must intervene when they do see it. Most staff tend to intervene with serious physical forms of bullying. They are less likely to intervene with more subtle forms of bullying. School leaders should clarify staff's role in intervening and provide them with guidelines and support for intervening.

Three Key Points of Clarification for Staff

School leaders should provide time at a staff meeting to clarify that all staff members are responsible for intervening for bullying. This understanding will reassure staff who take the risk of intervening. School leaders will need to address the reasons why staff are reluctant to intervene:

1. Some staff question their skills when intervening with an unfamiliar student. In addition to the basic guidelines for intervening, they need a backup plan and way to signal for immediate support from other staff or the principal.

2. Some staff might view intervening as requiring a lot of time and energy devoted to documentation, follow-up procedures, parent contact, or fear of criticism for their judgments. They should understand how intervening can be brief, concise, and effective.

3. Staff might worry about being challenged about intervening. They might also be concerned about needing sufficient evidence of bullying to justify intervening. They should see intervention not just as disciplining but also as a way to teach the students about how to treat each other.

School leaders can support and guide more consistent and effective staff intervention by helping them understand *two different types of interventions*.

Low-Intensity/High-Frequency Language-Based Occurrences

These incidents are ones that staff could overlook or ignore. They usually involve indirect or fleeting derogatory comments that students routinely make. Many students could respond to an adult's intervening with comments like "What's the big deal?" These derogatory comments can be overheard as students walk down a hallway. When staff are directed to intervene upon hearing these comments, they often think they will be intervening all the time and that there are bigger and better battles to fight.

Ironically, intervening on this level is the key to preventing the more blatant forms and serious forms of bullying. Intervening on this level is one of the most effective ways of changing the school climate and culture for the better. It is a way to unequivocally state the values and priorities of the school.

Wessler and Premble (2003) state that effective interventions have these common elements:

- Timeliness
- Consistency
- Firmness
- Respectfulness

To illustrate how these elements work in an intervention, they describe the following scenario:

Teachers often wonder how they should respond when they are walking through the hallways and hear a student use a slur that is not seemingly directed toward any particular student. Teachers tell me that in this situation they do not know the names of the students involved or even which group made the comment. My answer starts with what not to do. This is not the time to call the SWAT team . . . or to send the offending student to the principal's office . . . Rather this situation calls for the faculty member to send an immediate and clear message that he or she heard the comment and that the language used is not acceptable . . . The use of "I" statements can be very effective. Comments such as "I do not appreciate that kind of language" or "That word offends me" send a clear message that you find the language unacceptable. (p. 49)

Staff intervening do not have to raise their voice nor be condescending in any way toward those students. A simple, sincere, yet resolute tone says, "this is not how we talk to each other here." Such a statement tells the students that they are capable of and expected to raise their level of respect for others. If enough staff intervene this way, the school culture will turn toward the level of respect expected. Failing to intervene on these low-intensity instances conversely sends the message that the degrading language is acceptable. Unfortunately, the intensity and frequency of inappropriate language and behavior will only increase unless staff set high expectations and intervene when students fail to meet them.

School leaders need to help staff see that the time and effort invested in this type of intervention will pay dividends in preventing more harmful, insidious, and pervasive bullying in the school environment.

Physical/Blatant Bullying Occurrences

Although these instances are less frequent than the low-intensity occurrences, staff should have guidelines for how to intervene when the bullying is visible and nearby. The stopbullyingnow.gov provides some tips for how to intervene in these on-the-spot situations:

Immediately stop the bullying. Calmly but firmly tell the student who is bullying to stop and if necessary stand between the student bullying and the student who is bullied. Don't automatically send any students in the area away—have them stay where they are. Don't immediately discuss or ask the student(s) to explain what was happening.

Refer to the bullying behavior and how it is against the school rules and values. Calmly state what was witnessed and identify it as bullying. State that bullying is not acceptable in the school and is against the rules for how people are supposed to treat each other.

Support the bullied child in way that allows that student to "save face" and feel supported and safe from retaliation. Make it clear that the bullied student and the student who bullied are not equally responsible (don't tell them both to go to the principal's office). Don't start to discuss or process what just happened. Make sure the bullied student has staff support or can return to a safe place.

Include bystanders in the conversation and give them guidance about how they might appropriately intervene or get help next time. Depending on the circumstance, find time as close as possible to the incident to describe their behavior to them and how it affected the bullying. This can include sensitizing them to how the bullied students felt and providing strategies they can use in the future.

If appropriate, impose immediate consequences for the students who bully others. These consequences should at least temporarily keep the student(s) who bullied from proceeding as normal. They should be separated from the student who was bullied and the bystanders.

Do not require the students to meet and work things out. This would imply that this was a conflict and not bullying. Because bullying involves a power differential, these students cannot work it out.

This type of intervention will vary upon the location, the availability of other support staff, the time of the day, and many other variables. No one specific set of words or actions will sufficiently address every overt bullying situation. Staff need to have a few basic steps to follow, but it will be important to meet with them after the incident to talk about what happened.

CONSEQUENCES: CAVEATS

In many people's minds, rules and consequences are inseparable. Consequences become synonymous with penalties, punishment, or something negative. Some might even suggest that consequences need to hurt a bit in order to be effective. Rules without consequences applied by those in authority often are considered worthless. This type of thinking reflects the strongly held belief that consequences and the fear of them are the best way to address bullying. A teacher I knew once suggested that if severe enough consequences were given to a student who bullied, this example would deter others from bullying. This type of response would only exacerbate the problem. If fear and intimidation are the way to prevent bullying, then those in authority are using "bullying" to stop bullying.

Consequences are important, but they need to be used wisely and meaningfully by those in authority. Here are some caveats regarding the use of consequences:

Some people can break a rule and not have to receive an imposed consequence in order to learn from that experience. I doubt that there are staff who would automatically accept receiving an imposed consequence every time they broke a rule. If this holds true for adults, it holds true for students. For many students, just being held accountable for their actions by having to meet with a staff person and/or their parents is consequence enough for them to learn.

Students should understand the real consequence of their actions on others. Some students only learn the rule and why the rule exists after they break it. This should be a time for them to think more about the people affected by their action. The students who bullied should be more concerned about the other student than worrying about what is going to happen to them. They need to think more about the *we* (their relationship to others) and less about *me*.

Remember the "rational fallacy" of deterrence in relation to consequences. Those in authority don't catch most acts of bullying, even if they think they do. Students who bully very often think that they will not get caught so consequences don't matter to them. Some students bully impulsively—these students are often bully/victims. If they could stop and think about what they were doing, they would be less likely to bully in the first place. Emotions are a stronger factor in bullying than rational thought, so deterrence doesn't usually work. Most schools have rules and consequences, yet bullying persists, so deterrence in actual practice hasn't worked effectively.

Think about the 4 to 5 percent of bullying that adults see and 95 percent they don't see. Rodkin (2011) describes two types of students who bully: *socially marginalized* and *socially connected*. The socially marginalized students who bully have often been victims of bullying. Their bullying could stem from poor impulse control and a lack of social skills along with a desire to gain some status beyond being a victim.

The *socially connected* students who bully are often popular with students and teachers. They can be attractive, confident, and have strong social skills. Of these two groups, the socially marginalized students are probably the ones who are caught bullying. The socially connected students have figured out how to bully under the radar of adults. Adults are also more likely to monitor the socially marginalized students rather than the socially connected students. The socially marginalized students are at great risk for serious problems later in life. Consequences need to be judiciously applied to these students because they have already been victimized. Severe consequences for them could alienate them from the school. These socially marginalized students will need specialized interventions to change their behavior.

Rules 2, 3, and 4 of the recommended set are asking for positive behaviors. It would be difficult and make little sense to give students a negative consequence for failing to follow rules 2, 3, and 4. Students need to see that rules are not just to constrain or prevent negative behavior but are guides for acting in a more responsible and caring way. These rules are clear but not prescriptive. Students will need to make difficult decisions in often ambiguous situations. If they fall short, they need to be supported and not just criticized or made to feel bad about themselves.

The Three *I*'s of Using Consequences

I wanted the consequences I used with students who bullied to achieve the following goals:

- Directly address the bullying and communicate that it is unacceptable behavior in conflict with the school's values.
- Protect the student who was bullied from further acts of bullying and allow that student to feel safe.

- Do everything to help the student who bullied to stop bullying in the future and learn from the problem.
- Ensure that parents of the student who bullied are supportive of my decisions in order to convey a consistent message to their student about bullying.
- Educate the community about its responsibility to prevent and reduce bullying.

To meet these goals, the consequences had to be:

Individualized

I would take in consideration the following information about the student and the bullying:

- Age
- Length of time in the school
- Past history: How many times has this student been involved with bullying?
- Social status: How many friends, how popular?
- How the student is doing in school: academically, socially, conduct in the classroom
- Family background
- Student's relationship with the student who was bullied
- Staff's relationship with the student

My decision would also be based on the student's honesty, acceptance of responsibility, and remorse for the bullying. I would also check to see what the student's understanding of bullying was. I would confer the student's teacher for his or her reaction to the bullying and his or her thoughts about what would effective and meaningful for the student.

Incremental

These individual factors would definitely influence the decision I made about the appropriate consequence. If necessary, I would consult the parent and the teacher(s) to find the most effective and meaningful consequence that prevent the bullying from happening again.

Consequences could include but are not limited to

- Being accountable to the principal and parents for the behavior
- Completing a form to reflect on what happened
- Letter of apology to all relevant participants
- A positive task that would help the school
- A reading assignment related to bullying

- Plan or contract specifying future behavior
- Using a daily self-evaluation form that the student helped develop
- Assignment to a different classroom for a period of time
- Restricting the student's unstructured, less supervised time
- Change seating arrangements in classroom, cafeteria, school bus
- Suspension from the cafeteria, lunchroom, school bus
- Mandatory checking in with the principal or principal designee at the start or end of the day
- Daily report to parents
- Keeping daily reflection journal
- Ongoing meetings with the student and parents
- In-school suspension
- Out-of-school suspension
- Referral for additional services or evaluations

These consequences could be combined and spread out over a period of time. They would increase in intensity for repeated instances of bullying.

Insistent

Regardless of the particular consequence I chose, I made it very clear to the student who bullied that I would ultimately do whatever it took to keep students safe and stop bullying in the school. Students who bully need to have no doubt about the school leader's insistence that the school be a place where all students can learn. This insistent message teaches students that bullying is different from other behaviors that are against the rules.

I was prepared to ultimately suspend a student from school if that student persisted in spite of the consequences and other positive interventions being done. The parent of the child who was bullied has to be assured that the principal takes the bullying very seriously and will do whatever it takes to keep students safe.

GUIDELINES FOR MEETING WITH STUDENTS INVOLVED WITH BULLYING

Students are works in progress. They will break the rules, do thoughtless things, hurt other people, and make poor choices. They learn through trial and error. They do not get to rehearse before they act for real in life. School leaders have a great opportunity for supporting them through these difficult trial and error experiences. School leaders' goal should be that students learn from these problems and be better prepared for the next problem or challenge they face.

Consequences become meaningful through personal relationships; therefore, how consequences are communicated to students is sometimes even more important than the actual consequence. Students who bully should be viewed as capable of becoming positive leaders of the school community. Recruiting them to be part of the solution rather than part of the problem is an effective strategy.

These guidelines are designed primarily for students who bully but can be adapted for bystanders; they should help students learn from their mistakes:

• *Do your homework, gather relevant information*: Gather and organize the relevant information about what happened. The goal of doing homework is not to prove a case against a student but to have a clear and accurate (as possible) narrative for what really happened.

• *Present the narrative of what happened in a matter of fact way*. Simply state, "I am pretty sure this is what happened." Express concern about what happened and how it needs to stop. Tell the student to listen to the whole story before responding to it.

• *Inform students that it is in **their** best interest for their bullying behavior to stop (in addition to everyone's best interest)*. Obviously, it would be better for this student to think more about the other student first, but this step in the process will help the student make that shift in thinking later on.

• *Have the meeting be an opportunity for honesty and responsibility*. When consequences are automatic and too harsh, students choose the strategy that will best protect them: lying or denying what they did. They have nothing to lose and everything to gain by lying. Avoid putting them on the spot where they automatically defend themselves or plead their case. The goal should be to talk about a problem and learn from it.

• *"Reframe" the situation for the student*. Students approach a meeting like this with fear and defensiveness. It is understandable that they would want to protect themselves from the consequences for their actions. Let students know that there was a problem and that they made a mistake. Being honest and responsible is the best and only way for them to learn, which is the ultimate goal for the meeting.

• *Let them know that mistakes are part of life, without minimizing the seriousness of the mistake*. This guideline reflects the guiding principle of separating the person from the behavior. If students know that the bullying doesn't make them a "bad person" or a "bully," they will be more likely to accept responsibility for their actions. The student should be remorseful (regretting the act) but not guilty (condemning oneself).

- *Let students know the value of honesty and responsibility.* I would describe two scenarios to the students who bullied: I call their parents and report what happened but add that they were honest and accepted responsibility; or I call and report what happened but add that they weren't honest and didn't accept responsibility. I would ask the students to choose the scenario that their parents would prefer to hear. They usually choose the "honest" scenario, which helps them be honest.

- *Go back to the drawing board.* Use the circle of bullying to show the social dynamics of bullying. The circle of bullying diagram also illustrates how the bullying "rules" work in the social world.

- *Use positive presuppositions.* Since no one really knows what goes on inside someone's heart or mind, it is fair to give students the benefit of the doubt concerning their motives. Since most students don't even know their own motives, they depend on adults to help understand them. Saying something like: "I think knowing what you know now about the bullying and how hurtful it was, I think that you probably wouldn't have done it." A statement like "You are someone who could really help students do the right thing and help others" helps the students think differently about who they are.

- *Explain the purpose of the consequences and their connection to the problem.* Putting it simply, the goal of consequences should be to protect other students by making sure it doesn't happen again and to help the student learn not to do it again and learn better ways to act. I would often ask the student who bulled, "What do you think the consequence should be to help you learn not to bully?" Asking doesn't mean that I would change my decision, but it does get the student to think more about the real purpose of the discipline.

- *Leave no doubt that bullying is not acceptable in any way.*

- *Expect to hear the student tell about how he or she was bullied.* Don't be surprised to hear this twist of the story. Let the student briefly tell this story. I would usually calmly state that I wished I heard about it when it happened. I would have done my best to keep him or her safe. I would redirect the student back to the current incident.

- *Make sure that the parents of the students involved hear the school's version of events before the students give them their account.* This serves two purposes: it acknowledges the importance of informing parents as soon as possible, and it prevents having to change the parents' minds about what happened.

- *Use purposeful distractions as a way to more meaningful conversations.* I found this to be especially true with boys. A direct confrontation about the problem usually led to denials and avoidances. Letting students do something with their hands or talking to them about it while walking together often created better conditions for honest conversations. I would ask some students to draw a picture of what happened instead of being forced to admit it or explain it. Legos and Nerf balls were good to have on hand to use as diversions prior to or during conversations. *Some might think that I was rewarding students and that they would continue to bully as a result. I never had that happen. I found that this indirect way helped students be more honest and accept responsibility for what they did. This would decrease the likelihood of them bullying again.*

BULLYING: BLENDING IN OR STANDING OUT?

A teacher told me that he didn't think bullying was a problem in schools until he started working in a school where people treated each other with respect. He said that, although he didn't realize at the time, in his former school, bullying was so pervasive among all members of the school community that it wasn't seen as bullying. It was just the way things were.

It is ingrained in our culture to attribute behavior change more to rules and consequences than to cultural norms. Our experience, however, will tell us that cultural norms are the main determinants of behavior. In a high-class restaurant, is there a sign telling people to keep their voices low? If people walk into an environment that is littered, why would they be more likely to litter than if they walked into a clean and spotless environment?

When rules reflect values and principles, learning the rules means more than just following them. If students see the values and principles behind the rules consistently modeled in the words and actions of adults, they will internalize the rules and learn to govern their own behavior, even when adults are not there to enforce the rules.

All staff need to understand this process and have it be a goal for the school community. The process takes time, and that amount of time varies for each individual, but all staff must believe that all students are eventually capable of internalizing these values and learning to govern themselves.

It takes time to change cultural norms, but once they do change, the energy that otherwise would go into trying to control behavior can be redirected toward other activities like teaching and learning. Until cultural norms change, it can seem impossible to change behavior in any way other than rewarding or punishing behavior. This is why it is even more important to change adult behavior guided by principles rather than trying to change student behavior through other means of control.

SUMMARY

- Effective bullying prevention requires a comprehensive schoolwide approach based on building a positive and respectful school environment combined with specific practices designed to address bullying.
- The three-tier model used for RTI can be applied to bullying prevention, with the bottom tier consisting of practices to support autonomy, belonging, and competency and guiding principles; the next tier consisting of research-based bullying prevention practice; and the top tier consisting of intensive intervention for students with persistent problems.
- A set of clear and consistent rules specifically pertaining to bullying is an essential element of a schoolwide approach.
- The rules should be posted prominently throughout the school, but more importantly, they should reflect the values of the school.
- The rules should apply to every member of the school community. Staff should help students learn what they represent and what it means to follow them.
- Supervision strategically assigned, based on a needs assessment, can reduce and prevent bullying.
- In addition to just assigning staff to supervise areas, they should have guidelines and training for how to interact with students.
- Although most bullying occurs without adults witnessing it, supervisory staff will have to intervene in two types of situations: low-intensity/ language-based bullying and more blatant/physical bullying.
- For low-level/language-based interventions, staff must be timely, consistent, firm, and respectful. These interventions do not require lengthy or formal disciplinary procedures but can be brief and succinct statements indicating the expectations for how to act or speak in the school.
- For more physical/blatant bullying instances, staff need to follow some basic steps consisting of stopping the bullying, identifying it, protecting the bullied students, and holding the student who bullied and the bystanders accountable.
- Consequences for breaking the rules are important but should not be expected to deter future behavior or considered the main way of addressing bullying.
- School leaders need to use consequences appropriately by making sure they are individualized, incremental, and insistent.
- How consequences are explained and presented to students is as important as what the consequences are.
- When the rules, consequences, supervision, and intervention consistently reflect the values and principles of the school, the school's culture and climate will improve. Members of the community will positively influence each other's words and actions. Bullying, when it does occur, will stand out as a behavior that is incompatible with the culture of the school.

ACTIVITIES FOR "DISCIPLINE IN THE RIGHT CLIMATE"

ACTIVITY 1: GOING ALONG WITH THE CROWD

Purpose

People's behavior is highly influenced by the social norms. Research has even discovered that people have *mirror cells* that wire them to unconsciously imitate the movement and behaviors of others. It also reflects a basic human need to fit in or connect with others. This social psychology research has not typically changed how schools traditionally try to shape student behavior. Since effective bullying prevention ultimately means changing student behavior, schools usually rely on rewards and punishments as the way to get this change. To change this mindset, staff need to see examples of how social norms are the real determinants of behavior.

Content

A classic *Candid Camera* sequence (in black and white; Funt, 1962) on YouTube shows a *Candid Camera* power of conformity or elevator psychology experiment in which a person enters an elevator and mimics the behavior of actors placed there. This sequence is available on YouTube (http://www.youtube.com/watch?v=7rrNMS-iq8E) and lasts several minutes. Typically, people stand facing the front of the elevator. This sequence shows the placed actors facing the front of the elevator when a person enters. The placed actors slowly turn to face the back of the elevator for no apparent reason. The person who just entered the elevator observes this turning around and after a few seconds turns around, imitating the actors. A similar sequence happens with a different person who is wearing a hat. The placed actors not only turn around but also take their hats on and off. This second person imitates the turning and takes his hat off as the others do.

Procedure

Have the participants sit in groups of four to five and watch the clip together. After viewing the clip ask them to individually jot down their own reaction to it. After they have done that, ask them to share with one another what they thought of it. Have them discuss the following questions:

Has a similar thing ever happened to you? Explain.

What are examples of this phenomenon in our society?

Are there examples of this at school? Explain.

How could this mirroring be used for positive change in the school?

Ask someone from each group to summarize the thoughts of the group. Facilitate a whole-group discussion and, if possible, select one behavior that they think they could change using this idea of social norms and mirroring.

Variation 1 on Activity 1

Use another clip from YouTube called "The Asch Conformity Experiment" (www.youtube.com/watch?v=VgDx5g9ql1g) (Gitlow, 1997). The phenomenon is sometimes also called "The Diffusion of Responsibility Effect."

ACTIVITY 2: "WHAT LAW WOULD YOU BREAK?"

Purpose

Most people follow the rules and attribute behavior to the fact that there are rules and consequences for breaking them. This activity is designed to generate a discussion about what does constrain or direct people's behavior.

Content

Ask participants to think about what law they would break if there was no consequence for breaking it. If they think of one (most probably won't) ask them to think of why they would. Why is it that most of them probably can't think of too many laws they would break? What really determines what they do or don't do in their life?

Procedure

After the participants have had a chance to reflect on the questions, ask for volunteers to share their answers and their thoughts. Facilitate a large-group discussion if possible.

Ask the group if there are rules in the school that might not be necessary. How would students respond if certain rules were eliminated? Why would they react that way? What could be done to get them to act responsibly without the constraints of rules and consequences?

OUTCOMES

1. Since bullying is a social problem that manifests itself in many ways depending on a particular school environment, staff will need to be creative in how to effectively address it. They need to reflect on many disciplinary practices that are not sufficient for the complex problem of bullying.

2. Getting staff to think a little differently can build their collective capacity to generate unique and creative approaches to the problem of bullying.

14

Beyond the School Building

Parents, the School Bus, and the Digital World

"But in the end it comes down to a matter of respect, and the simplest way that respect is communicated is through tone of voice."

—Malcolm Gladwell (2005, p. 43)

WHO'S TO BLAME?

Once a group of school monitors "hijacked" my bullying prevention workshop. The monitors worked in a school district with many needs and problems. They were hard working people who cared about the students they served. They were, however, "mad as hell and couldn't take it anymore." They had a very tough job and didn't need to add bullying prevention to their job description. They "knew" the answer to this problem: parents just needed to raise their children better. The workshop simply became a forum for them to vent their anger and frustration, and all I could do was listen.

On the other side, I have heard angry parents complain about schools' failure to stop bullying. They are convinced that harsh disciplinary measures for the bullies are the only effective way to address the problem. They often threaten schools who fail to take such actions with lawsuits for being negligent. Schools are places where the *us* against *them* mentality can be locked in place fairly easily.

LEADING FROM BETWEEN A ROCK AND A HARD PLACE

It is intolerable for bullying in schools to continue unabatedly. Parents are rightfully angry and upset if their child is persistently bullied. School staff are under greater scrutiny than ever to fix problems that seem beyond their control. They become defensive and ironically feel bullied by critical parents. School leaders face the challenge of bringing these groups together.

School leaders must also now implement laws, regulations, and procedures designed to solve the problem of bullying. (They also know that these new laws were created because schools have failed to solve the problem.) How can school leaders who are barely surviving themselves lead the school community to any type of successful resolution concerning the problem of bullying?

NO ONE IS TO BLAME, BUT WE ALL ARE RESPONSIBLE

There is one undeniable fact about bullying: it is too complex and insidious a problem to require anything less than the commitment and cooperation of the school community. School leaders must correct the misconceptions that can divide the community. School leaders must help their staff understand how the social needs of students can override even the most effective parenting. They must also help parents understand how discipline alone cannot adequately address the problem of bullying.

Laws, regulations, programs, curricula, rules, consequences, and strategies become meaningful tools when they are in the hands of the whole community committed to working together. School leaders can, however, only control one thing: what they say and do in all of their interactions with others. They are in the best position to bring people together or drive them further apart.

SCHOOL LEADERS' MAIN TASK: FROM FINGER-POINTING TO WORKING TOGETHER

When bullying persists in schools despite the enactment of laws and policies, it is very understandable for each of the different groups of people concerned with the problem to blame another group for the problem. Ironically, no group alone can effectively address the problem. Each group must cooperate and communicate in order for substantial progress to be made in preventing and reducing the frequency, intensity, and duration of bullying in schools. Figures 14.1 and 14.2 illustrate this point.

Figure 14.1 Who Is To Blame?

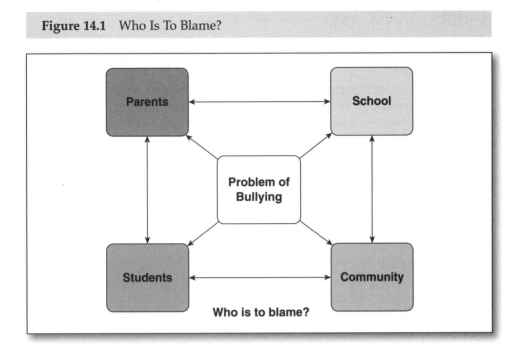

Figure 14.2 All Are responsible

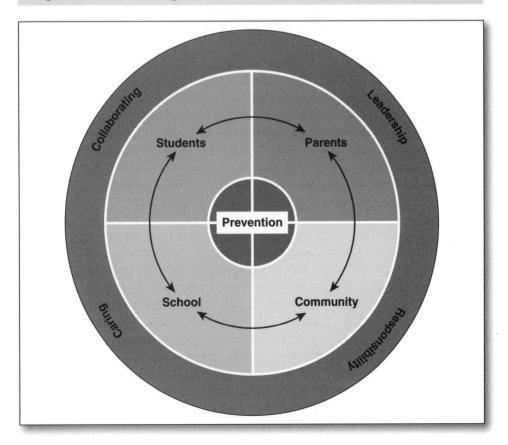

A PARALLEL CASE

Doctors are expected to help people get better and face consequences when they don't. In his book *Blink* (2005), Malcolm Gladwell explores the research of why some doctors get sued for malpractice and some don't. These research findings can be instructive for school leaders who face similar expectations concerning the emotional well-being of students. The differences among those doctors were not related to their medical skills or experience but rather to how they interacted with their patients.

> The surgeons who had never been sued spent more than three minutes longer with each patient than those who had been sued. They were more likely to make "orienting" comments, such as "First I'll examine you, and then we will talk the problem over" or "I will leave time for your questions"—which help patients get a sense of what the visit is supposed to accomplish and when they ought to ask questions. They were more likely to engage in active listening, saying things as "Go on, tell me more about that," and they were far more likely to laugh and be funny during the visit. Interestingly, there was no difference in the amount or quality of information that they gave their patients . . . The difference was entirely in how they talked to their patients. (p. 43)

On a personal note, several years ago, I contracted a severe case of pneumonia that was not easy to diagnose. I was hospitalized for almost three weeks. I clearly recall my doctor telling me that he didn't know what was wrong with me and how he felt bad because he couldn't directly help me but needed to bring in specialists. Ironically, at that moment, my trust in him soared because I knew he cared and he was honest with me.

IMPLICATIONS FOR SCHOOL LEADERS

School leaders often don't realize that even the most aggressive parents approach them with some fear and trepidation. School leaders can make decisions that could conflict with what parents consider to be best for their child. Often, parents subconsciously overcompensate for this sense of vulnerability by coming on strong from the start of an interaction with a school leader. In short, parents often approach school leaders thinking they will have to fight for their child. School leaders' initial words or gestures either confirms or corrects this expectation. Regardless of whether a child was bullied or did the bullying, school leaders need to approach parents with sensitivity toward their vulnerability.

GUIDELINES FOR RECEIVING COMPLAINTS

• *No matter how tired, do not convey an "Oh no" tone of voice.* Many complaints are made at the end of a long day at work, too often it seems on a Friday afternoon or before a school vacation. School leaders need to take a deep breath and listen closely to any complaint made at any time.

• *Hear the emotion and the content of the complaint but separate them in your mind.* Expect parents to be emotional. Don't tell them to calm down. Listening closely and accepting the emotion is the best way to help them calm down. Acknowledge the emotional nature of the complaint with phrases such as "I can see how this would be very upsetting, and I want to make sure I understand what happened, so let's go through it step by step."

• *Don't rush; give parents your time.* Conveying impatience will only lengthen the time spent on the problem. School leaders who invest the necessary time listening to the complaint will be questioned and challenged less on the resolution of the complaint.

• *Express concern over how the students are feeling.* This concern does not mean agreeing that the student was bullied. It is acceptable to give the student and the parent the benefit of the doubt at this point.

• *Take responsibility for looking into the problem at school.* Don't suggest having the complaining parent call the parent of the student who possibly bullied their child. Take responsibility for the complaint because it is a school problem. Emphasize that working together is the best approach: the parent was responsible for alerting you, and you are responsible for looking into it.

• *VERY IMPORTANT: Ask what the parents want as an outcome of the whole process.* Indicate that you will be asking their child what they want or need to happen as a result of the whole process. It could be that the parent and the student have not thought about this. School leaders need to know what parents and students expect. In most cases, the ultimate goal is for the bullying to stop, not just that the student who bullied is punished. *This clarification is important at the start of the process.*

• *Thank the parents for calling and for caring enough to call.*

• *Thank them for the trust that they had in the school.*

• *Thank them for helping you do your job.*

• *Double check to make sure you have the right information.*

• *Explain the next steps and what they can expect from you (a return call within twenty-four hours). Make sure you have the best method, e.g., email, phone call to get back in touch.*

- *Let them know that it is OK for them to call with additional information.*

- *Remind them that you will need to speak with their child.*

In sum, how to listen to a parental complaint? Think of **practicing TEA Time**:

T = Thank them for calling.

E = Empathize with them.

A = Acknowledge the problem and its impact.

TIME: Give your time and attention no matter how busy you are.

GUIDELINES FOR RESPONDING TO THE COMPLAINT

When school leaders respond promptly to a complaint and report back to the parent, they demonstrate that student safety is a high priority for the school. Parents are much more likely to accept a report that doesn't match their complaint when the school leader is prompt and sincere in reporting back to them.

Outline the steps taken in gathering the information. Parents need to know how the information was obtained and how thorough the process was in obtaining it.

Do not refer to the students by name in reporting the version of what happened. Most parents respect students' confidentiality and realize that school leaders are obligated to protect it.

Share the most accurate version of the narrative but indicate areas of uncertainty. Make sure that parents do not interpret the report as an implication that their child was not telling the truth. Students' perception of events is their truth, and it probably will not be accurate on all points.

The facts of the complaint and the facts that were gathered don't have to match in order for positive steps to be taken. School leaders can speak to the students involved in the situation and use it as an opportunity to restate the school's expectations and rules and their responsibilities. Even without sufficient proof that bullying occurred, the students who might have bullied can learn the limits and expectations for their behavior. These are positive steps that can stop the bullying and prevent it from reoccurring.

*If the bullying complaint turns out to be **conflict**, take the opportunity to explain the difference without diminishing the value of the parents making the complaint.* Helping members of the community learn the distinction between bullying and conflict should be a goal for all school leaders. Remember it is better to have a bullying complaint turn out to be conflict than not to have a complaint and have the bullying continue.

If the parent is not satisfied with the report, ask for a face-to-face meeting to talk about the situation. I often would explicitly state that I wish I could give the report that the parent wanted me to give but that I could only report what I found. Sometimes your best effort will not be enough for some parents. It is better to accept that fact rather than defend yourself or convince the parents that your report is accurate.

Focus on the future and the steps being taken to stop and prevent the bullying. It may be difficult for some parent to accept any outcome other than the punishment of the student who bullied their child. School leaders need to articulate how the school's approach to bullying prevention is more comprehensive and effective than discipline alone. Provide specific information about actions taken to protect the bullied student in the future.

Summarize the process and its outcome in a brief letter to the parent. This summary should also be part of the documentation kept for school records. Giving the parent who made the complaint a printed copy of the summary shows that complaints are taken seriously. State your appreciation for the parent taking the time to complain.

GUIDELINES FOR COMMUNICATING WITH THE PARENT OF A STUDENT WHO BULLIED

School leaders' communication skills are put to test when they call the parents of a student who bullied another student. The educational mindset and the guiding principles of bullying prevention have to be reflected in the words and actions of the school leader for this interaction to be positive and productive. Most of the guidelines I listed in the previous chapter on communicating with students who bullied can be applied to communicating with their parents. School leaders' words and tone of voice must override sensitivities that parents of students who bullied will most likely have. These sensitivities are the following:

- Parents can think that criticism of their child's behavior is criticism of their child as a person. They don't want their student labeled as "bad," a "criminal," or a "bully."
- Parents can interpret the call from the school leader about the problem as an implicit criticism of the job they have done as a parent.
- Parents can think that the school leader expects them to fix the problem for the school, i.e., punish their child to make sure it doesn't happen again.
- Parents can fear that the school leader will be negative about their student from that point on.
- Parents can fear that their child is not being treated fairly. They could think that the other student is getting away with something.

Before making the phone call, school leaders need to put themselves in the shoes of the parents. Any success I had in communicating with parents was based on my empathy for them. As a parent, I did not receive a lot of calls from school about something my children did wrong, but the few I did receive taught me how the recipients of those calls feel. I also remember the school leaders who were empathetic and the ones who just followed standard operating procedure.

To override these sensitivities, school leaders must act on a different set of assumptions:

- The student is a good person who made a mistake, and all people make mistakes.
- The parents and the school need to work together to help the student learn from the mistake. It is in the student's best interest to learn from the mistake.
- The student is capable of learning not just to stop the negative behavior but also to do better things.
- The parent and school must collaborate about what the student needs to learn.
- The student must know that the parent and the school are sending the same message. They are working together and support each other in helping the student learn not to bully.

Using those assumptions, school leaders can increase parents receptivity to their message by doing the following:

- Acknowledge that hearing the principal's voice is stressful.
- Acknowledge that hearing from the principal about a problem is not easy to do. If possible at some point in the conversation, share your own experiences as a parent in receiving this type of call.
- State up front, "I need your help."
- State the problem with a calm and understanding tone of voice.
- Explicitly state that you want to help the student. Ask the parents what they think would help their child.
- Don't make consequences the focal point of the conversation.
- State what your ultimate positive outcome for the whole process is.
- If necessary, arrange for a meeting with parents and the student to develop a plan to help the student learn from the problem.
- Thank the parents for their help and cooperation.

School leaders might accurately predict some parents reaction to the complaint and decide to meet in person rather than over the phone. Caution: Never use e-mails for this type of communication—parents need to be able to ask questions and respond to this type of information.

COMMUNICATING WITH PARENTS OF BYSTANDERS

Many parents of students who were bystanders will wonder why they are even being contacted. This would be a good opportunity to reiterate the school's values and rules regarding bullying. (The guidelines for contacting the parents of the student who bullied can be applied when interacting with these parents.)

Most parents probably do not understand the key role bystanders play in bullying prevention, so school leaders can educate them about it. Since it is so vital that bystanders know the important role they play in bullying, parental support for sending this message to them is essential for it to *stick*. All parents want their children to do more than just follow the rules; they want them to be leaders and people who care. School leaders who can reframe the problem of bullying as an opportunity for students to change and learn better ways of interacting with others are turning the culture and climate in the right direction.

Helpful Background Knowledge for Parents

Obviously the more that parents understand about a comprehensive schoolwide approach to bullying prevention, the more productive and positive any conversation with them will be. Having parents on the bullying prevention team is essential. Most of the information and resources that the team receives should be shared with all the parents in the school. The bullying prevention team can develop plans for how to share this information. The key points that parents should know as soon as possible should include the following:

- The social nature of bullying and the role of bystanders
- Information about human development and roles of peers in a child's life
- The key elements of a comprehensive schoolwide approach and how those elements work together
- The differences between bullying and conflict
- The complex and elusive nature of bullying and how discipline alone is not effective in addressing it
- How their involvement and support is essential

Other areas that could be helpful would be

- How to develop resiliency in children
- Helpful social and emotional skills for students
- Positive approaches to parenting and the negative effects of punitive approaches to discipline

- How to coach students to be empowered bystanders
- How to listen to their child's complaint
- Responsible use of the Internet and other digital issues

Learning by Doing: Parents and Staff Working Together

Staff and parents can work together to develop guidelines for making a complaint about bullying. The guidelines would include how to listen to a student's complaint and how to communicate the information to the school. Parents and staff working together could list the expectations they have for each other when communicating about bullying. All of this information could be included in a pamphlet on bullying prevention and/or on the school's website.

THE SCHOOL BUS

School leaders have a hard enough time dealing with problems within the school building. Their reluctance to confront problems that occur miles away from school is very understandable. What happens on the school bus, however, is carried into the school building. Students who get off the bus after being bullied are not ready to learn. Students who worry about what will happen on the school bus on the way home will have difficulty attending to lessons at the end of the school day.

In the school building, traditional external methods of controlling some types of student behavior using rewards and consequences can work. These controls however do not transfer to the school bus. Bullying prevention on the school bus is primarily dependent on empowered bystanders taking responsibility and for what happens on the bus.

I have written a book, *Peaceful School Bus* (Dillon, 2008), based on a program developed at our school. Although it was a successful program at our school and has been used successfully in many other schools across the country, school leaders can do many other things to improve life on the school bus without using the Peaceful School Bus Program.

School Environment and the Bus Environment

The first and most important step in addressing the unique needs of the bus environment is realizing how the environments differ (see Table 14.1). Staff must also understand how students view the bus and how they think adults view the bus. These perceptions have a big influence on how students behave on the bus. When students view the bus route group as a community, bystanders are more likely to accept responsibility for intervening or reporting.

Table 14.1   Comparison of Environments: School Building and Bus

School Building	School Bus
Students are grouped by age.	Students are in one large mixed-age group.
Staff focused on students	Driver has to drive the bus.
External controls under adult supervision can be effective.	External controls from school don't extend to bus.
Internal control not always necessary	Internal control only real option
Most bullying is unnoticed by adults.	Even easier to conceal than in building
Purpose and importance of school clear in students' mind	Bus is a means to an end—something to get you to school.
Many environmental options for behavior change	Contained space with few options
Adults are adjacent to students.	Driver can be far away and occupied with driving the bus.
Timely response to behavior possible	Response to behavior can be days away
Traditional approaches to behavioral management can work.	Traditional approaches are not effective.
Bystanders can remove themselves as an audience to the bullying.	Students who bully have a captive audience on the bus.

Common Ground for the School and the Bus

It is difficult for school staff and transportation staff to work collaboratively to prevent problems. Instead, they typically communicate after problems have already happened. If they were able to talk without having a pressing problem, school staff and transportation staff would discover that they share a set of common beliefs. These common beliefs could form the basis for creative responses to the bus problems.

Here are a set of common beliefs that transportation staff and school staff probably would agree with:

- The school day begins and ends on the school bus.
- Students need to feel safe in order to learn.
- What happens on the bus affects what happens in school.
- The students on a school bus can be a community, not just a group.

- School staff and transportation staff want what is best for students.
- Working together on problems is more effective than working separately.
- Learning to navigate the social world on the bus is especially challenging.
- Prevention is preferable to reaction.
- The current state of bus behavior needs improvement.
- Students need adults to find better approaches for addressing bus problems.

The Right Direction for the School Bus: Intentionally Communicate Common Beliefs

Students need outward signs to know what adults value. If they don't see and hear those outward signs, they will often assume the value doesn't exist. For example, if the bus driver is seldom seen talking to teachers or the principal, students could assume that they don't communicate nor do they value communicating with each other. When students realize that what happens on the bus is likely to be communicated to school staff, the level of accountability for their behavior increases. This alone will not eliminate inappropriate behavior on the bus but will add some level of restraint to how they act on the bus.

If members of the school staff and members from the transportation department could meet briefly to prevent bus problems rather than just react to them, student behavior on the bus could significantly improve. The task of such a group would be simple: generate ideas that would cost nothing and require little time and would intentionally communicate those commonly held beliefs. Each school could have a different set of ideas based on their needs and resources.

Here are some examples of *no cost/little time* ideas that could improve life on the school bus:

- Raise the status of the bus driver in the eyes of the students by posting pictures of the drivers in the school building, introducing them at assemblies, and having some special bus driver appreciation activities in the school.
- Make sure that the drivers come into the building on a regular basis and are seen talking to teachers or the principal.
- Have a meeting with the bus drivers to review the guiding principles of bullying prevention and the rules against bullying.
- Have the principal invite the bus drivers into the school a few times a year for coffee and donuts.
- Ask for teacher volunteers to be a bus liaison for each bus driver: one person in addition to the principal that the driver could contact and consult for support.

- Have bus drivers share hobbies or interests with students in the building.
- Have the principal or teachers take a short ride on the bus with the students, even if it is around the block.
- Provide bus drivers with a printed invitation from the principal informing them that the principal is never too busy to hear from them. It is better for a driver to inform the principal about a small problem happening rather than wait for it to expand into a more serious one.
- Post the bullying rules on the school bus and have teachers explain to students how they apply on the bus.
- Take a group photo of the bus driver and the students on that bus route. Post all the photos on a bulletin board in the school.
- Have students write thank you notes to the bus drivers.
- Have students make posters or write newsletters for improving life on the school bus.

CHALLENGES WITH THE DIGITAL WORLD

There are many resources available on cyberbullying and other issues related to digital media and technology. Although this problem presents different challenges for school leaders, the basic approach to this problem is very consistent with the key concepts, principles, and practices for bullying prevention in general. The most significant difference is that the traditional approaches that have proved ineffective within the school are even *less* effective in the digital world. Schools' ability to externally control student behavior is *very* limited, and all students know it.

Go to the Right Source

School staff have a heightened sense of anxiety over students and the digital world. School staff know that students know more than they know in this domain. Adults' attempts to control student behavior often exacerbate the problem of cyberbullying. Looking for answers, school leaders are faced with a great array of commercial products and services available that promise solutions to this problem. These solutions might sound good but often are not based on any research nor do they come from reliable sources. School leaders must be knowledgeable consumers when they are looking for resources. I have found some excellent resources that provide accurate and reliable information:

- *Cyber Bullying: Bullying in the Digital Age* (2005) by Robin Kowalski, Susan Limber, and Patricia Agatston provides current research on cyberbulling, recommendations for parents and educators, and a review of laws and policies.

- *The Cyberbullying Research Center* (www.cyberbullying.us): Sameer Hinduja and Justin Patchin, both university professors, coordinate this research center that offers accurate statistics on the prevalence of cyberbullying. It also provides up-to-date information about the nature, extent, causes, and consequences of cyberbullying among adolescents.
- *The Center for Safe and Responsible Internet Use* (csriu.org): Nancy Willard, the executive director, is an educator and a lawyer who provides an excellent and accessible analysis of the law and the current research on bullying (Willard, n.d.; Willard, 2005).

CYBERBULLYING: THE SCHOOL'S RESPONSIBILITY AND AUTHORITY

Since most cyberbullying occurs off-campus, school officials are often confused about both their authority and their responsibility for responding to incidents related to digital technology.

Nancy Willard (2011) summarizes the legal authority that schools have related to cyberbullying:

> School officials have the legal authority to respond to student off campus speech in situations where this speech has caused, or there are particular reasons to believe that it will cause a substantial disruption at school or interference with the right of students to be secure. This might involve the threat of violent altercations between students, significant interference with the delivery of instruction or a situation where there has been a significant interference with the ability of any student to receive an education. It is important to have policy provisions that outline this authority to provide notice to students. (p. 8)

Although the communication might have occurred off site, the impact of that communication can cause harm to students that interferes with their ability to learn. Schools also have the authority to investigate and respond to students who have used district equipment inappropriately or have communicated inappropriately using a district website or network.

The field memo from the Civil Right Division of the Federal Department of Education (U.S. Department of Education, 2010) referred to in Chapter 12 pertains to cyberbullying also. Schools cannot simply wait and see if cyberbullying occurs and then determine if it impacts student learning. They also cannot address the problem with disciplinary actions directed solely toward the students who bullied. Schools need to assess, monitor, and take preventive measures to ensure that students can feel safe, secure, and able to learn in school.

When to Involve Law Enforcement

There are some instances when the improper use of technology violates criminal law. In those instances, school leaders do need to consult with their school lawyers and contact law enforcement officials. Here are the areas when school leaders should consider involving law enforcement (Willard, 2011):

- Death threats or other forms of violence to people or property
- Excessive intimidation or extortion
- Evidence of sexual exploitation
- Harassment or stalking
- Hate-based crimes
- Creating for dissemination material considered to be harmful to minors or any type of child pornography
- Invasion of privacy or taking an image of someone in a place where privacy is expected

A Useful Analogy: Driver's Education and Cyber Education

Adults are understandably anxious when they perceive the potential for harm and the degree of freedom that students have in the digital world. In response to the problem, school officials often resort to scare tactics and tighter controls on the use of digital technology by students.

There are however some key points to remember regarding students and technology:

- Most students are responsible users of technology.
- Students who bully using technology are even more confident in their ability to elude and outmaneuver any adult attempt to stifle or control it.
- There is not a new class of students who are bullied. Most students who are bullied online have also been bullied in traditional ways.
- Their digital life is inseparable from their social life, so the fear of losing access to technology is similar to that of losing all their friends.
- Students fear the loss of access to technology as consequence to any report they make about its misuse. This fear suppresses their reporting of problems. It decreases the likelihood of them communicating to adults about it for any reason.
- Technology has many benefits to students that should not be overlooked.
- Schools also have a responsibility to prepare students to succeed in a world where technology is pervasive and essential for any job.

If an educational approach with a goal of empowering students seems like too great of a risk to take with technology, adults just need to reflect on the risk involved when an adolescent is given a license to drive. This is an almost universal opportunity that is provided for young people. When a person sits behind the wheel, he or she has the freedom to be "irresponsible." Adults are only able to give young people that freedom because they have been preparing them for driving since they were infants.

Most young people become responsible drivers because of the education they received. They are also required to demonstrate their competence in order to have the privilege to drive: meeting the requirements for getting a license.

These are the key points to remember regarding the development of a responsible driver that could also be applied to being a responsible user of technology:

- The technical aspects of driving can be mastered rather easily with time and practice, but judgment and responsibility are what ultimately makes good drivers.
- Driver's education starts when a baby is put in a car seat and first sees his or her parents buckle their seat belts.
- Children watch how their parents drive and hopefully see appropriate and responsible driving habits.
- Good driving habits can and should be taught and practiced. They need to become automatic and consistent behaviors.
- Laws and the enforcement of them set appropriate limits for drivers. Driving responsibly, however, requires more than just obeying the posted laws.
- Strong cultural taboos against highly dangerous behaviors like drunk driving require a combination of laws being established and publicized, knowledge of potential dangers, established alternative strategies like designated drivers, and a general perception of disapproval of that behavior by most peers.

The same conditions that are in place to educate responsible drivers can be put into place for educating responsible users of technology. *Cyber education* can be as effective as *driver's education* if its one key difference is acknowledged: the children have learned the technical skills of the digital world before the adults have. Instead of backing off from the challenge of preparing students for the use of technology, adults must realize that they do have something important to teach them: responsibility, respect, and judgment in communicating with others.

For cyber education to be successful, the following conditions are necessary:

- It has to start early and be integrated into all uses of technology.
- Students need to be taught about responsible use and allowed to discuss the issues related to it on a regular basis. Avoid having "responsible use" be a policy or procedure just handed to them.

- Utilize the technical knowledge that students have about how to handle challenging social-digital situations.
- Increase student ownership in the problem and involve them in developing guidelines for using technology responsibly.
- Make sure that students know that what other students think about the right way to use technology.
- Provide a clear and accessible procedure for reporting anything inappropriate.
- Provide students with specific things to do or say should they encounter cyberbullying in any form.
- Invest the time required for students to internalize the values behind the rules.
- Expect students to be responsible but also realize that they will make mistakes.
- Build trust to keep the lines of communication open between the adult world and the student world.
- Educate parents about the school's responsible use of technology policy and how the school's antibullying policies apply to the use of technology.

The technological world has developed so rapidly and has become so pervasive in everyone's life that it is difficult to reflect on our relationship with technology. Malcolm Gladwell (2002) shares this perspective on our current state of affairs:

> We have given teens more money, so they can construct their own social and material world more easily. We have given them time to spend among themselves—less time in the company of adults. We have given them e-mail and beepers and most of all cell phones, so they can fill in all the dead spots in their day—dead spots that might have been filled with the voices of adults—with the voices of their peers. (p. 271)

Young people, regardless of their skill or expertise, still need adults to guide them in how to be human and live a good life. School leaders, staff, and parents all share this same responsibility: to make sure that adult voices are still heard, valued, and heeded by young people. The best intervention for cyberbullying, however, is the least technical: having adults invest in relationships and fostering a climate of trust with our students.

SUMMARY

- School leaders must correct misconceptions that can divide members of the school community.
- When it comes to bullying prevention, no one is to blame, and everyone is responsible.

- School leaders must welcome and accept parental complaints as a way of helping them do their job.
- School leaders must have empathy when communicating with parents of students who have bullied others.
- What happens on the school bus affects what happens in the school.
- School leaders must build collaborative and supportive relationships with transportation staff.
- School leaders have the authority and responsibility to address cyberbullying that occurs off-site, if it affects student learning.
- Students must be taught responsible use of technology. They need to be involved in formulating the school's efforts to address cyberbullying.

ACTIVITIES TO SUPPORT CONCEPTS IN "BEYOND THE SCHOOL BUILDING"

ACTIVITY 1: PARENT–TEACHER TENSION

Purpose

Parents and teachers want what is best for students, yet the emotional nature of student problems can unfortunately push parents and teachers apart rather then bring them together. Being able to watch a dramatized version of a parent–teacher conflict can help them reflect on their own experiences.

Content

There is a scene in the movie *Pay It Forward* (Leder, 2000) available on YouTube   (www.youtube.com/watch?v=_yZEi-LOBaI&feature=plcp) under parent/teacher conflict. A teacher, played by Kevin Spacey, is confronted by a single mother, played by Helen Hunt, of a student in his class. She is angry about a homework assignment that she thinks encourages her son to do dangerous things. Caught off guard by her confrontation, the teacher points out how the mother was wrong. The conflict escalates, and they both get increasingly defensive and angry.

Procedure

Have the participants sit in groups of four to five. If it is a mixed group of parents and staff, make sure that there is an equal number of school staff and parents in each group. Designate a facilitator, recorder, reporter, materials manager, and timekeeper for each group. Show the video and have the participants briefly write down their reaction to the clip. After all the participants are finished writing, each person can take turns briefly sharing the reaction.

Following the sharing, the group can respond to the following questions and tasks:

What contributed to the meeting getting off to a bad start?

What words and actions of the teacher contributed to increasing the intensity of the conflict?

How did the parent share her concern?

Why do you think that parent came on so strong?

What assumptions did the parent think the teacher had about her?

What assumptions did the teacher think the parent had about him?

List three recommendations for the teacher on how to handle a conflict with a parent.

List three recommendations for the parent on how to handle a conflict with a teacher.

After each small group has completed the discussion, have the reporter from each group share the recommendations for the parent and the teacher.

Option

Have a subcommittee draft guidelines for parent–teacher conferences based on the recommendations for this meeting.

ACTIVITY 2: THE DIGITAL WORLD FROM THE STUDENT PERSPECTIVE

Purpose

One clear dividing line of experience between students and school staff is their use of the digital media/technology. Those who are not familiar with various uses of technology generally often have a negative view of it. Their fear and lack of control over what students can do digitally exacerbates the gap between students and adults. Students think that adults ignore the positive aspects of technology and therefore will never understand their world. They often fear that any problem with technology will result in adults taking it away from them.

Content

Have the members of the staff that have embraced technology and integrated it into their lives present its positive aspects to the rest of the staff. This could include demonstrations of applications, websites, smart phones, or tablet devices.

Procedures

If possible, have one staff person who has embraced technology pair up with one who hasn't. Ask them to interview each other about their own views about technology and its impact on our culture and society. This should not be a debate about technology but rather an opportunity for reflection. Following these paired conversations, have the whole group discuss implications for bridging the technological gap between students and staff to increase trust and cooperation.

OUTCOMES

1. Staff should realize that, since parents are inherently emotional, they need to listen calmly and respond in a way to *defuse* the situation rather than *ignite it*.

2. Staff should reflect on their own fears regarding technology and find creative ways to use it rather than fight it or ban it as the only way to address the problems associated with it.

15

Beyond Bullying Prevention

Climate Change for the Better

"Change in education is easy to propose, hard to implement and extraordinarily difficult to sustain."

—Andy Hargreaves and Dean Fink (2006, p. 1)

"Many of life's failures are experienced by people who did not realize how close they were to success when they gave up."

—Thomas Edison

IT TAKES GENERATIONS

The year before the Peaceful School Bus Program started, the bus drivers made fifty-eight behavioral referrals to my office. Within six years, the number of referrals was consistently below nine per year. In my last year as principal, the tenth year of the program, there were three referrals.

The key component of the program was fostering positive relationships between older and younger students. Older students were challenged to care for and support younger students. They were expected to be leaders and were told that they were *needed* to be leaders on the bus. As the fifth-grade students over the years slowly started to act more as leaders and less as bosses, the younger students were treated better and did not need to get their "revenge" when they finally became fifth graders. They were ready to become leaders like the students who were their leaders. Over time, the social norms of the bus gradually shifted to reflect the behavior of responsible students. They became more influential than the students who bullied.

The behavioral referrals decreased dramatically because the program was in place for a full generation of students; it took six years for kindergarten students to become fifth-grade students. The program did take time to work, but once it did, it sustained itself because all members of the school community experienced and benefitted from its success. There was a collective commitment to make it an integral part of our school.

THE MISSING KEY INGREDIENT

My idea for this book originated from my observation of another school's attempt to recreate the Peaceful School Bus Program. They faithfully followed the procedures and activities of the program for one year but didn't see any significant improvement in bus behavior. The staff decided that the logistical problems of implementing the program were not worth the time and effort, so it was discontinued. Instead, they decided to keep students in their classrooms and periodically have the classroom teachers review the rules of the bus with them. The staff didn't understand the key element of the program, which was to turn the bus route group itself into a community and foster positive relationships between the older and younger students.

The staff at our school understood the underlying principles of the programs and knew that progress would take time. As the principal of the school, I was able to explain these principles and help staff see past the inconveniences that can tend to dominate any change initiative. The other school just wanted a program that would solve their bus problem, and when it didn't, there was no reason to continue it. *(This is not meant to disparage the other school. They should be commended for wanting to improve their bus situation; many schools don't even try.)* From these two experiences, it was clear to me that success was much more a product of leadership (shared leadership) than it was of a program.

THE FLYWHEEL OF BULLYING PREVENTION

Jim Collins (2001) comments on the process of true success:

In building a great institution, there is no single defining action, no grand program, no killer innovation, no solitary lucky break, no miracle moment. Rather our research showed that it feels like turning a giant, heavy flywheel. Pushing with great effort—days, weeks, and months of work, with almost no perceptible progress—you finally get the flywheel to inch forward. But you don't stop. You keep pushing, and with persistent effort, you eventually get the flywheel to complete an entire turn. You don't stop. You keep pushing, in an intelligent direction, and the fly-wheel moves a bit faster . . . Then at some point—breakthrough! Each turn builds upon previous work, compounding your invest-ment of effort. The flywheel moves with almost unstoppable momentum. This is how you build greatness. (p. 23)

Note that the last sentence does not say "This is how you solve a prob-lem" but rather how you become "great." The irony of bullying preven-tion is that if a school persists in an "intelligent direction" to address the problem, it will do more than "stop bullying": it will become a better place for everyone. School leaders need to reveal this secret to the school community, because the shared sense of moving forward together toward something special is the key to sustaining success. We didn't stop the Peaceful School Bus once the referrals went down to three per year; it became part of our identity as a school—an identity that we were all proud of.

THE RIGHT HABITS FOR SUCCESS

Effective bullying prevention, although initially guided by moral purpose, commitment, and determination, must establish the necessary procedures and practices that become part of how the school routinely operates. There will always be new problems and challenges that will require creativity and commitment from the school community. Effective bullying preven-tion requires a balance of established routines and procedures (infrastruc-ture) with a commitment to continuous growth and improvement.

The Essential Routines of Bullying Prevention: Services, Ongoing Evaluation, and Traditions

Schools that sustain their success have processes in place that will per-form three key functions:

1. Proactively address the needs of students at risk (*services*)

2. Provide meaningful feedback on progress (*ongoing evaluation*)

3. Integrate bullying prevention into the customs and traditions of the school (*curriculum, classroom, and schoolwide activities*)

SERVICES

All students are affected by bullying; however, there are some students who have characteristics that make them at risk for being a persistent bully or victim. Schools should actively identify these at-risk students and offer services and interventions to address their needs. Many of these students need intensive training in social skills, anger management, self-regulation skills, and positive problem solving. There are also students from difficult home environments with families that require a lot of support and guidance. These are the type of intensive interventions represented in the three-tier model of bullying prevention shown in Chapter 13.

School counselors, psychologists, and socials workers can help teachers improve their communication skills and support them in developing more democratic classrooms within the school. This type of classroom is a preventive strategy for the students who are the *socially connected* bullies: "Classrooms with more egalitarian social status hierarchies, strong group norms in support of academic achievement and prosocial behavior, and positive social ties among children should deprive many socially connected bullies of the peer regard they require" (Rodkin, 2011).

At a time of significant budget cuts, school leaders must articulate how investments in school social work, counseling, and psychological services will ultimately save time and money and better serve the entire school community. These services should not be considered extras and therefore vulnerable to budget cuts. School leaders need to reaffirm the connection between feeling safe and higher levels of learning for all students.

ONGOING EVALUATION OF BULLYING PREVENTION

Data Collection

The school's bullying prevention team should collect data on bullying on a yearly basis. The time period for collecting the data should be put on the school calendar and become a regular part of a school's required annual activities. Just as the original survey data were organized, analyzed, and presented, the yearly data should also be treated the same way.

This ongoing evaluation of the school bullying prevention allows for the school community to recognize and celebrate progress. This data become the basis for setting new goals and adjusting plans and strategies. In addition to survey data, schools could elect to conduct annual focus groups. These groups would hopefully yield success stories that the survey data can't portray.

Schools may also consider using two surveys and alternating the administration of them on a yearly basis. One survey could be longer and more comprehensive and the other one shorter and more targeted toward specific aspects of bullying.

Monitoring and Recording of Specific Bullying Incidents

Another important source of data is the actual recording and tracking of bullying incidents. Following a consistent protocol for investigating, resolving, and recording incidents is essential for meeting district and state requirements for accurate reporting.

Protocol for Responding to Bullying Complaints: Four Steps

Step One: Initiate the Report Process. If a staff member witnesses or hears of a potential incident of bullying:

- Staff member completes a *brief incident report form* indicating what happened, when and where it happened, and who was involved. This should be brief and concise. Completing the form signals the start of the process.
- Staff receiving a complaint from a student who was bullied should be sensitive to the needs of the student. Staff should acknowledge the student's courage for reporting the incident. They should inform the student that the complaint will be taken seriously.
- Staff should also make sure that the student is safe in returning to school activities.
- The principal or principal's designee should be notified as soon as possible.
- If an anonymous report is received, the principal or principal designee will complete the brief incident report form with whatever information is available in the complaint.

Step Two: Conducting the Investigation. The principal or staff designated to investigate the incidents should review the brief incident form and talk to the staff person who completed it.

If the report warrants an investigation, a more detailed report form should be used.

This form should have space for the following:

- The definition of bullying being used by the school
- The type of bullying being reported (physical, verbal, indirect, cyberbullying)
- Location and time of the incident

- Name of student issuing the complaint indicating if the student was the victim or a bystander
- Name of students who possibly bullied
- Name of bystanders involved
- Details of incident

The form should provide space for a summary of discussions with the people involved with the incident.

There should be a checklist listing steps to follow:

- Interviews conducted
- Persons contacted (staff, parents, other administrators)
- Dates and times of interviews and contacts
- Reminder to tell students about retaliation and confidentiality

There should be a list of the parents/guardians called, including the date and time of the call.

It should include space for a summary of the findings.

There should be a check box to indicate if it was bullying. *(Since some complaints turn out to be conflict and not bullying, checking a box indicating that bullying actually occurred will make it easy to review these forms later on.)*

It should include space for descriptions of actions taken in response to the bullying:

- Include steps to protect the victims, formative discipline taken with student(s) who bullied, communication with teachers, referrals to counseling, or other services.
- Plans to monitor the situation

Step Three: Initiating the Action Plan

- Follow through on decisions made regarding whom to contact, corrective/disciplinary action, protective measures, referrals, etc.

Step Four: Finalize the Report/ Monitoring the Plan

- Make sure all the information is accurate.
- Update information in response to the plan of action taken.
- Collect the forms; distribute and file them according to the school's procedures.
- Principal and other staff typically involved with investigations should meet twice a year to review these files.
- Provide written summary of actions taken to parents whose students were involved with the bullying incident.
- Share incident reports (without names) with bullying prevention team.

This protocol should be adapted to each school's policy regarding bullying and discipline.

Anonymous Reporting

Many resources on bullying prevention recommend establishing a procedure for anonymous reporting of bullying incidents. As a general rule, knowing about bullying incidents is highly preferable to not knowing, so any method of reporting should be considered.

At the elementary school where I was principal, we did not have an established and publicized method for anonymously reporting bullying. We felt that, by building strong classroom communities and by having a full time social worker available, students would feel safe enough to report to a person. We also emphasized the importance of telling parents, so students who were reluctant to report at school knew they should tell someone. *(A question on our survey asked students who were bullied two to three times per month if they had told an adult about the bullying. After three years of implementing our bullying prevention program, 100 percent of these students indicated that they had.)*

By receiving reports personally, we were able to obtain the information that helped us investigate more effectively. Anonymous reports can be unclear and difficult to interpret. They also can be used to falsely accuse students of bullying or to mislead staff about the actual incidents of bullying.

If anonymous reporting is going to be publicized and used in school, students should receive guidance and training in how to report. Students should be warned of the dangers and consequences for false reporting. Hopefully, as a school makes a concerted and sincere effort to address bullying, students will feel safer about reporting and will not need to do so anonymously.

INTEGRATING BULLYING PREVENTION WITH THE CURRICULUM, CUSTOMS, AND TRADITIONS OF THE SCHOOL

In the words of Deal and Peterson (2009),

> School cultures are complex webs of traditions and rituals built up over time as teachers, students, parents and administrators work together and deal with crises and accomplishments. Cultural patterns are highly enduring, have a powerful impact on performance, and shape the ways people think, act, and feel. Everything, and we do mean everything, in the organization is affected by the culture and its particular form and features. (p. 7)

CURRICULUM

Health

There are many curricula available that can teach students about many topics related to bullying prevention. Many schools have health curricula that address bullying, conflict resolution, problem solving, empathy, and other social and emotional skills. Some curricula are specifically designed for bullying prevention; others include bullying prevention as one topic among others. School leaders should review what is available with the bullying prevention team and select programs that are based on the best available research. Even the best bullying prevention curriculum can only be effective if it is implemented as part of a schoolwide comprehensive approach that educates all members of the school community, not just students.

Character Education

There are character education programs that promote values that are incompatible with bullying. These programs can support bullying prevention efforts but cannot be the only *way* to address bullying. Teaching a unit lesson on respect similar to an academic unit will not instill respectful behaviors in students. It would be like reading about how to play a sport and then expecting to be able to play it. Students need real opportunities to practice character and also need to see it consistently practiced by all the adults in their world.

Social Studies

There is nothing more central to the topic of citizenship than issues of responsibility and respect about how members of community treat each other. Teachers can help students understand how the rights and responsibilities of being a citizen apply to bullying prevention and respecting their school community.

One of the basic goals of public education is to develop informed citizens. Integrating bullying prevention into social studies should be a natural fit and does not require adding on already overloaded curricula. Being a responsible citizen is being an empowered bystander.

English Language Arts

Bullying prevention should also be integrated into English language arts curricula. There are many excellent books available at all reading levels that address issues related to bullying and navigating the social world. Students are not only interested in but are hungry for stories that reflect the questions, challenges, and confusion that they face every day. These stories help them figure out who they are and where they fit in the world.

Math and Science

Statistical information of survey data from the school itself or from national studies can be studied and analyzed. The research on how our brain operates and the discoveries of the ways that people are hardwired for social interaction and learning should be of interest to students. There is fascinating research in social psychology that can intrigue students about human nature and why people do what they do. This information can become a reference point for talking about bystander behavior and why it is so difficult to report bullying.

Service Learning

Students can research topics related to the needs of the community and then convert their knowledge into service projects. For example, they can study the topic of poverty and then conduct a canned goods drive for a community food pantry. Working together on projects can build relationships among students who might otherwise have little positive contact with each other.

CUSTOMS AND TRADITIONS: CLASSROOM AND SCHOOL

Classroom Level

Class Meetings

One requirement of some bullying prevention programs is to have a weekly classroom meeting. The purpose of this recommended practice is to create a sense of community and to give students a forum to discuss problems related to bullying or any other relevant issue.

Many teachers balk at this requirement because they will have to teach their class differently and perhaps have difficulty managing the behavior of the class. If students have been used to sitting quietly in rows and instructed to just listen to the teacher, they will have trouble adjusting to this new seating arrangement and set of expectations. If teachers don't understand the purpose of the meeting and don't have support for developing the skills for making this shift in their management approach, they will either fail to have these meetings or will just go through the motions of having them. School leaders should help teachers see beyond just compliance with this requirement and focus instead on the purpose and meaning behind a class meeting.

The most effective teachers create a strong sense of community in their class. Students should value their membership in their classroom community and feel connected to one another. The simple act of sitting in a circle and facing each other at least once a day tells students that they are connected to each other. Not sitting and facing each other but rather sitting in rows facing the teacher or the board sends an opposite message—that school is a place where you just have to look out for yourself.

The bully prevention team can support teachers by developing a list of options that can achieve the similar goals and purpose of class meetings.

Alternatives to Class Meetings

Think-Pair-Share: This is an alternative to calling on volunteer raised hands. Teachers pose a question and provide a few seconds for students to think. Two students then share their thoughts with each other. Teachers can then randomly call on the pairs to share their responses with the whole class.

Energizers: These are activities interjected throughout the lesson to allow students to get up and move. A teacher could play music and instruct the students to, when the music stops, share their thoughts with the closest student. There are many other variations on this type of activity that can be found in variety of teacher resources.

Getting-acquainted activities: These activities allow students to get to know each other and discover common interests and experiences. For example, Find Somebody Who (Craigen, J., & Ward, C., 2004) is an activity where students are given a sheet of paper with statements such as the following:

Find somebody who

went to the beach on summer vacation _____

has more than one pet _____

likes to play basketball _____

has read every Harry Potter book _____

Students go around the room to find other students who have had similar experiences and write the name of the student next to the item.

As students get to know each other and trust is established in the classroom, the teacher can direct the discussion to topics related to how people treat each other or what to do when faced with a bullying situation.

Welcoming new students: Since students who enter the class during the school year can often have difficulty fitting in or making new friends, classes can develop an orientation program for them. This is an opportunity to talk about community and build empathy for others by responding to a statement like: "If I were a brand new student, how would I feel and what would I need to adjust to a new school?" Students can develop a sequence of events to familiarize new students to the classroom.

PLANNING FOR SUBSTITUTE TEACHERS

To create a sense of ownership among the students, the teacher should facilitate a discussion with them about how to welcome and support substitute teachers. Each student can have a role in developing and implementing a plan to ensure that the class can learn even when the regular teacher is not present.

RITUALS FOR COMINGS AND GOINGS

Classrooms rituals designed to start and end the day can give all students a sense of security. They can build a class identity and community. Teachers can facilitate discussions and involve the students in designing these rituals.

SCHOOLWIDE CUSTOMS AND TRADITIONS

School Themes

Our school decided to have an annual theme that could unite the school community. Our building cabinet working with the staff, students, and Parent Teacher Association (PTA) would select a theme based on a topic that could create common learning experiences across the grade levels. Over the years, we selected themes such as the following:

"Lynnwood Is Working Together for Peace"

"Kindness Counts at Lynnwood"

"Lynnwood Follows the Golden Rule"

"Lynnwood Makes Healthy Choices"

"Lynnwood Goes Around the World With Books"

"Lynnwood Is Making Connections"

Once a theme was selected, a theme steering committee would brainstorm a range of activities that could be done schoolwide. There could be two or three events that would involve the entire school. Grade levels would pick their own activities related to the theme, and individual classrooms could integrate the theme into lessons. Our librarian would select books related to the theme and offer a different one for each grade level to read. Speakers from the community would be invited to present to the students on the topics related to the theme. These themes allowed us to extend and expand on the antibullying message and connect it to positive ways of serving each other and the community.

"Share and Celebrate" Assemblies

This monthly event supported the school theme and brought the entire school community together on a regular basis. These assemblies typically occurred on a Friday afternoon about an hour before dismissal. They provided an opportunity for any classroom to share what they had been learning about. For example, a class might have done research on North American explorers; the teacher would find a way to have each student share one part of what they learned in front of the entire student body.

There were certain standard features of the assemblies:

- Saying the Pledge of Allegiance and singing a patriotic song at the start of the assembly
- Students sitting on the floor in the gym to keep it informal and different than a special assembly
- Fifth-grade students being the emcees and ushers wearing special "Share and Celebrate" t-shirts
- Singing "Happy Birthday" to everyone born in that month
- Announcing upcoming events of the month
- Welcoming new students and staff
- Celebrating schoolwide achievements
- Sharing information about school theme-related activities

These assemblies gave every student an opportunity to stand in front of the school community and share and celebrate what they learned. They strengthened our school community and created pride in our school.

Promoting Interage Activities When Older
Student Can Help Younger Students

Our school had fourth- and fifth-grade classes that "adopted" kindergarten and first-grade classes. Older students on a regular basis would read to younger students. They could also assist them at arrival and dismissal times. Older and younger students would work together on community service projects.

Creating and Posting Schoolwide Tools for Solving Problems (in Addition to the Bullying Prevention Rules)

Common Conflict Resolution Strategy

We wanted to give student some common strategies that they could readily access in challenging social situations. Since student-to-student conflict is inevitable, we provided a simple way to resolve the conflict: Talk, Walk, and Scissors.

There were posters put up around the school to remind students of this strategy. Students could try to talk about the problem. If talking didn't work, they could walk away from it. If those two ways didn't work, they could try rock-paper-scissors to decide who would win the conflict. This didn't work every time, but even if it worked some of the time, it could reduce the number of nonpeaceful solutions.

Problem-Solving Procedures

We tried having a simple problem-solving procedure that students could use both individually, in pairs, or as a class. We used an ABCD model:

Ask about the problem.

Brainstorm solutions.

Choose the best solution.

Do it.

Posters with this ABCD sequence were in classrooms.

Reporting and Tattling Distinction

Reporting is when you want to get someone or yourself out of trouble.

Tattling is when you want to get someone into trouble. (Morrison & Marachi, 2011)

Posting this simple way of determining what to do provides a great visual cue as reminder to students who want to do the right thing but have trouble knowing the difference between reporting and tattling.

Response to Bullying

These are simple suggestions by Rigby (2008, p. 187) for students to try if they are being bullied. Students should be told that these don't always work but could help them in some situations. *(Number 5 should be emphasized as a strategy if the others don't work, and it can also be used after the bullying incident.)*

1. Ignore

2. Walk away

3. Talk friendly

4. Talk firmly

5. Report

These five strategies could be put on an open hand symbol with each finger having a strategy.

Improving the School Climate

These are just a few examples of schoolwide activities. Each school's bullying prevention team could customize these activities with the goal of strengthening the ties among all the members of the school community.

Schools should be places people want to go to and don't want to leave. I heard a speaker respond to a question about how to *measure* a school climate by asking, "Do the kids run into the building faster than they run out it?" Let's accept the opportunity of bullying prevention to make schools places where all students feel cared for and valued. These are the type of places that people will want to run into.

SUMMARY

- Successful bullying prevention takes time and requires the sustained efforts of each member of the school community.
- Leadership is the essential element for the positive changes in climate and culture to be sustained and integrated into the life of the school.
- Schools need to establish specifically designed routines and procedures designed to provide intensive services to students at risk.
- Data in many forms need to be collected on a regular basis to monitor progress and be the basis for ongoing goal setting and planning.
- A procedure/protocol for investigating and recording incidents of bullying needs to be established and implemented.
- There are many ways to integrate a bullying prevention message into already existing curricula.
- Bullying prevention can be integrated into many classroom and schoolwide activities.

- Bullying prevention can be a positive opportunity not just to address a serious problem but also to improve and even transform the school community for everyone.

FINAL THOUGHTS

This book was not designed to give school leaders the answer to preventing and reducing bullying. I wish I could do that, but I can't. I hope, however, that this is book can guide you on your journey to make schools a better place for students to learn.

The problem of bullying in schools is complex and elusive. Schools face enormous challenges and opportunities yet receive less support financially and less confidence from the public it serves. Schools leaders are pressured to do more with less and face consequences for not meeting higher and higher standards. In spite of this, I have great reason to hope and believe that not only can schools keep all students safe, but they can become places where students thrive and end up leaving prepared to learn more and lead a great life. My source of hope rests in some simple fundamental truths that I have discovered in my almost forty years as an educator:

- All people want to do well. No student enters schools not wanting to succeed. No teacher wants to do a bad job. We all really want the same things.

- Schools have all the knowledge, skills, creativity, and resources they need to be the type of schools they want to be.

- Schools just need to find a way to bring people together in the right way to harness their knowledge and skills and direct it toward some common goals.

- All people can lead and want to lead. We move forward when we lead each other in the same direction and learn as we go.

- Many small changes in the right direction done over time can really transform a school.

- Schools should be places where everyone feels at home and can be who they really are.

We discover our wisdom, our heart, and our courage in the process of caring for and helping each other. The change necessary for effective bullying prevention comes from the work we do together to serve our students. We develop the will to prevent bullying from connecting to our moral purpose of improving the lives of children. We develop the necessary skill to prevent bullying by learning from each step we take together with that common purpose. We make sure that we have the infrastructure in place to sustain the school culture and climate developed from our commitment and hard work devoted to that purpose.

Our Beginning and Our End

"Faith is taking the first step even when you don't see the whole staircase."

—Martin Luther King, Jr.

Our starting point and our ending point are the same: making the life of each student a little better each day. Bullying prevention is nothing more than making a commitment to doing everything possible to ensure that each student walks into school unafraid and that while in school reaches his or her full potential. If the people in a school rally around that simple idea and commit themselves to helping each other achieve that goal, they will: change is not just possible it is inevitable. It is as simple or as hard as that. I hope that this book can help you take that first step in the right direction and guide your community as you walk together.

Appendix

Bullying Prevention Resources

OLWEUS BULLYING PREVENTION PROGRAM (OBPP)

This program is one of the few evidence-based programs being implemented in schools today. It incorporates all of the ten recommended practices from the stopbullyingnow.gov website. The program is based on the book *Bullying at Schools* by Dr. Dan Olweus. He was one of the first researchers to investigate bullying in schools and its effects on school environments and individuals. His research indicated that effective bullying prevention required a schoolwide comprehensive approach involving education, professional development, policies and rules, data collection, interventions, and parent/community outreach.

Hazelden has published a schoolwide guide and a classroom guide for implementing the program. In order to maintain program fidelity, school teams need to be trained by certified Olweus trainers and use the appropriate program materials. Hazelden has many excellent resources for supporting all the elements of the OBPP.

Clemson University's Institute on Family and Neighborhood Life oversees the OBPP program and coordinates the training of trainers and the dissemination of the model in the United States. The OBPP should be commended for the pioneering work they have done and the leadership they have provided to the field of bullying prevention.

There are three main websites for information on the OBPP:

www.clemson.edu/Olweus

www.olweus.org

www.hazelden.org

PrevNET

This is an excellent resource on bullying prevention based in Canada. It is a network of researchers, nongovernmental, and governmental agencies dedicated to stopping bullying. It also recommends a comprehensive schoolwide approach to the problem without promoting a specific program. All bullying prevention efforts are based on four pillars: education, assessment, intervention, and policy.

TEACHSAFESCHOOLS.ORG

This website's mission is to help school personnel develop a supportive, safe, and inviting learning environment where students can thrive and be successful. It provides evidence-based information and techniques to assist the school community in the prevention of school violence. In addition to information about bullying prevention, this site provides resources specifically for school leaders.

BOOKS

There are many excellent books available on bullying, and the websites mentioned above are reliable sources for finding useful publications that can be used for study groups and professional development. I do cite specific books related to various topics in bullying prevention within the chapters. Those books are reliable and useful resources for school leaders, staff, and parents. I list these two books in this section because they don't appear to be as readily available or as well known as many of the other books in the field of bullying prevention.

Bullying Prevention and Intervention: Realistic Strategies for Schools (2009) by Susan Swearer, Dorothy Espelage, and Scott Napolitano

In addition to the books recommended on these websites, I found this particular book very helpful. It is a concise and accessible resource that covers all the critical elements of effective bullying prevention. It discusses the problems of researching bullying prevention in schools yet points school leaders in the right direction for getting started and sustaining effective efforts addressing the problem. It makes a strong and convincing case for viewing bullying in a social-ecological context.

The Respectful School (2003) by Stephen Wessler and William Premble

Implementing effective bullying prevention on the secondary level presents many challenges. This book articulates the reasons for these challenges and provides some straight-forward principles and practices for overcoming them. I particularly liked the focus on changing adult words and actions rather than prescribing what *should* be done to the students.

RESOURCES ON LEADERSHIP AND THE CHANGE PROCESS

The Works of Michael Fullan

Anyone wanting to understand and navigate the change process must read the works of Michael Fullan. He explores this complex process in a clear and cogent way, providing guiding principles and sensible approaches for anyone in a leadership position. His work is grounded in a deep respect for people and an affirmation of the moral purpose of education. *The Six Secrets of Change* (2008), *Change Leader* (2011a), and *Leading in a Culture of Change* (2001) would be excellent choices for book study groups.

Made to Stick (2008) and *Switch* (2010) by Chip and Dan Heath

These books are very easy to read and provide a variety of entertaining examples to make their points about creating lasting and memorable change in all areas of life.

Practical Wisdom (2010) by Barry Schwartz and Kenneth Sharpe

This book explores how our culture has shifted from valuing the wisdom gained from the experience of living and working together to an overreliance on rules and regulations as the solution to our complex problems.

The Works of Malcolm Gladwell

Malcolm Gladwell skillfully translates the research of social psychology into fascinating stories and anecdotes that illustrate how people think, act, and influence each other. *The Tipping Point* (2002), *Blink* (2005), and *The Outliers* (2008) provide great food for thought for getting staff to look at problems differently.

Drive (2010) by Daniel Pink and *Why We Do What We Do* (1996) by Edward Deci and Richard Flaste

These two books explore the differences between extrinsic and intrinsic motivation in all aspects of life. Since most schools rely on extrinsic motivation, emphasizing rules, rewards, and consequences to change student behavior, it can be very difficult to get staff to consider alternative ways to solve any school problem. Getting staff to discuss and reflect on the critical distinction between these different types of motivation can be an effective way to create an openness to more creative approaches to addressing school problems.

The Research of Amy Edmondson

Dr. Amy Edmondson of Harvard Business School is doing fascinating research analyzing leadership and learning in business environments. She makes many of the theories and key principles of effective change operational and amenable to research. Although the research was done outside of schools, her findings are very applicable to education. Her work is not yet consolidated into one publication, so I recommend investing the time to find the articles listed in References.

Mindset (2006) by Carol Dweck

This book and the research behind it have profound implications for how we educate our students. Since educators talk to students, they need to understand how the words they use affect how students learn, and more importantly, view themselves. Getting educators to use words reflecting a *growth mindset* rather than a *fixed mindset* can have a tremendous positive impact on student learning and achievement. When students see effort as the key element of success, they will be more likely to invest their time and energy in becoming more empowered bystanders.

References

Anspaugh, D. (Director). (1986). *Hoosiers* [Motion picture]. United States: Metro-Goldwyn-Mayer. Retrieved from www.youtube.com/watch?v=9Cdc13CU9Fc

Asher, W. (Director). (1952). Switching jobs [Television series episode]. In D. Arnaz (Executive producer), *I love Lucy*. United States: Columbia Broadcasting System. Retrieved from www.youtube.com/watch?v=8NPzLBSBzPI

Ayers, W., Dohren, B., & Ayers, R. (Eds.). (2001). *Zero tolerance: Resisting the drive for punishment in our schools*. New York, NY: The New Press.

Bregman, P. (2007). *Point B: A short guide to leading a big change*. New York, NY: Space for Change.

Brooks, D. (2011, September 13) [op. ed.]. If it feels right. *New York Times*. Retrieved from www.nytimes.com/2011/09/13/opinion/if-it-feels-right.html?_r=1&ref=davidbrooks

Chabris, C., & Simons, D. (2009). *The invisible gorilla: How our intuitions deceive us*. New York, NY: Broadway Paperbacks.

Cohn, A., & Canter, A. (n.d.). *Bullying: What schools and parents can do*. Retrieved February 22, 2005, from www.guidancechannel.com/default.aspx?M=a&index=508&cat=50

Collins, J. (2001). *Good to great*. New York, NY: HarperCollins.

Collins, J. (2005). *Good to great for the social sector*. New York, NY: HarperCollins.

Covey, S. (1990). *The 7 habits of highly effective people*. New York, NY: Free Press.

Craig, W. (2007). *Bullying is a relationship problem*. Retrieved from http://qspace.library.queensu.ca/handle/1974/968

Craigen, J., & Ward, C. (2004). *What's this got to do with anything?* San Clemente, CA: Kagan Cooperative Leaning.

Curwin, R., Mendler, A., & Mendler, B. (2008). *Discipline with dignity* (3rd ed.). Alexandria, VA: ASCD.

Deal, T., & Peterson, K. (2009). *Shaping school culture: Pitfalls, paradoxes, & promises*. San Francisco, CA: Jossey-Bass.

Deci, E., & Flaste, R. (1996). *Why we do what we do: Understanding self-motivation*. New York, NY: Penguin Group USA.

Dewey, J. (1985). *Democracy and education*. Carbondale: Southern Illinois University Press.

Dillon, J. (2008). *Peaceful school bus: A program for grades K–12*. Center City, MN: Hazelden.

Dillon, J. (2010). No place for bullying. *Principal Magazine, 90*(1), 20–23.

Dweck, C. (2006). *Mindset: The new psychology of success*. New York, NY: Ballantine Books.

Edmondson, A. (2008, July/August). The competitive imperative of learning. *Harvard Business Review,* 60–67.

Edmondson, A., Bohmer, R., & Pisano, G. (2001, October). Speeding up team learning. *Harvard Business Review,* 125–132.

Edmondson, A., & Cha, S. (2002, November). When company values backfire. *Harvard Business Review,* 18–19.

Edmondson, A., & Nembhard, I. (2009). Product development and learning in project teams: The challenges are the benefits. *Journal of Product Innovation Management, 26,* 123–138.

Edmondson, A, & Smith, D. M. (2006). Too hot to handle? *California Management Review, 49*(1), 6–31.

Engel, S., & Sandstrom, M. (2010, July 22nd). There's only one way to stop a bully. *New York Times.*

Farrington, D. P., & Ttofi, M. M. (2009). School-based programs to reduce bullying and victimization. *Campbell Systematic Reviews, 6,* 1–147.

Focus group. (n.d.). In *Wikipedia.* Retrieved March 15, 2012, from http://en.wiki pedia.org/wiki/Focus_group

Fox, L., Dunlap, G., Hemmeter, M. L., Joseph, G. E., & Strain, P. S. (2003). The teaching pyramid: A model for supporting social competence and preventing challenging behavior in young children. *Young Children* 58 (July): 49.

Fritz, R. (1984). *The path of least resistance.* New York, NY: Random House.

Fritz, R. (2010). Supercharging the creative process. Retrieved from www.robertfritz .com/index.php?content=writingnr&news_id=181

Frost, R. (1969). In E. C. Lathem (Ed.), *The poetry of Robert Frost: The collected poems, complete and unbridged.* New York, NY: Henry Holt and Company.

Fullan, M. (2001). *Leading in a culture of change.* San Franscisco, CA: Jossey-Bass.

Fullan, M. (2003). *The moral imperative of school leadership.* Thousand Oaks, CA: Corwin.

Fullan, M. (2007). *The new meaning of educational change* (4th ed.). New York, NY: Teachers College Press.

Fullan, M. (2008). *The six secrets of change.* Thousand Oaks, CA: Corwin.

Fullan, M. (2010a). *All systems go.* Thousand Oaks, CA: Corwin.

Fullan, M. (2010b). *Motion leadership: The skinny on becoming change savvy.* Thousand Oaks, CA: Corwin.

Fullan, M. (2010c). *Turnaround leadership.* San Francisco, CA: Jossey-Bass.

Fullan, M. (2011a). *Change leader.* San Francisco, CA: Jossey-Bass.

Fullan, M. (2011b) Choosing the wrong drivers for whole system reform. Retrieved from www.michaelfullan.ca

Funt, A. A. (Director). (1962). Face the rear [Television series episode]. In A. A. Funt (Producer), *Candid Camera.* United States: Columbia Broadcasting System. Retrieved from www.youtube.com/watch?v=aX1gL5Zqkao

Garrity, G., Jens, K., Porter, W., Sager, N., & Short-Camilli, C. (2000). *Bully-proofing your school: A comprehensive approach for elementary schools* (2nd ed.). Frederick, CO: Sopris West.

Garvin, D., Edmondson, A., & Gino, F. (2008, March). Is yours a learning organization. *Harvard Business Review,* 109–135.

Gitlow, A. (Director). (1997). Follow the Leader [Television program episode]. In F. Rothenberg (Producer), *Dateline.* United States: National Broadcasting Company. Retrieved from www.youtube.com/watch?v=VgDx5g9ql1g

Gladwell, M. (2002). *The tipping point.* New York, NY: Little, Brown.

Gladwell, M. (2005). *Blink.* New York, NY: Little, Brown.

Gladwell, M. (2008). *The outliers.* New York, NY: Little, Brown.

Goleman, D., Boysatziz, R., & McKee, A. (2002). *Primal leadership.* Boston, MA: Harvard Business School Press.

Goodman, R. (Director). (2002, February 15). *The "in-crowd" and social cruelty with John Stossel* [Television series on DVD]. New York, NY: ABC News.

Hamburger, M. E., Basile, K. C., & Vivolo, A. M. (Eds.). (2011). *Measuring bullying victimization, perpetration, and bystander experiences: A compendium of assessment tools.* Atlanta, GA: Centers for Disease Control and Prevention, National Center for Injury Prevention and Control. Retrieved from www.cdc.gov/ViolencePrevention/pdf/BullyCompendium-a.pdf

Hargreaves, A., & Fink, D. (2006). *Sustainable leadership.* San Francisco, CA: Jossey-Bass.

Hawkins, D. L., Pepler, D. J., & Craig, W. (2001). Naturalistic observation of peer intervention in bullying. *Social Development, 10*(4), 512–527.

Heath, C., & Heath, D. (2008). *Made to stick.* New York, NY: Random House.

Heath, C., & Heath, D. (2010). *Switch: How to change things when change is hard.* New York, NY: Broadway Books.

Heifetz, R., & Linsky, M. (2004). When leadership spells danger. *Educational Leadership, 61*(7), 33–37.

Heifetz, R., Grashow, A., & Linsky, M. (2009). *The practice of adaptive leadership.* Cambridge, MA: Harvard Business Press.

Hoover, J., & Oliver, R. (1996). *The bullying prevention handbook: A guide for principals, teachers and counselors.* Bloomington, IN: National Education Service.

Howard, R.(Director). (1995). *Apollo 13* [Motion picture]. United States: Universal Pictures. Retrieved from www.youtube.com/watch?v=hLZZ_y1xdJg

Hughes, J. (Director). (1985). *The Breakfast club* [Motion picture]. United States: Universal Pictures. Retrieved from www.youtube.com/watch?v=bTeYncx1xmI

Humberman, M. (1983). Recipes for busy kitchens. *Knowledge: Creation, Diffusion, Utilization, 4,* 478–510.

Johnston, J. (Director). (1999). *October sky* [Motion picture]. United States: Universal Pictures. Retrieved from www.youtube.com/watch?v=uMREOwM S4Ys&feature=youtu.be

Johnston, P. (2004). *Choice words: How our language affects children's learning.* Portland, ME: Stenhouse Publishers.

Kazdin, A., & Rotella, C. (2009, August 11). Bullies: They can be stopped, but it takes a village. Retrieved from www.slate.com/id/2249424

Kegan, R., & Lahey, L. (2001). *How the way we talk can change the way we work.* San Francisco, CA: Jossey-Bass.

Kegan, R., & Lahey, L. (2009). *Immunity to change: How to overcome it and unlock the potential in yourself and your organization.* Boston, MA: Harvard Business Press.

Khosropour, S. C., & Walsh, J. (2000). *That's not teasing—That's bullying: A study of fifth grades conceptualization of bullying and teasing.* Paper presented at the annual conference of the American Educational Research Association, Seattle, Washington.

Kish-Gephart, J., Detert, J., Trevino, L. K., & Edmondson, A. (2009). Silenced by fear: The nature, sources, and consequences of fear at work. *Research in Organizational Behavior, 29,* 163–193.

Kotter, J. (2008). *A sense of urgency.* Boston, MA: Harvard Business Press.

Kouzes, J., & Posner, B. (2010). *The truth about leadership: The no-fads, heart-of-the-matter facts you need to know.* San Francisco, CA: Jossey-Bass.

Kowalski, R., Limber, S., & Agatston, P. (2005). *Cyber bullying: Bullying in the digital age.* Malden, MA: Blackwell Publishing.

Lazarus, P. (2001). Breaking the code of silence: What schools can do about it. *Communique, 29*(7), 28–29.

Leder, M. (Director). (2000). *Pay it forward* [Motion picture]. United States: Warner Brothers. Retrieved from www.youtube.com/watch?v=_yZEi-LOBaI&feature=plcp

Leithwood, K., Louis, K., Anderson, S., & Wahlstrom, K. (2010). *Learning from leadership: Investigating the links to improved student learning.* New York, NY: Wallace Foundation.

Macklem, G. (2003). *Bullying and teasing: Social power in children's groups.* New York, NY: Kluwer Academic/Plenum Publishers.

McGregor, D. (1960). *The human side of enterprise.* New York, NY: McGraw-Hill.

McNamara, C. (2006). *Field guide to nonprofit program design, marketing and evaluation.* Minneapolis, MN: Authentic Consulting, LLC.

Mindset. (n.d.). In *Wikipedia.* Retrieved from http://en.wikipedia.org/wiki/Mindset

Morrison, B., & Marachi, R. (2011, March 16). *Understanding and responding to school bullying.* Retrieved from http://safesupportiveschools.ed.gov/index.php?id=9&eid=16

Keller, L. (Director). (2011a). My kid would never bully (girls' group) [Television program episode]. In A. Orr (Producer), *Dateline.* United States: National Broadcasting Company. Retrieved from www.youtube.com/watch?v=MDa9jTgRa0k

Keller, L. (Director). (2011b). My kid would never bully (boys' group) [Television program episode]. In A. Orr (Producer), *Dateline.* United States: National Broadcasting Company. Retrieved from www.youtube.com/ watch?v=yPKqpn3O6NQ

Oliver, C., & Candappa, M. (2007). Bullying and the politics of telling. *Oxford Review of Education, 33*(1), 71–86.

Olweus, D. (1993). *Bullying at school.* Malden, MA: Blackwell Publishing.

Olweus, D., Limber, S. Flex, V., Mullin, N., Riese, J., & Snyder, M. (2007). *Olweus bullying prevention program teacher guide.* Center City, MN: Hazelden.

Oz, F. (Director). (1991). *What about Bob?* [Motion picture]. United States: Touchstone Pictures. Retrieved from www.youtube.com/watch?v=1dWk0eHBOvk&feature=youtu.be

Parker-Roerden, L., Rudewick, D., & Gorton, D. (2007). *Direct from the field: A guide to bullying prevention.* Retrieved from www.mass.gov/eohhs/docs/dph/comhealth/violence/bullying-prevent-guide.pdf

Partnership for the 21st Century. (n.d.). Life and career skills. Retrieved from www.p21.0rg/index.php?option=com_content&task=view&id=266&Itemid=120

Patall, E., Cooper, H., & Robinson, J. (2008). The effects of choice on intrinsic motivation and related outcomes: A meta-analysis of research findings. *Psychological Bulletin, 134*(2), 270–300.

Payne, A. (Director). (1999). *Election* [Motion picture]. United States: Paramount Pictures. Retrieved from www.youtube.com/watch?v=tcgvP8v3W54&feature=youtu.be

Pepler, D. (2007). *Relationship solutions for relationship problems.* Retrieved from http://qspace.library.queensu.ca/handle/1974/968

Petrosino, A., Guckenberg, S., DeVoe, J., & Hanson, T. (2010). *What characteristics of bullying, bullying victims and schools are associated with increased reporting of bullying to school officials?* [Issues and Answers Report, REL 2010-No. 092]. Retrieved from http://ies.ed.gov/ncee/edlab

Pickeral, T., Evans, L., Hughes, W., & Hutchinson, D. (2009). *School climate guide for district policymakers and educational leaders.* New York, NY: Center for Social and Emotional Education.

Pink, D. (2010a). *Drive: The surprising truth about what motivates us.* New York, NY: Riverhead Books.

Pink, D. (2010b). *Two questions that can change your life* [Video file]. Retrieved from www.danpink.com/archives/2010/01/2questionsvideo

Piper, T. (Writer/Director). (2006). *The Becel Broken Escalator Ad* [Extended 2-minute version of 30-second advertising spot]. Adapted by Brenda Surminsky (Producer), Ogilvy Canada, from Joan Bell (Producer), *Broken Escalator*, Steam Films. Toronto, Canada: Becel Margarine. Retrieved from www.youtube.com/watch?v=47rQkTPWW2I

Pollack, W., Modzeleski, W., & Rooney, G. (2008). *Prior knowledge of potential school-based violence: Information students learn may prevent a targeted attack.* Report from the U.S. Secret Service and U.S. Departement of Education. Retrieved from www.secretservice.gov/ntac/bystander_study.pdf

Rigby, K. (2001). *Stop the bullying: A handbook for teachers.* Ontario, Canada: Pembroke Publishers.

Rigby, K. (2008). *Children and bullying: How parents and educators can reduce bullying at school.* Malden, MA: Blackwell Publishing.

Rigby, K., & Johnson, B. (2006/2007). Playground heroes. *Greater Good.* Retrieved from http://greatergood.berkeley.edu/article/item/playground_heroes?

Rodkin, P. (2011). Bullying—And the power of peers. *Educational Leadership, 69*(1), 10–17.

Salmivalli, C. (2010). Bullying and the peer group: A review. *Aggression and Violent Behavior, 15,* 112–130.

Schulz, K. (2010). *Being wrong: Adventures in the margin of error.* New York, NY: HarperCollins.

Schwartz, B., & Sharpe, K. (2010). *Practical wisdom: The right way to do the right thing.* New York, NY: Riverhead Books.

Shapiro, M. (Producer). (2003, April 25th) [NBA playoff game]. *Mo Cheeks National Anthem.* Portland Trailblazers versus Dallas Mavericks. On ESPN. United States: National Broadcasting Company. Retrieved from www.youtube.com/watch?v=q4880PJnO2E

Simons, D. [profsimons]. (2010, March 10). *Selective attention test* [Video file]. Retrieved from www.youtube.com/watch?feature=player_embedded&v=vJG698U2Mvo

Smith, J. D. (2007). *School climate and bonding: Pathways to resolving bullying.* Retrieved from http://qspace.library.queensu.ca/handle/1974/968

Smith, P., Pepler, D., & Rigby, K. (Eds.). (2004). *Bullying in schools: How successful can interventions be?* Cambridge, UK: Cambridge University Press.

Sparks, D. (2002, Summer). Inner conflicts, inner strengths: Interview with Robert Kegan and Lisa Lahey. *JSD,* 66–71.

Sullivan, K., Cleary, M., & Sullivan, G. (2004). *Bullying in secondary schools: What it looks like and how to manage it.* Thousand Oaks, CA: Corwin.

Surowiecki, J. (2005). *The wisdom of crowds.* New York, NY: Anchor Books.

Swearer, S. (2010). *Risk factors for and outcomes of bullying and victimization.* Retrieved from www.stopbullying.gov/ . . . /white_house_conference_materials.pdf

Swearer, S., Espelage, D., & Napolitano, S. (2009). *Bullying prevention and intervention: Realistic strategies for schools.* New York, NY: Guilford Press.

Swearer, S., Espelage, D., Vaillancourt, T., & Hymel, S. (2010). What can be done about school bullying: Linking research to educational practice. *Educational Researcher, 39*(1), 38–47.

TED2005. (2005). *Richard St. John's 8 secrets of success* [Video file]. Retrieved from www.ted.com/talks/lang/en/richard_st_john_s_8_secrets_of_success.html

TED2011. (2011). Barry Schwartz: *Using our practical wisdom* [Video file]. Retrieved from http://www.ted.com/talks/lang/en/barry_schwartz_using_our_practical_wisdom.html

TEDxToronto 2010. (2010, October). Dave Meslin: *The antidote to apathy* [Video file]. Retrieved from www.ted.com/talks/dave_meslin_the_antidote_to_apathy.html

Thornberg, R. (2010). A student in distress: Moral frames and bystander behavior in school. *Elementary School Journal, 110*(4), 585–608.

Trainor, D. O. (Director). (1997). The Comeback [Television Series episode]. In J. Seinfeld, G. Sharpiro, H. West (Executive Producers), *Seinfeld.* United States: National Broadcasting Company. Retrieved from www.youtube.com/watch?v=c2eCXhbYWVU&feature=youtu.be

Turner, C., & Greco, T. (1998). *The personality compass: A new way to understand people.* Salisbury, England: Element Books.

U.S. Department of Education. (2010). Dear colleague letter on bullying and harassment. Retrieved from http://www2.ed.gov/about/offices/list/oct/colleagues-201010.html

U.S. Department of Education. (2011). Anti-bullying policies: Examples of provisions in state laws. Retrieved from http://www2.ed.gov/policy/gen/guild/secletter/101215.html

vooktv. (2010, June 11). Carol Dweck: *The effect of praise on mindsets* [Video file]. Retrieved from www.youtube.com/watch?v=TTXrV0_3UjY

Wessler, S., & Premble, W. (2003). The respectful school: How educators and students can conquer hate and harassment. Alexandria, VA: ASCD.

Willard, N., (n.d.). *Educator's guide to cyberbullying, cyberthreats and sexting.* Retrieved from http://csriu.org/cyberbully/documents/educatorsguide.pdf

Willard, N. (2005). *Cyberbullying guidance for school leaders.* Retrieved from http://csriu.org/cyberbully/documents/educatorsguide.pdf

Willard, N. (2011). *Cyberbullying, sexting, and predators, oh my! Addressing youth risk in the digital age in a positive and restorative manner.* Retrieved from http://csriu.org/documents/documents/IssueBrief.pdf

Wood, S. (Director). (1935). *A night at the opera* [Motion picture]. United States: Metro-Goldwyn-Mayer. Clip retrieved from www.youtube.com/watch?v=10xHIFtLzp0&feature=youtu.be

Zemeckis, R. (Director). (1994). *Forrest Gump* [Motion picture]. United States: Paramount Pictures. Clip retrieved from www.youtube.com/watch?feature=endscreen&NR=1&v=nKubwgJK8q8

Index

CORWIN

A SAGE Company

The Corwin logo—a raven striding across an open book—represents the union of courage and learning. Corwin is committed to improving education for all learners by publishing books and other professional development resources for those serving the field of PreK–12 education. By providing practical, hands-on materials, Corwin continues to carry out the promise of its motto: **"Helping Educators Do Their Work Better."**